Before Disaster Strikes

Professional Review

Lori E. Burger, CPM®
John N. Gallagher, CPM®
Richard F. Muhlebach, CPM®
Cher Zucker-Maltese, CPM®

Caroline Scoulas
Senior Editor
Education Publishing

Before Disaster Strikes

Developing an
Emergency Procedures Manual

Third Edition

IREM **Institute of Real Estate Management**

CHICAGO

1 2 3 4 5 6 7 8 9 10 Printing / Year 14 13 12 11 10 09 08 07 06 05

Publisher's Preface

This revision of *Before Disaster Strikes: Developing an Emergency Procedures Manual* was undertaken to update the guidelines provided in earlier editions, expand the array of emergency situations to be considered, and provide a comprehensive listing of potential resources. New chapters have been added on natural gas leaks, explosions, hazardous materials incidents, volcanic eruptions, landslides, and terrorist acts. Wherever potential information sources could be identified, these have been cited in the text and included in the list of Additional Resources at the back of the book.

Before Disaster Strikes is not itself an emergency procedures manual. Rather, it is designed to help property managers work through the process of identifying types of emergency situations and developing property-specific responses to them. It does this by suggesting questions to ask, actions to consider, and information resources that may be helpful.

Not all suggestions will apply to every property. Some managers may need to seek out more specific information to address unique situations. For some aspects of emergency planning—e.g., security, medical emergencies, fragile occupant populations (children, disabled persons, the elderly)—it may be desirable or appropriate to consult with knowledgeable professionals. Advice of legal counsel may be needed in regard to potential liabilities.

The accompanying CD-ROM contains digital files for the Emergency Planning Forms printed in the back of this book. These are provided in both Excel and MS Word formats. Also included are the forms presented within the chapters and the Risk Assessment Questionnaire (appendix). These are provided as Word files only. The forms in this book and on the CD should be considered as tools to help the property manager start the information collection process. All of the Excel and Word files can be modified to tailor the contents to the information needs of a specific property. For example, the Resident Emergency Information Request form from Chapter 9 may be adaptable for use in collecting similar types of information about commercial tenants' employees. The CD also includes a PDF file, *Coping with an Attack: A Quick Guide to Dealing with Biological, Chemical, and "Dirty Bomb" Attacks*, that summarizes preparations for and responses to these types of terrorist acts.

Throughout this book, there are references to organizations and to specific web sites. Readers are encouraged to explore the Internet sources—but to use caution. Many sources include good information, but their intended audience is the professionals who respond to emergencies—fire and police departments, etc.—and some of the recommended actions may not be appropriate (or feasible) for implementation in the private sector. It is also important to seek out multiple sources. In particular, the web sites for the Federal Emergency Management Agency (www.fema.gov) and the American Red Cross (www.redcross.org) address a wide spectrum of emergencies including fire, power outages, earthquakes, and terrorist attacks as well as various types of weather disasters. Those organizations have also partnered with the National Oceanic and Atmospheric Administration to publish weather emergency information, which is available for download from the National Weather Service web site at www.nws.noaa.gov.

Because of continuing technological advances and increasing emphasis on preparedness among business owners and government agencies at all levels, property managers may be well advised to review emergency plans and procedures on a regular schedule and to check with local authorities and knowledgeable professionals about new emergency response strategies.

About This Book

Before Disaster Strikes: Developing an Emergency Procedures Manual offers guidelines for planning and implementing emergency procedures for managed properties. Throughout this book, reference to an emergency plan or emergency procedures assumes a single plan for a unique property. While a real estate management company may develop a basic emergency procedures guideline, it should be understood that such a guideline will need to be modified for each property the firm manages.

Chapter 1 provides an overview to help readers understand the scope of emergency planning. Chapters 2 through 7 cover the basic components of an emergency plan—determining who among management staff will have specific responsibilities in an emergency situation, assessing a property's security needs to identify vulnerabilities and minimize risks, developing an evacuation plan, resuming operations after an emergency, having a plan to address public relations, and documenting emergency incidents and responses. Chapter 8 discusses the purpose and contents of an emergency procedures manual. It also addresses emergency procedures for building occupants and developing an occupant emergency handbook.

Chapters 9 through 13 address emergency planning for specific types of properties, pointing out the ways residential and commercial properties differ from each other in regard to emergency planning needs, especially evacuation of the property. While the basic evacuation plan will be specific for fire as required by local ordinances, other types of emergencies—a power outage, a criminal act, stormy weather—may necessitate a different approach to evacuation. The chapters on specific types of emergencies indicate some of the challenges they pose.

Chapters 14 through 23 suggest responses to emergency situations that relate to buildings. These include fire, power outages, elevator emergencies, water leaks, natural gas leaks, medical emergencies, crime on the property, bomb threats, explosions, and hazardous materials incidents. The chapters on water and gas leaks also look at these types of emergencies as urban infrastructure failures. Bomb threats and hazardous materials incidents might also be part of planned terrorist acts.

Chapters 24 through 29 address preparations for and responses to weather-related emergencies—tornadoes, hurricanes, winter storms, floods, drought, and wild fires. Chapters 30 through 32 suggest responses to geologic upheavals such as earthquakes, volcanic eruptions, and landslides. Chapter 33 covers emergencies related to nuclear power plant accidents, and Chapter 34 outlines what to do in the event of a nuclear attack. Chapter 35 outlines possible responses to releases of biological and/or chemical agents and the use of radioactive materials in a "dirty bomb." Currently, these are considered likely components of terrorist acts.

Note: While this guideline is intended to be comprehensive, it cannot be all-inclusive. If there is a perceived need to plan for situations that are not discussed in *Before Disaster Strikes*—e.g., kidnapping, hostage-taking, civil disorder—it may be wise to seek direction from local, state, and federal law enforcement agencies or consult with a security professional who is knowledgeable about the specific type of incident.

Acknowledgments

The Institute of Real Estate Management gratefully acknowledges the contributions of the following individuals who read the manuscript, provided insights from their experience in real estate management and emergency planning, suggested additional topics to be covered, identified information resources, and generally shaped the content of this book: **Lori E. Burger, CPM®, PCAM, CCAM**, Vice President of Eugene Burger Management Corporation in Rohnert Park, California; **John N. Gallagher, CPM®**, Senior Vice President of Polinger Shannon & Luchs Company, AMO®, in Chevy Chase, Maryland; **Richard F. Muhlebach, CPM®, SCSM, RPA, CRE**, Senior Managing Director of Kennedy Wilson Properties Northwest in Bellevue, Washington; and **Cher R. Zucker-Maltese, CPM®**, Vice President of Corporate Real Estate at Prudential Financial in Newark, New Jersey. Special thanks also to **David J. Mistick, CPM®**, President of Insurance Restoration Services in Pittsburgh, Pennsylvania, who provided updated versions of the emergency planning forms included at the back of this book and on the accompanying CD-ROM and granted permission for those forms to be used by readers of *Before Disaster Strikes*.

Contents

Emergency Planning for Specific Property Types

Illustrations

Emergency Planning Forms

Before Disaster Strikes
Developing an Emergency Procedures Manual

1

The Scope of
Emergency Planning

Every property, regardless of size or function, should have an emergency procedures plan that addresses the property's unique needs. The plan should spell out how the property staff will respond to different types of emergencies. In developing emergency procedures, the property manager has two primary responsibilities:

1. To protect the lives of the building's occupants and others on the premises and
2. To protect the property owner's investment.

A thorough and well-designed emergency procedures plan enables the property staff to be prepared *before* a disaster occurs, in order to minimize and perhaps prevent injuries to people and damage to property. *Before Disaster Strikes* offers guidance in constructing such a plan.

Preparing an emergency procedures plan requires extensive research and teamwork. The planning involves in-depth knowledge of the property and its occupants, the neighborhood, and the community in which the property is located. A property manager cannot create a comprehensive, well-conceived plan alone. It must be formulated in cooperation with an *emergency planning team* which may be comprised of the property owner, police and fire department officials, disaster recovery contractors, outside service contractors, and community service agencies, as well as the property's on-site management staff and the management firm's office staff. The property owner's insurance carrier may make available written materials or identify consulting resources that can be helpful. State and federal governmental agencies may also be consulted. Individuals and organizations provide their expertise in specialized areas to help determine what is needed for the emergency procedures plan. However, not all of the members of this planning team will be involved with the implementation of the plan if a disaster should occur.

An emergency procedures plan also includes an Emergency Management Team (or emergency response team) which actually sees the plan through to completion in an emergency situation. This team will be comprised primarily of management staff personnel with participation by commercial tenants' employees as appropriate (see Chapter 2). Members of this team may have participated in the emergency planning process. As the planning process progresses, you will want to formulate an emergency procedures manual (see Chapter 8), which will be an important reference guide for the Emergency Management Team in the event of an emergency.

Property managers should also be aware that there may be specific requirements for an emergency procedures plan. In particular, the Occupational Safety and Health Administration (OSHA) requires businesses that employ more than ten workers to have a written action plan in place. Such an emergency action plan is to cover "designated actions that employers and employees must take to ensure safety from fire and other emergencies," including:

- Procedures for reporting emergencies,
- Alarm systems,
- Evacuating the premises under different circumstances,
- Emergency escape procedures and escape route assignments,
- Procedures for employees who remain on site after an alarm sounds,
- Procedures to account for employees,
- Rescue and medical duties,
- Contacts for further information, and
- Training of personnel.

Particulars of the OSHA regulations can be found in the *Code of Federal Regulations* at 29 CFR 1910.38, Employee Emergency Plans and Fire Prevention Plans. The OSHA Plan components above are described in *Introduction to Employee Fire and Life Safety* published by the National Fire Protection Association. Additional guidance can be found in the OSHA publication, *How to Plan for Workplace Emergencies and Evacuations,* which can be downloaded from the Internet at www.osha.gov. There is also an e-tool on the OSHA web site to help small, low-hazard service and retail businesses implement an emergency action plan.

Individuals who manage properties that house governmental agencies should be aware that the Government Services Administration (GSA) requires the agencies to have an Occupant Emergency Program (OEP) for evacuation of occupied space in response to fire, explosion, severe weather, and other emergencies. The GSA has published an *Occupant Emergency Program Guide* (on the Internet at www.gsa .gov), which provides comprehensive guidelines that can be adapted for use in the private sector. Emergency plan templates are available in publications from a company called Emergency Planning Services; their Internet site is www.epserve.com.

Preparing an emergency procedures plan involves six steps:

1. Developing the emergency planning and management teams,
2. Identifying potential emergencies and the probabilities of their occurring,
3. Adopting preventive measures to avert emergencies,
4. Planning responses to specific types of emergencies,
5. Developing procedures for debriefing the Emergency Management Team and others involved after an incident, and
6. Preparing for an emergency by rehearsing and testing the plan.

An emergency procedures plan should also address recovery from emergencies, including restoration of the property and resumption of operations (see Chapter 5).

An emergency response plan will not come into being overnight. Before a plan can be developed, there must be an assessment of vulnerabilities and an evaluation of capabilities. This should include how and how quickly a public fire department or other first responder is likely to respond and any obstacles (physical barriers, traffic patterns, etc.) that may hinder a rapid response. The plan will evolve through several drafts and reviews before it is printed and distributed. It will take time to train the personnel who will be responsible for implementing specific procedures in the event of an emergency. Also, it may be necessary or desirable to coordinate your planning with outside emergency responders such as the fire department. The accompanying box identifies some of the actions and decisions needed to guide the emergency planning process.

Once established, the plan should be reviewed periodically and updated as appropriate. Being prepared will facilitate an appropriate response and make it easier

Emergency Planning Actions and Decisions

- Identify federal, state, and local laws, as well as your own corporate policies, that impact emergency procedures planning. Relevant laws for a property's location may include, but are not limited to, fire codes, building codes, environmental regulations, seismic safety codes, transportation regulations, occupational safety and health regulations, and zoning ordinances.
- Identify who will alert staff and building occupants of an emergency situation. This may take the form of a telephone "tree" or flow chart.
- Determine where staff should report in an emergency (if they are called to the site).
- Determine which entrance the responding agency or public units will use.
- Determine where external emergency response personnel will set up a "command center" on site.
- Determine where occupants should assemble after an evacuation.
- Determine what procedures should be followed if authorities' instructions are to shelter in place.
- Determine where and to whom agencies will report.
- Determine how public and agency officials will be identified. What kind of identification will authorities require to allow key personnel to be admitted into the facility during a crisis?
- Determine the needs of disabled and non-English-speaking persons. Assign tenant or emergency team "partners" to these persons to assist them in an evacuation.
- Determine who on staff will respond to media inquiries.
- Determine who on staff will be in charge until a fire chief or other person of authority assumes command of the site as well as who will be the point of contact for responding agencies.
- Determine where relevant records will be stored (on site and off site).
- Ensure that the property owner is informed of and approves the emergency procedures plan for the property. This is especially important if the owner has not been actively involved in developing the procedures.

You should also have backups or alternatives for the chain of command, communications means and methods, gathering places, exits, and other aspects of the plan. In other words, develop "plan B" to be implemented in the event an emergency disrupts part or all of "plan A."

Note: The foregoing list is not all-encompassing. Evaluation of a particular property may suggest other actions to be taken and/or decisions to be made.

to recover from an emergency. Additional guidance is available in a publication from the Federal Emergency Management Agency (FEMA) titled *Emergency Management Guide for Business and Industry,* which outlines a step-by-step approach to emergency planning, response, and recovery for companies of all sizes.

Note: *Before Disaster Strikes* includes sample forms that can be used to facilitate emergency procedures planning. Print versions are presented at the back of this book. The same forms are provided in Microsoft Word and Excel formats on the accompanying compact disk (CD) so they can be tailored to the needs of the property and the plan.

What Is an Emergency?

At the outset, the manager needs to work with the property staff and others to identify the specific types of situations and events for which emergency procedures are needed. Loosely defined, an *emergency* is an event or occurrence that disrupts the normal flow of a property's operations, often resulting in danger to occupants and visitors as well as damage to buildings.

Many people consider only fire and natural disasters such as earthquakes, tornadoes, and floods when they think of potential emergencies. However, property managers must consider a wide range of natural and man-made disasters when developing emergency procedures. (Information relevant to planning for specific emergencies is presented in separate chapters.) Depending on the type of property and where it is located, emergency procedures may be needed to address some or all of the following:

Weather-related disasters
- Tornadoes
- Hurricanes
- Floods
- Drought
- Wildfires
- Landslides
- Severe thunderstorms
- Severe winter weather—heavy snow, extreme cold
- Heat waves

Other natural disasters
- Earthquakes
- Tidal waves
- Volcanic eruptions

Man-made emergencies
- Arson and fire-related accidents
- Power outages
- Hazardous materials incidents
- Hostage situations
- Civil disorder
- Crime—assault, theft, robbery, vandalism
- Bomb threats
- Explosions
- Medical crises
- Terrorist acts

This list is not all-encompassing. The possibilities are endless. Regardless of what type of emergency arises, all emergencies have in common the need for a prepared property manager and an Emergency Management Team whose members are trained to respond. A planned response to specific emergencies will provide a frame of reference for responding to emergencies that had not been anticipated.

What Is Emergency Management?

Emergency management is the process of preparing for, mitigating, responding to, and recovering from an emergency. Training, conducting drills, testing equipment, and coordinating activities with community agencies and the community at large are important related functions.

To be successful, emergency management requires decisive leadership from the property manager. The manager sets the tone by authorizing an emergency response and directing the actions of the Emergency Management Team. There are numerous benefits to having a well-designed emergency management plan:

- It may minimize the risk of injuries to people and lessen the extent of property damage and business interruption losses.
- It facilitates compliance with federal, state, and local regulations.
- It enhances a property owner's and a management company's ability to recover from financial losses and physical damage to equipment and the managed property.
- It reduces susceptibility to criminal liability in the event of an incident.
- It may reduce insurance premiums.

Emergency Planning

In order to prepare an emergency management plan, you will need to gather specific information about the property to facilitate identification of emergencies that are likely to arise. Other preparatory steps include identifying and implementing preventive measures that can avert certain types of emergencies, ensuring compliance with applicable laws, assignment of emergency-specific responsibilities to property staff, maintaining accurate property records, and stocking emergency equipment. It is also important to identify external resources that can help with the planning process as well as those that respond directly in emergency situations.

An emergency plan should address how information about an emergency will be communicated to those who need to know. It should also include strategies for resuming operations after an emergency and providing information to the media and the general public—i.e., public relations. (Specific recovery and PR strategies are discussed in Chapters 5 and 6, respectively.)

Information about the Property

One of the manager's initial steps should be to gather as much information as possible about the property and to become knowledgeable about its surroundings. Knowing all you can about a property and its neighborhood allows for an effective response to emergencies with minimal human injury and property loss. Five characteristics affect the likelihood that certain types of emergencies will occur.

1. Geographic location
2. Immediate surroundings
3. Property type
4. Size and construction
5. Occupancy profile

A review of the property's leases, especially for any requirements for residents or commercial tenants to maintain specific types of insurance coverages, is also in order.

Geographic Location   Certain areas of the country are more prone to specific natural disasters than others, and property managers must plan accordingly. On the West Coast, for example, earthquakes are a major concern. Earthquakes on or near the sea coast may cause tsunamis or tidal waves. Earthquakes can also occur in other areas of the country. In fact, earthquakes have been experienced in at least 33 states, with the nation's largest fault line running through Missouri and Illinois.

In the western United States, canyon and forest fires can threaten occupied properties. In the Southeast and South and along the Eastern Seaboard, the most serious concerns are hurricanes and resultant flooding, while the Midwest and North are more likely to experience tornadoes and other violent storms.

Severe winter weather—excessive snowfall, extremely cold temperatures—can be a problem in northern states that are generally prepared for snow and cold. It can be devastating in areas outside the Snow Belt where such weather does not occur routinely.

Drought can occur almost anywhere in the United States, and periods of drought can last for years. In areas experiencing drought, water conservation measures may restrict personal and business usages. There is also increased potential for wildfires and greater difficulty fighting all types of fires.

What this points out is that a property's geographic location will play a central role in determining some of the contingencies to be included in an emergency plan. It is wise to seek outside guidance in compiling your list of potential emergencies. For instance, the National Weather Service, in conjunction with FEMA and the American Red Cross, has published preparedness guides specific for winter storms, hurricanes, and thunderstorms; the latter includes tornadoes and lightning. The National Weather Service web site (www.nws.noaa.gov) includes historical weather data as well as daily weather alerts and downloadable preparedness guidelines for a variety of weather-related emergencies. The American Red Cross web site (www.redcross .org) includes similar guidelines.

Other locational information should also be noted:

- Is the property situated on a flood plain? If so, what type of flood plain?
- Does the area have a history of flooding?
- Is the area near a fault line?
- Are there any state and local laws in effect regarding earthquakes, flooding, and the like?
- What are the chances of tornadoes or hurricanes?

Lightning strikes follow patterns in some areas, and this may also be a locational factor to consider. The probability of a weather-related disaster occurring in a specific area can be researched at www.fema.gov/library/dizandemer.shtm where FEMA publishes "general disaster statistics" and maps.

Immediate Surroundings   Just as relevant in planning emergency procedures is the neighborhood and community surrounding your property. The following suggest problems for which emergency procedures might be needed based on a property's surroundings.

- *Crime*—Buildings located in major urban areas are more likely to have a higher volume of pedestrian traffic than similar buildings in suburban or rural areas, and this often increases the probability of theft or assault.

- *Hazardous materials incidents*—Proximity to a chemical factory can result in exposure to chemicals released to the environment if there is a manufacturing accident. Hazardous materials (chemicals, wastes) are transported by train and truck, and there are occasional accidents with spills. Thus, being located close to railroad tracks and interstate highways may increase the likelihood of an emergency related to such a spill.

- *Nuclear incidents*—An incident at a nuclear power-generating plant can result in radiation exposure.

- *Explosion*—If a neighboring property houses a business that uses combustible materials—a fireworks manufacturer, for example—it is likely that an explosion on that site would have repercussions for adjacent properties, including explosion damage and fire.

- *Civil disturbances*—Buildings that house embassies, international businesses, governmental agencies, politically oriented organizations, or nonprofit entities have an increased likelihood of experiencing demonstrations and civil disturbances, which can spill over to nearby properties. Such tenancies may also attract bomb threats or hostage situations that can necessitate evacuating a wide area around a building.

Another consideration is whether neighboring properties might be potential targets of terrorism. Examples of likely targets include nuclear and other power-generating plants, government nuclear and biological facilities, military bases, oil refineries and gas pipelines, airports, railroad stations, offices of U.S. government agencies or foreign governments, and corporate headquarters of controversial businesses. Public monuments may also be targets. If such entities/facilities are in your immediate vicinity or within a narrow surrounding radius, any terrorist attack on them could affect the nearby property you manage.

Environmental hazards are an ever-present and growing concern. Property managers should be alert for potential effects of hazardous materials at neighboring properties as well as the ones they manage. It may be wise for an emergency plan to address potential long-term environmental dangers such as air and water pollution and toxic chemical spills. Water contamination is a problem whether it results from sabotage or a simple water main break. Other environmental hazards to consider are bloodborne pathogens, Legionnaire's disease, and anthrax.

While asbestos, lead-based paint, toxic mold, and radon may be addressed in emergency procedures, there are protocols for testing and abating or removing these hazardous materials that go beyond emergency exposure situations. The presence of such materials should be identified during management take-over inspections—or they may be discovered during preparations for renovation or rehabilitation—and their potential hazards should be addressed appropriately as part of the property's management. Exposure to asbestos, lead-based paint, toxic mold, or radon is most likely to result in a medical emergency relating to inhalation or ingestion.

An invisible part of a property's surroundings is the underground and above ground facilities maintained by the municipality. If water mains and sewers are old or poorly maintained, they can rupture, disrupting vital services and possibly causing flooding. Telephone trunk lines and electrical main lines are usually buried under streets. Damage to them can mean service disruptions while the damage is assessed as well as the inconvenience of reconstruction after repairs are made. Gas service can be disrupted by construction work and other excavations. Gas leaks can lead to fires and/or explosions, and the leaking gas can cause illness.

Contingency plans for road construction, utility installations, and nearby development work may also be worth considering, especially for buildings in areas of new development, urban renewal, or major road works. While not emergencies in themselves, these represent potential for situations to arise that require an emergency response. Other contingencies to consider are infrastructure failures (collapse of a bridge or tunnel, wash out of a road), which can make it difficult to safely enter and exit the property. Planning would include alternate routes to your managed property and ways to minimize service disruptions on site. Contingency planning should also take into account potential obstacles that can limit access or otherwise hinder outside responders. Railroad tracks, dead-end streets, cul-de-sacs, and locations of on-street fire hydrants are examples of these.

Background research will be needed to determine what potential threats your immediate surroundings may pose. Local police and fire department representatives can provide background information on the types of emergencies that are most likely to occur (e.g., crime rates, environmental hazards). Information on infectious agents can be obtained from the Centers for Disease Control and Prevention (CDC). Information on workplace hazards, including bloodborne pathogens, can be found on the OSHA web site at www.osha.gov or at www.cdc.gov/niosh.

Property Type The use of the property also plays a significant role in what is included in the emergency plan. Residential properties, office buildings, medical office buildings, industrial properties, and shopping centers and other retail properties all have their own particular needs for emergency management planning. For commercial properties, it is appropriate to ask questions such as these:

- Is there anything especially vulnerable in or on the property?
- What types of hazardous materials are present on the property?
- What types of hazardous materials are used by commercial tenants in their business activities?
- What types of hazardous wastes are created by tenants in their business activities?
- Are hazardous materials being stored, used, and disposed of properly?

Emergency planning for specific property types is discussed elsewhere in this book.

Note: *Before Disaster Strikes* focuses specifically on professionally managed investment real estate. Emergency procedures for other types of properties are beyond the scope of this book.

Size and Construction The size of the building often determines the complexity of the emergency plan. One-story commercial buildings and small residential properties where there is a single entrance to each apartment do not require complex evacuation procedures. However, expansive enclosed malls and multistory office buildings call for sophisticated planning and extensive training of commercial tenants' employees. Similarly, the type of construction—wood frame, steel girder, brick, or a combination of these—determines whether and how well a building will withstand a disaster. The manner of construction may also be a consideration. High-rise buildings may have an exterior skin attached with clips that can erode. Terra cotta finishes have been known to become detached, causing injuries to pedestrians and vehicles below. The finishes themselves can deteriorate over time. In Chicago, repeated exposure to high levels of noise from lakefront air shows has been cited as a contributor to cracks in building exterior finishes. Residential properties often include balconies or porches, which can pose hazards if they are not constructed properly. Items used and stored outside on balconies can cause damage to the building and injuries to people if they are blown away.

Note: The Emergency Management Team will need to become familiar with the building's layout, mechanical equipment, and emergency equipment, as well as its structure. This knowledge will be critical in the event of an evacuation and if team members are responsible to escort occupants to safety. A complete record of information about the property should be included in the emergency procedures manual. *Before Disaster Strikes* includes sample forms that can be used to record information for this purpose. (See the Emergency Planning Forms at the back of this book and the files on the accompanying CD.)

Occupancy Profile The property's occupancy must be considered in emergency procedures planning, so it is important to know who is living in a residential property (a resident profile) and what types of businesses are on the premises of commercial properties (tenant mix).

Residential Property In multifamily housing, there is likely to be a mix of young and old residents, varying from infants to senior citizens. Some may be disabled. These residents may not hear radio warnings or emergency announcements, or they may not be capable of evacuating on their own. Ramps may be required for easy ingress

Property Insurance Requirements

In addition to the basic property casualty and liability insurance coverages a property owner may carry, there may be special coverages that are required or desired. Rent loss insurance should be considered if it is not currently carried.

Flood insurance is available through the National Flood Insurance Program (see Chapter 27). Special earthquake coverage can also be obtained. Many lenders require owners to carry flood or earthquake insurance in areas prone to these types of events. Insurance premiums are high and large deductibles are required.

As a consequence of September 11, 2001, lenders may want some form of terrorism insurance on prominent buildings. The Terrorism Risk Insurance Act, which became law in 2002, requires insurance carriers to offer such coverage to their customers. Discussion with a competent insurance professional is suggested, especially in regard to the need for terrorism insurance, what this coverage costs, and the types of exclusions that apply.

Consultation with an insurance professional is also advisable to review the adequacy of current coverages and ensure understanding of specific requirements that relate to disaster prevention. For example, there may be a requirement to implement specific preventive measures to minimize the possibility of fire in the event water is shut off to a building during rehabilitation or other construction work.

and egress by people who are physically disabled. At a large property, management may ask for resident-volunteers who will accept responsibility for assisting elderly or disabled residents during an evacuation. In housing designed for the elderly, difficulty evacuating the building by themselves will be the rule rather than the exception.

Commercial Property   The tenancies of office buildings, shopping centers, and industrial properties are business entities. Emergency procedures must focus on the tenants' employees and may involve those employees in overseeing evacuations of their co-workers. People with physical disabilities or limitations are an increasing component of the work force, so it is important to know which workers are disabled and need assistance to evacuate the building. It may also be necessary to provide for evacuation of assistive animals. In addition to tenants' employees, retail properties have the added concern of shoppers who may include infants and small children as well as disabled persons and the elderly. At office buildings and industrial properties, visitors to the tenants' premises should also be considered. Day care centers may be located in any type of property; the presence of children in a commercial setting requires specific emergency planning for them.

Lease Insurance Requirements   The property manager may wish to conduct a comprehensive review of all of the leases to identify specifics of insurance requirements. As part of this analysis, the following questions could be asked:

- Who is responsible for insuring the leased premises?
- Who is responsible for insuring the building (to the extent that it differs from the leased premises)?
- What are the insurance amounts called for in the lease? How much damage does there have to be before the leased premises is considered uninhabitable?

**Emergency Incident Prevention—
Suggested Action Items**

- Post signs by wet floors, open holes, and defects in floors and floor coverings; have barriers available if possible.
- Avoid using extension cords.
- Do not overload electrical outlets.
- Keep all doorways, aisles, hallways, and stairs clear for easy egress.
- Store heavy items on lower shelves.
- Install clips and latches on cabinet doors.
- Secure bolts or fasteners, or both, on ventilator hoods and roof fans.
- Use tempered glass on balcony and shower doors.
- Make sure all stairwells and elevators have emergency lighting in good working order.
- Make sure stairwells include floor identification and that multiple stairwells are clearly identified by reference to a directional base (e.g., northwest vs southeast; front vs rear).
- Install fire alarm systems, fire extinguishers, smoke and heat detectors, and automatic sprinklers in accordance with local fire ordinances; carbon monoxide (CO) detectors may be mandated for residential properties.
- Change batteries in battery-operated alarms and detectors on a regular schedule; install and periodically test battery backup for hard-wired alarm systems.

- What duty does the lessee have to pay rent if the leased premises is not habitable?
- How will commercial tenants be affected from a business standpoint in the event of a large-scale natural disaster? Are they required to carry business interruption insurance?
- Does the lease require the tenant to include the landlord as an additional insured?

Also to be considered is the amount and type of general liability insurance carried by the property owner, the management company, and the tenants.

Preventive Measures

Central to any emergency procedures plan are effective measures designed to avert potential crises or minimize the effects of specific incidents. Property managers can adopt an emergency prevention strategy that will make a managed property less vulnerable to crime and vandalism and more secure in the event of a natural or manmade disaster. The accompanying box lists some actions that can be taken to prevent emergency incidents. A separate Risk Assessment Questionnaire is included at the back of this book. Security is addressed in Chapter 3.

Compliance with Applicable laws

Be sure to take into account all local laws and building codes when developing the emergency procedures plan. For example, a number of cities require buildings of a

---

Emergency Incident Prevention—Suggested Action Items (*continued*)

- Conduct fire drills annually or as required by local laws.
- Post evacuation route maps and signs in prominent locations.
- Keep all valves, switches, drains, and sewer plugs clear of sand, dirt, rocks, and debris.
- Regularly inspect housekeeping and storage areas to make sure they are clear of combustible items and hazardous materials.
- Post "no smoking" signs in accordance with local ordinances.
- Enforce "no smoking" ordinances. (Where smoking is allowed—e.g., designated areas in commercial buildings—instruct maintenance staff to never empty ashtrays into wastebaskets; conversely, never dispose of paper in ashtrays.)
- Keep all vehicles fueled and in good repair.
- Report any abandoned cars in the building's parking lot to the appropriate authorities.
- Maintain a comprehensive profile of all critical utility controls and system activators (e.g., maps showing locations of valves and on/off controls). Keep these areas properly secured.
- Keep an updated "as-built" drawing of the property easily accessible on the premises and in the fire control room if the building is so equipped.
- Make sure that exit signs have a backup power source to ensure visibility when needed. Test the alternative power source periodically.
- Keep emergency exit doors in proper working order.

---

certain size to have an approved emergency plan and to conduct annual fire drills. (Many municipalities require an emergency plan before a building is granted a certificate of occupancy.) Many communities require buildings to have smoke detectors and/or sprinkler systems. A City of Chicago ordinance mandates the installation of carbon monoxide detectors in residential dwellings. There may be requirements to automatically unlock fire doors to stairwells when the fire alarm is activated (if those doors are locked for security reasons).

Also determine state and local requirements for reporting emergencies and add them to your emergency procedures manual. Input from police or fire officials would be beneficial in developing evacuation plans and evaluating drills. It is important as well to establish procedures for turning over control of an emergency situation to the appropriate authorities.

Personnel Assignments

Once the manager has determined the various emergency risks for the property, the duties and responsibilities of the Emergency Management Team must be established. The Emergency Management Team carries out the emergency procedures plan at the direction of the property manager. Some or all members of the property management staff will participate on the Emergency Management Team. In office buildings and other commercial properties, tenants' employees may be asked to assume specific roles in implementing evacuation procedures. Everyone involved must have a clear understanding of their assigned duties and responsibilities.

Staff and Emergency Management Team assignments include responsibility for stocking and maintaining safety equipment and emergency supplies; covering, removing, or securing equipment; closing or barricading doors and windows; shutting down equipment; containing material spills; and performing a facility shutdown when necessary. Their responsibilities will also extend to safely evacuating occupants of the building.

Personnel will require specific training for many of these emergency assignments. Emergency training should include how and when to use fire extinguishers and other means to combat small fires and prevent fire from spreading. However, fires can easily get out of control, so the fire department should always be notified. The fire department will assume command of the situation upon its arrival.

Property Records

Successful emergency plans depend on maintaining extensive and accurate records about the property. This includes "as built" drawings that clearly show the locations of mechanical equipment, utility (electricity, water, gas) shutoffs, power mains, standpipes, emergency generators, elevators, stairwells, roof access, telephones and other communication systems, and life-safety equipment.

Ensure safekeeping of these records by storing a second set in a secure off-site location, or committing them to a computer-aided design (CAD or AutoCAD) file, and updating them as necessary. This duplicate set of records should be readily accessible so that it can be given to emergency crews if on-site records are misplaced, damaged, or otherwise not available. An alternative is to use a fireproof box or vault at or near the entrance to the building to store pertinent information. Public agencies such as fire and police departments should be provided with keys. Yet another option is to arrange for records to be held in a nearby building or storage facility. Such arrangements may be reciprocal.

In addition to paper records, having electronic backup files may be useful, especially for lists of personnel, emergency contacts and equipment, and the other contents of the property's emergency procedures manual. Consider storing an additional "master" copy on CD or on a USB flash drive that can be plugged into a laptop or other computer. Keeping a copy of the emergency procedures manual on a dedicated laptop computer or personal digital assistant (PDA) is another approach. There are also computer-aided facility management (CAFM) systems that might be considered. These modular software programs include emergency preparedness as well as leasing, operations and maintenance, and other property management functions, and they can be tailored to a property's information management needs.

A large Emergency Management Team will likely have more than one person assigned to specific positions or roles. Minimally, the team should include individuals assigned as alternates for leadership roles. Because a team leader may be alone when the emergency occurs or may even be working from a home telephone or cell phone, copies of specific records that are pertinent to the emergency plan should be distributed to leaders and alternate leaders of the primary emergency team.

A comprehensive, current listing of occupants should also be maintained. This list should indicate how many people occupy the property as residents or commercial tenants' employees, which units or suites are vacant, and which occupants may need help during an evacuation. The latter should identify individuals with disabilities and include the type of disability and level of assistance needed. It is also wise to maintain a list of occupants who may keep potentially dangerous or flammable materials on the property and what those materials are.

After-hours contacts for all occupants (residents, commercial tenants' representatives), contractors, and Emergency Management Team members are a must. Keep in mind the frequency of changes in tenancy. Occupant lists and emergency contact

Records Storage

The emergency plan and emergency procedures manual need to be available in the event of an emergency. Other property records—the business records needed for day-to-day operations—will be needed to resume operations after an emergency. These records should also be backed up and stored. Because of advances in digital technology, there are web sites where data can be stored and accessed from any computer. AmeriVault (www.amerivault.com) and Precision Online Backup (www.precisionbackup.com) are two of many examples that can be found with an Internet search for online data backup.

Managers may also wish to explore other possibilities for off-site data storage. These include use of magnetic media to back up computer data, retention of hardcopy records, or both. Information on the different methods of off-site storage and how to select a service provider using competitive bids is outlined on the web site of the Contingency Planning and Management Group at www.contingencyplanning.com/Tools/BCP Handbook/purchaseplans/offsitestorage.asp.

lists must be updated regularly, as inaccurate information can hinder actions of the management staff and could be devastating if an occupant cannot be contacted for an evacuation.

Current listings of contract services with home and cell phone numbers of contact persons can prove to be invaluable during emergencies when you have a special need. Temporary telephone services, for example, can provide vital communications; and portable sewage containment services—Porta-Potty is only one of many brand names—are merciful aids when sewage lines rupture or toilet facilities are otherwise inaccessible.

Discussion with the property's insurance carrier about emergency and recovery service providers may identify vendors the insurer knows and works with. Using those companies can save considerable time and effort in restoring the property after an emergency. Networking with other property managers is another way to identify reliable sources for emergency-related services. Otherwise, check your local Yellow Pages telephone directory and contact several potential sources for each type of service. As with any contracting, you should know who you are dealing with, what services they provide, and the approximate cost.

Emergency Equipment

Having the proper tools and equipment ready and available in an emergency can save property and lives. Equipment should be specifically designed for emergencies and capable of handling the size of building and number of occupants. It should be stocked in a location that is easily accessible by the management staff. The accompanying box (pp. 14–15) lists items that should be considered when emergency equipment is being stocked. Items should be stocked as they apply to your property's specific needs. A separate box lists the contents of a comprehensive emergency first aid kit. Members of the Emergency Management Team should be prepared to administer first aid to those who are injured and waiting for medical assistance to arrive.

Emergency Equipment and Supplies

Basic Emergency Equipment and Tools
Fire extinguishers
Portable fire escape and ordinary ladders
Auxiliary pump with hoses
Adjustable wrench and other tools
Crowbar

Personnel Safety and Protective Equipment
Plastic hard hats
Rubber boots
Safety goggles
Safety belts
Safety gloves
Reflective vests
Rain slickers
Rope
Face masks (to protect from soot and dust)
Earplugs

Emergency Lighting and Power
Flashlights with batteries
Candles and stick matches
Flares
Gasoline or propane-powered emergency generators
Fuel for auxiliary power generators

Communications Devices*
Two-way radios with extra batteries
Cellular phones
Bullhorn or megaphone
Battery-operated radio with extra batteries (ideal radio will include weather channels)

Property Cleanup and Protection
Emergency caution tape
Water evaporation spray to dry electrical contacts to prevent corrosive damage
Brooms and shovels for removing glass and debris
Wet-dry vacuum cleaner
Plywood
Barricades
Chains and locks

A comprehensive emergency procedures plan should include an inventory of emergency equipment and supplies and a schedule for checking and replacing items. For example, first aid kit items should be replenished after supplies are used. Aspirin and other items that may be ingested should be replaced when their labeled shelf life expires. Food and water should also be checked periodically for positive package seals and expiration dates; damaged and out-of-date items should be replaced.

Emergency Equipment and Supplies *(continued)*
First Aid and Personal Comfort
Emergency first aid kit†
Automatic external defibrillator (AED)
Stretcher
Collapsible wheelchair(s)
Evacuation chair(s)
Plastic bags and garbage cans for use as toilets
Cots and blankets
Bottled drinking water (for 72 hours)
Canned goods and dried food (for 72 hours)
Manual can opener
Portable stove

Adjunct Equipment / Record Keeping
Masking tape
Duct tape
Scissors or knife
Clipboard
Paper and pens
Cardboard and markers for hand-lettered signs
Emergency record-keeping forms

Planning for specific emergencies may suggest additions to this list.

* Communication technologies now include text-messaging and photographic capabilities in cell phones, making these devices increasingly useful. Personal digital assistants (PDAs) may also be useful in an emergency situation.

† Suggested contents of an emergency first aid kit are listed separately.

It is also a good idea to include a means of visually documenting damage that results from an emergency. While a video camera with a stock of videocassettes may be ideal, it may be more practical to work with a still camera. You will need a supply of film, flashbulbs, and batteries for such an item although there are disposable, single-use cameras that might serve the purpose. As an alternative, you might want to consider a digital camera with sufficient capacity to store multiple images. You may need a supply of digital storage media for the camera (e.g., floppy disks, flash sticks, CDs) if there is no internal "memory." A camera cell phone may also prove useful in an emergency. Digital photographs should be downloaded to a computer as soon as possible.

Periodic testing of installed emergency equipment (e.g., alarms, communication systems, sprinklers, and emergency lighting) should be conducted, as should verification of the location of essential keys to common area facilities and occupants' leased spaces. Keys should be properly identified as to the locks they open.

You may want to prepare an emergency checklist for the storage, care, and use of materials that are considered hazardous or may require special handling and disposal. Container labels and related material safety data sheets (MSDSs) provide guidelines. You should also know your state and local regulations for the handling of hazardous wastes generated at a property by staff, contractors, and occupants.

Contents of an Emergency First Aid Kit

Sterile adhesive bandages in various sizes
Sterile gauze pads (2″ and 4″)
Sterile roll bandages (2″ and 3″)
Latex gloves
Triangular (cloth) bandages for slings
Splints
Scissors
Tweezers
Adhesive tape
Safety pins (assorted sizes)
Soap or other cleansing agent
Betadine microbicide (liquid or packaged swabs or wipes)
Antiseptic solution
Rubbing alcohol
Moist towellettes
Antiseptic wipes
Cotton balls and cotton swabs
Thermometer
Tongue depressors
Petroleum jelly or other lubricant
Aspirin or non-aspirin pain relievers
Antidiarrheal medication
Syrup of ipecac or other recommended emetic
Activated charcoal
Chemical cold packs
Chemical hot packs
Thermal blankets
Bloodborne pathogens kit

Eye drops or eye wash and treatment for burns may be appropriate additions; consult a pharmacist or physician for recommendations. Also, preparation for specific emergencies may reveal other items to add to a first aid kit. (See discussions of types of emergencies elsewhere in this book.) Prepackaged first aid kits can be purchased, but they often need to be supplemented with specific components and to ensure adequate quantities of bandages and other items. A physician or pharmacist may be able to advise about specific quantities of materials to stockpile. To protect first aid items from dust and contamination, storage in a portable, sealable box or container is advisable.

Guidelines for creating a first aid kit can be found on the American Red Cross web site at www.redcross.org or the FEMA web site (www.fema.gov). The guidelines may only be part of preparations to address specific types of emergencies.

Several companies have developed bloodborne pathogen kits that include absorbent materials, personal protective equipment, waste disposal bags and labels, and other items to facilitate proper cleanup and disposal of spilled blood or body fluids.

Emergency Communications

Even if exhaustive preparations and emergency plans have been made, a disaster can catch even the most-prepared manager off guard. Creating the emergency plan is essential, but how that plan is implemented can affect the safety of people in the building and the amount of property damage that results. An emergency can occur at any time of the day or night. The plan should specify how information about an emergency is to be disseminated under different types of circumstances.

Note: Installation of fire alarm pull stations that sound a bell or claxon indicating a fire or other reason to evacuate the building is usually required under local fire codes. There may also be requirements for such alarms to include strobe lights as an additional signal as well as to alert hearing-impaired individuals. However, as the name implies, these types of alarms have to be "pulled" to initiate an alarm, and use of fire alarms for non-fire emergencies may be regulated under local fire codes. While smoke, fire, and heat detectors automatically sound an alarm under specific conditions related to fire, they are not viable alarms in non-fire emergencies. Because of these limitations, it is important to have planned ways to communicate emergency information to building occupants, including whether evacuation is necessary and what to do after they evacuate the building (see Chapter 4).

Alerting the Emergency Management Team   Whether informed of the emergency by an occupant, by a staff member, or through self-discovery, the property manager must act decisively. The first step is to activate the Emergency Management Team.

Team members should be equipped with an appropriate means of quick communication. Pagers, two-way radios, or cellular phones may be carried. Walkie-talkies and CB radios are other possibilities. If telephone lines and cell services are overwhelmed, walkie-talkies may be a better way to communicate within a building. During off-hours, access to an answering service may also be desirable. The answering service may be responsible to make the first calls to the property manager and other Emergency Management Team leaders. The success of the emergency plan depends on prompt and accurate notification of team members and the unimpeded flow of information among them.

Special circumstances should also be considered. A management company with widely dispersed properties may encounter a situation where property managers in a distant state are unable to contact their properties because local communications are disrupted or cell phone services are overwhelmed. However, if long-distance service is available, the manager may be able to call the management company and the company may be able to contact staff at the property directly then get back to the manager. That way information and instructions can be relayed between the manager and his or her property until local communication services are restored.

If the Emergency Management Team includes tenants' employees, the plan should provide for those individuals to be included in alerts during working hours. The roles of tenants' employees will usually be stratified (see Chapter 2), with some serving in leadership positions (floor leaders or floor wardens). To expedite alerting tenants about an emergency, it is useful to have floor wardens or other key tenant contacts sign in each day when they enter the building. In an emergency, this sign-in record will indicate which tenants have someone in the building to guide their employees to safety and which do not.

Make sure that the plan includes details about transporting staff to the emergency site and that alternate methods are available to alert staff when telephone lines are down and roads are closed. There should also be contingency plans for notifying families of property staff about the status of personnel on the premises, especially when an emergency requires search and recovery operations. The emergency procedures manual may include standard announcements to be used by the person who is disseminating information and directions to the Emergency Management Team (see Chapter 4 for more information about communications procedures.)

Alerting Building Occupants   Once alerted, the Emergency Management Team should inform the property's occupants and others on the premises that an emergency is taking place and instruct them to relocate to a place of safety. (In some emergency situations, authorities may recommend that people shelter in place. This is discussed in Chapter 23.)

The form of this communication will depend on a number of variables, most notably the type and size of the property, the occupant profile, the size of the management team, and the type of emergency. The emergency procedures plan should address who will alert which occupants and how. Again, if commercial tenants' employees are part of the Emergency Management Team, those contacts would be given specific instructions to guide their co-workers to safety.

If the property has a public address (PA) system, the designated spokesperson can announce to those on the property, or in the affected area, the emergency steps that should be taken. A PA system is even more helpful if it allows management to contact only certain areas of the building as required at different times, such as in fire drills or evacuations in which only specific locations are affected.

If there is no PA system, the team members and the property's security personnel, if available, can be assigned to notify occupants about the type of emergency and the appropriate response. Some properties establish " telephone trees" among occupants, with each person instructed to call another person or group of people.

A word of caution: Use of a PA system is not always the best means of communication. It truly depends on the emergency situation. For example, if it is known that a terrorist is in a high-rise, an announcement over the PA system could make the person flee the location. In this type of situation, a fax tree would be more appropriate because it would alert building occupants to the situation and suggest action for them to take, without the terrorist knowing about it.

Informing Ownership, Local Authorities, and Insurance Companies   In the event of an emergency, the property manager should inform the owner of the property immediately. Keeping the owner informed not only is expected in an owner-manager relationship, but also may protect the property manager from potentially dangerous miscommunications and liability.

If the owner does not actively participate in the emergency planning process, the owner should be informed about emergency plans and procedures as they are developed as well as during and after an emergency. Information to be shared includes plans for minimizing potential damage and responding to specific emergencies as well as possible outcomes from different emergency scenarios. The owner should also receive a copy of the emergency procedures manual and regular updates to it.

You should also inform local authorities (e.g., police, fire department) immediately. They will provide valuable assistance during an emergency. Many properties install a direct phone link to the fire department in case their property's alarm sounds. In some states, this is required. Similarly, many states have laws requiring fire control panels that alert either the property's engineers, if they are in the building, or an off-site monitoring service. Whoever receives the alert is responsible to contact the fire department.

When an emergency occurs, contact your insurance agent and/or the insurance carrier's claims office as soon as possible. Inform him or her that you are taking necessary measures to protect the property. Your insurance representative may advise you of specific measures to take to prevent further damage and will be better able to quickly process your claim.

Note: Many insurance companies have training materials and sample loss prevention forms they will share with their customers.

External Resources

Federal Agencies
- Federal Emergency Management Agency (FEMA)
- National Weather Service (NWS)
- U.S. Department of Homeland Security (DHS)
- U.S. Environmental Protection Agency (EPA)
- U.S. Fire Administration (USFA), part of FEMA
- Occupational Safety and Health Administration (OSHA)
- U.S. Department of Housing and Urban Development (HUD)
- U.S. Citizenship and Immigration Services (USCIS)*

State Government Agencies
- State emergency management agency
- State department of natural resources or environmental protection agency
- Civil defense department/agency
- Department of children and family services
- Department on aging

Local Government Agencies
- Department of emergency services
- Fire department
- Police department
- Bomb squad
- Department of human services/welfare
- Department of public health
- Civil defense department/agency

Private Agencies
- Hospital and/or urgent care center
- Ambulance service
- American Red Cross
- Salvation Army
- Services for the blind and disabled
- Services for senior citizens
- Child abuse and neglect services
- Suicide prevention services
- Anti-Cruelty Society or other animal welfare agencies
- Religious and charitable organizations that provide relief assistance
- Counseling services, including grief counseling

External Resources

It is very likely that some occupants will need assistance that exceeds what the property manager or the emergency team can provide, especially in a major disaster. Fortunately, a number of government, community, religious, and charitable organizations are available to assist with disaster planning and can help you and your management team prepare to survive a crisis.

These groups can provide such services as food service for emergency workers as well as the victims, emergency medical attention, temporary shelter, child protection assistance, treatment for poisoning, and psychological counseling. Repre-

---

External Resources *(continued)*

Local Yellow Pages telephone directories include separate sections listing contact information for city, state, and federal government agencies, including local contacts for state and federal agencies. Federal and state agencies may have separate departments for different categories of activities or emergencies (e.g., the U.S. EPA Department of Waste Management regarding hazardous wastes). Most major cities, individual states, and federal agencies have their own web pages on the Internet; these can be resources for specific emergency information as well as agency contacts.

Because the names of state and local agencies can vary, this list suggests the types of services likely to be sought at those levels of government. Some services may be provided in the form of a telephone hotline (e.g., a suicide hotline). The American Red Cross and the Salvation Army have local chapters in major cities and locations serving geographic areas outside the cities. In large metropolitan areas, there is likely to be some overlap among governmental agencies and private entities although they often work together to provide emergency services. (See separate discussion of the Coordinated Assistance Network.)

A great deal of weather-related disaster preparedness information is coordinated among FEMA, NWS, DHS, and the American Red Cross. Emergency-specific information from FEMA, DHS, and NWS is often available on state web sites.

Many nationwide social service agencies as well as local organizations and health care providers (physicians as well as hospitals) are listed on the Internet at the Information & Referral Resource Network (www.ir-net.com), which is a collection of links to the respective entities' web pages. Links to U.S. government agencies are also included.

Contact information for a number of federal agencies and national organizations is provided in the list of Additional Resources at the back of this book.

* Formerly the U.S. Immigration and Naturalization Service (INS); USCIS is part of the Department of Homeland Security.

---

sentatives of these organizations should be contacted when the plan is being prepared so that management knows what services are available for disaster victims. The accompanying box (pp. 19–20) provides additional information. Contact information for organizations, including local or regional contacts for federal agencies, should be included in the emergency procedures manual.

Other Considerations

There are costs involved in emergency planning and implementation. How much you spend will depend in large part on how comprehensive a plan you develop. There will be upfront costs for emergency equipment and printing of emergency procedures manuals. There will be ongoing costs for training, testing equipment, and maintaining stockpiles of things like first aid supplies, water, and foodstuffs. It may be necessary or desirable to purchase reference or training materials. A building with a complex tenancy may warrant employing an emergency planning consultant.

Coordinated Disaster Assistance

In the wake of 9/11, a number of nonprofit entities have collaborated to establish the Coordinated Assistance Network (CAN) whose aim is to share information and expedite assistance to people in a disaster. The founders include five national organizations:

- Alliance of Information & Referral Systems (www.airs.org)
- American Red Cross (www.redcross.org)
- National Voluntary Organizations Active in Disaster (www.nvoad.org)
- The Salvation Army (www.salvationarmy.org)
- United Way of America (www.unitedway.org)

plus two local New York organizations:

9/11 United Services Group (www.9-11usg.org)
Safe Horizon (www.safehorizon.org)

A special telephone number has been provided by the United Way and AIRS as a centralized contact point. In communities participating in this initiative, people need only dial 211 to register for disaster relief. There are 128 active 211 systems in 28 states, and the number continues to grow. (See www.211.org/status/html.) Alternatively, the relief agencies can be contacted directly through their respective disaster lines.

    The agencies use one central data base, so disaster victims need only register once. Personnel who take the registration give out direct phone numbers for individual agencies responding to the particular disaster. Agency personnel can access the data base; they do not need to collect the victim's information over and over again. This means specific assistance can be provided more quickly.

There could be capital expenses to upgrade existing systems (e.g., sprinklers; fire doors) or to install new ones to comply with local codes. It may be desirable to establish accounting codes for specific expenses related to development of the emergency plan and emergency procedures manual (e.g., reference and resource materials), printing the manual and updating its contents, purchase of emergency equipment and supplies, and expenses likely to be incurred in responding to emergencies (boardup and other related services).

    There are also potential liabilities to consider. Actions taken in an emergency may cause or result in injury despite someone's intention to be helpful. Inadequate or improper training may render an emergency plan ineffective. These are among the reasons to clarify insurance coverages and to seek guidance from proper authorities such as local police and fire departments and federal agencies. Also, an attorney can advise whether there are laws regarding public access or other issues that might affect your actions and/or liabilities in an emergency. Liabilities may arise if you do *not* have an emergency plan in place or do not implement a plan to protect people and property. You should also find out if your state has a Good Samaritan law (see Chapter 19).

    Another way to limit liability is to limit the scope of the emergency plan. You might develop specific procedures related to the building and its equipment, fire and life safety issues, and evacuation procedures. However, instead of preparing comprehensive plans for building occupants, you might encourage them to develop their own plans and procedures for other (non-fire) emergencies. Commercial tenants should have their own emergency plans for their businesses so that they can take care of their equipment in an emergency and resume operations afterward. You might consider suggesting to them some of the resources identified in *Before Disaster Strikes* to facilitate their individual planning. They should also have plans for communicating with their employees' families regarding the status or condition of personnel who are on the premises during an emergency. Residents should make their own preparations for contacting family members, supplies of food and water, a designated place for family members to gather, and alternative shelter. The American Red Cross, National Weather Service, and FEMA web sites include information on emergency planning for individuals and families.

An emergency plan will only work if the information in it is current. Staff assignments to the Emergency Management Team will change as employees are promoted or leave the organization. The same factors affect lists of tenant contacts in commercial buildings. If equipment is changed or relocated, the particulars in the emergency plan must be updated accordingly. The plan may also need to be revised from time to time at the direction of the fire department or other authorities.

The test of an emergency plan is how it works in actual practice. After an emergency has passed, the property manager should assemble the Emergency Management Team and review their response to the emergency, not only to determine which emergency procedures worked successfully and which did not, but also to identify needs that had not been anticipated. This will allow the team to respond to future emergencies more efficiently, possibly minimizing the extent of bodily injury and property damage.

The Basics of
an Emergency Plan

2

The
Emergency Management Team

Critical to emergency planning is assembling the Emergency Management Team. This team will be called upon to carry out your property's emergency procedures plan. The team members are appointed to protect and safeguard your property and the lives of the people occupying it by performing their assigned responsibilities before, during, and after an emergency. They should be equipped to respond to various life- and property-threatening crises and prepared to help restore normal operations as soon as possible. Most—perhaps all—of the team members will be property staff. They know the property, where they can and should turn for help, and how to respond quickly to unexpected and dangerous conditions.

Note: Readers who would like additional specific guidance in structuring an emergency management team may wish to seek out information and training on the Incident Command System (ICS) developed by the National Fire Service and adopted for use by business and industry as well as government. The ICS is built around five major management activities—command, operations, planning, logistics, and finance. A brief description of the ICS can be found in "The Incident Command System: A Proven Tool for the Management of Emergency Operations," published online by the International Foundation for Protection Officers (IFPO) at www.ifpo.org/articlebank/incident_command_system.htm. The Emergency Management Institute offers interactive web-based training in the Incident Command System that includes an examination. It is also possible to print hard copies of instructional materials for self study and take an examination online. The interactive course and printed materials can be accessed on the Internet at www.training.fema.gov/emiweb/is/is195.asp.

Assembling the Team

Usually the manager of the property will lead the Emergency Management Team. However, a property manager who is unable to handle emergency situations should not assume this leadership role. In some situations, the property manager may delegate this duty to another staff member—e.g., an on-site manager or chief engineer. Throughout this book references to the team leader assume this role is performed by the property manager.

There should be a clear line of authority between the team leader and the team members. The team leader should be available to team members at all times and have an understanding of the property's layout and emergency procedures plan in order to be able to provide clear and decisive direction at a moment's notice.

The team leader assigns the appropriate duties and responsibilities to each team member. (Note: A team mission statement may be created to reinforce the company's commitment to emergency management.)

The Emergency Management Team will carry out the emergency plan and take immediate action to assist occupants, lead them to safety, and help secure the property. Depending on the size and staffing of the property, this team should consist of the property manager/team leader, the on-site management staff, the administrative and maintenance staff, and, in some cases, occupants of the property. In a high-rise office building, for example, tenants' employees may be involved in evacuation procedures. The types of roles and responsibilities assigned to tenants' employees may include some or all of the following:

- *Fire warden or area captain*—This person coordinates the evacuation process for a particular floor or a specific area of the building. An assistant fire warden or area captain may also be appointed so there will be a backup if the primary person is not available.

- *Floor leader*—This person makes sure everyone knows where stairwells are and is responsible for orderly evacuation of his or her work area. The assigned individual may represent a single tenant on a floor or an entire multi-tenant floor. In some situations, there may be more than one floor leader for a tenant or floor, or the floor leader and fire warden functions may be combined.

- *Searcher*—There is usually more than one searcher who makes sure all areas of a floor, including rest rooms, have been evacuated. The emergency procedures manual may require those who work in private offices to close their doors as they leave, but this responsibility may be assigned to the searchers. To indicate that a room or enclosed area has been checked, a Post-it® note or other easily removable adhesive label may be applied on the closed door about 12 inches above the floor.

- *Stairwell monitor*—On each floor, there should be one monitor for each stairwell to ensure that people evacuating a floor stay to one side so that firefighters can also use the stairwells. These monitors should prevent people from entering a stairwell that is filled with smoke, directing them to another way out.

- *Elevator monitor*—In a building with multiple banks of elevators, it may be appropriate to assign a monitor on each floor for each bank of elevators that stops there. This monitor is responsible to direct people *away from* the elevators. It is important to keep people from entering elevators because (1) they might not work at all or (2) a working elevator might stop on a burning floor because a heat-sensitive call button was activated. In an emergency, elevator service should be stopped immediately, and the elevators should be returned to the ground floor for use by firefighters (if appropriate).

- *Handicap aide*—A tenant that employs a number of disabled workers may need several handicap aides; on a floor where there are no disabled workers, there may be no need for such an aide. Handicap aides are responsible for moving disabled workers to safe areas in stairwells where they can be rescued by firefighters. Building management should ask tenants to provide detailed information about their employees who are disabled—including their names, the location of their work space in the tenant's premises, and the nature of their disability—to assist in emergency evacuation planning for the tenant and for the building. (Note: Information about disabilities should be considered confidential and made available to members of the Emergency Management Team only.)

BUILDING EMERGENCY RESPONSE TEAM ASSIGNMENTS

Floor	Tenant Name	Area Captain	Asst. Captain	Searcher(s)	Stairwell Monitor	Elevator Monitor	Handicap Aid

An example of a form that can be used to list names of tenants and their employees who have been given emergency response assignments is provided on the previous page.

While titles may vary regionally, the roles noted here are representative. It is best to work with the local fire department in identifying the roles and responsibilities of tenants' employees who will be involved with emergency evacuation of a specific building. The local fire department may recommend additional or different roles for them, and the department's guidance should be followed. (Note: Although this approach is more likely to be used in a high-rise office building, the same principle may be applied at a large residential property where resident volunteers might assume specific roles as appropriate.)

Tenants' employees who are assigned to specific roles will need to be trained—and periodically retrained—so they will be prepared to respond when evacuation is necessary. They also need to be clearly identified as team members during an evacuation. Colored T-shirts or baseball caps with the property name and the name of the team have been used successfully. Color-coded vests might also be considered. If Emergency Management Team will be used exclusively to refer to property management staff members, tenants' employees might be referred to as a special emergency evacuation team.

To expedite evacuation of multitenant floors or tenant offices with multiple entrances, a member of the evacuation team should have a master key that will open all the corridor doors on the floor. In buildings in some areas, all doors to the common or core areas that are kept locked (e.g., stairwell doors for security reasons) must open when the fire alarm is activated. This is accomplished by using electromagnetic locks that are wired directly to the fire alarm system for such activation. The locks will also open when electric current to the door lock is cut (e.g., a power outage). Stairwell doors, lobby doors, and sometimes corridor doors to tenant suites are required to open this way. (Interior office doors and locks are the tenant's responsibility.)

The emergency plan should also identify a support team that comprises certain specialists who will not respond to every emergency at the property but may be called on for backup assistance. This team may include some or all of the following:

- Contractors and suppliers, including electricians, plumbers, elevator and HVAC contractors, boardup services, and glass companies
- Disaster recovery contractors specifically trained and equipped to minimize loss and fast-track restoration of the building and contents
- The building's architect and structural, mechanical, and electrical engineers
- Utility company representatives
- Police and fire department representatives, possibly including hazardous materials and bomb/arson specialists
- Representatives from the local building department
- Contract security services
- Representatives from the property's insurance company
- Attorneys for the property owner and manager
- Resident and/or commercial tenant representatives
- Government and charitable agencies
- A consultant or representative from a disaster restoration firm
- A professional public relations representative
- A representative of the firm whose communication systems and equipment are used in the building
- The on-site staffs of adjacent properties

At large properties, security personnel may be employed directly. In which case, additional (outside) security may be needed in an emergency. However, if security personnel on site are contract workers, the contractual arrangements should be checked to ensure that those workers are permitted to have an emergency response role. Also check whether the contract prohibits you from contracting elsewhere for additional security personnel in an emergency situation. If after-hours janitorial services are provided by contract workers, those workers will need emergency evacuation training for their own safety and as an adjunct to the Emergency Management Team. It may be necessary to call upon them to help ensure that any tenants' employees working in the building after hours are evacuated safely.

Duties of Team Members

Each team member should be assigned specific duties, and the duties should be explained in the property's emergency procedures manual. Remember that not all team members may be available when an emergency arises, so each individual should understand the entire emergency plan. One member may be alone to direct the action during an emergency until the team can be assembled.

Members of the team will carry out any number of important duties, such as conducting evacuations, cooperating with public agencies (fire, police, etc.), communicating with building occupants, or providing first aid to injured parties. Again, it is important that each member of the team not only know his or her duties in an emergency, but also be familiar with the duties of other team members in case he or she must assume another's responsibilities when an emergency occurs.

The property manager, as team leader, will be charged with directing the actions of the entire team. The team leader should therefore know what actions to take for each type of emergency and what tasks have been assigned or need to be assigned to various team members. During an emergency, it is important for all communications to flow from the leader, and that all team members remain in contact with the team leader for further instructions.

In addition, the Emergency Management Team should include assignments of alternates for each team member/role. The emergency procedures manual should state who is in charge if the property manager/team leader is unavailable and then assign alternates for each position on the team.

Training the Team

Once the emergency procedures for the property have been written and the team has been assembled, the team must be trained to carry out the plan. The plan must be reviewed, studied, and practiced by the members of the team in order for them to respond effectively to emergencies. Training begins with a tour of the property conducted by the property manager and/or building engineer. Although many team members might think they know the property well, it is unlikely that they do, and during the property tour they should be encouraged to think of the property in light of crisis situations.

Attention should be focused on the features that are of particular relevance in an emergency, such as the overall layout of the property; the configuration of individual floors: the location of stairwells, entrances, and exits; roof and basement access; mechanical equipment; emergency equipment; stored chemicals and hazardous waste; location of essential keys; telephones and other communications equipment; and life-safety equipment. It is vital that team members know where utility shutoffs are located and how to use them. Labeling switches allows for easy identification. Team members should know where fire extinguishers are located and how to operate them, as well as the locations of fire alarms, emergency telephones, and other emergency supplies and equipment. In buildings with elevators, team members should know where elevator controls are located and what is needed to manually shutdown elevators and return them to the lobby level if this becomes necessary. They also need to know whom to contact to dispose of hazardous materials. Knowledge of the area surrounding the building (streets, parks, alternate access routes) is also essential to their training.

As part of the training process, the property manager should invite representatives of the fire and/or police departments to provide information on evacuation procedures, how to safely move disabled and elderly persons, and how to keep children calm and cooperative during a crisis. Training should also be provided on specific emergency procedures—i.e., how some procedures, including evacuation, may differ because of the type of emergency. There may be specific seminars and courses offered by outside entities that can be considered as well—for example, first aid training from the American Red Cross. An Emergency Management Team may meet periodically to review and discuss changes to the emergency plan and to specific emergency procedures in order to maintain a constant sense of mission and ensure that procedural instructions are current.

To ensure easy access to written emergency response procedures, provide *two copies* of the plan to all team members and on-site personnel (one copy to be kept in their work areas and one at their homes). It may be desirable to have information accessible in digital form that staff can download to a PDA or laptop computer.

Having information available in an abbreviated form may also be desirable. At some properties, management staff are given wallet-sized cards containing key emergency procedures information, including evacuation routes and points of assembly for building evacuees. They may be asked to keep these cards with the cards that identify them as staff members. If such cards are prepared, it may be desirable or appropriate to distribute them to all building occupants.

To ensure that occupants are aware of the property's emergency procedures, refer to them in property newsletters and mailings and include the information on the property web site (if there is one). The frequency of such communications depends upon many factors, including the size, type, and location of the building. For instance, the management staff and occupants of a high-rise building may need more frequent training than the manager and merchants at a small strip center. It may also be appropriate to offer periodic presentations from the fire department or police. Respectively these might cover fire prevention and fire safety or personal safety and security. These types of communications are in addition to emergency procedures information provided to occupants in a separate handbook (see Chapter 8).

Drills

Scheduled drills enable team members to instinctively respond to emergencies and build confidence within the Emergency Management Team and among the building's occupants. In addition, drills give the property manager the opportunity to evaluate the emergency plan, identify weaknesses, and make corrections before a real-life emergency arises.

Initially, drills should be announced in advance to give team members a chance to walk through their roles. Later, the property manager may schedule surprise drills to evaluate team performance. Separate drills can be scheduled for building occupants and the Emergency Management Team.

Many municipalities have ordinances covering practice evacuations and other safety procedures, including how often drills should be conducted. These ordinances may only apply to buildings of a certain size or height (e.g., mid- and high-rise). Local ordinances regarding evacuations and practice drills should be checked to ensure that plans for your managed property comply with them. Emergency procedures requirements may be posted on a city's web site.

The property manager should meet with the building's occupants to explain the significance of practice evacuations and other drills. By encouraging the cooperation of everyone in the building and stressing what could happen if occupants are not prepared for emergencies, the manager can make these drills a valuable part of a building's emergency procedures plan.

Drill Performance Review

Immediately after an emergency drill, the Emergency Management Team should be assembled to critique the plan and the team's performance. Questions you may wish to consider in your evaluation include:

- Do members of the Emergency Management Team understand their respective responsibilities? Have new team members been adequately trained?
- Are there problem areas and resource shortfalls? If so, they must be identified and addressed.
- Is the plan reflecting structural changes in the facility (including the leased premises)?
- Are photographs, blueprints of the property, and other records and documents up to date?
- Are the names, telephone numbers, and responsibilities of the team members up to date?
- Does the plan consider ongoing changes in the occupant profile?

The property manager should encourage everyone to speak freely at these review sessions—to point out areas that need improvement and to applaud good performance. If parts of the plan did not work effectively, the plan should be revised and the staff should be retrained accordingly. It could also be beneficial to have a "suggestion box" for others in the building who participated in the drill but were not members of the Emergency Management Team; they may have observed something about which the team should know.

In addition to evaluating and possibly modifying your emergency procedures plan after each training drill, it is imperative to evaluate it under the following circumstances:

- After each actual emergency,
- When personnel responsibilities change (e.g., via promotion or reassignment),
- When the layout of the facility changes,
- When policies and procedures change, and
- When annual audits of the property's maintenance and emergency equipment are conducted.

Some cities stage mock disasters with mass casualties to test their emergency response capabilities—fire department, police department, 911 system, paramedics, trauma centers, etc.—and help work out problems with responses. Usually there is some level of civilian participation as volunteers (victims). It may be worthwhile to participate in such events to observe how different types of emergency situations are likely to be handled. If your city does this, it could be helpful in training and evaluating your property's Emergency Management Team.

3

Security

Security is an important component of emergency preparedness because any type of emergency situation is likely to make the property vulnerable to breaches of security. If the building does not have any security devices or programs—door locks are a given—it may be desirable to perform a security survey or hire a professional to conduct a security audit.

For purposes of emergency planning, the objective of a security survey should be to identify vulnerabilities that can create opportunities for criminal activity as well as anticipate vulnerabilities that are likely to arise in the context of an emergency. Some questions to consider are:

- How will security be maintained for the building and its occupancy in a fire? An earthquake? A weather emergency?
- Are there preventive strategies that should be implemented now?
- What strategies should be incorporated into emergency procedures?

If a property employs a large staff, it may be sufficient to modify personnel assignments during emergencies. For example, garage attendants may have a security role in controlling egress during an evacuation. When additional security presence is needed (e.g., during periods of heightened alert), security personnel may serve as "greeters" in office building lobbies. After an emergency, it may be necessary or appropriate to hire security guards to patrol damaged portions of the building until reconstruction can be started and then to protect the site during construction (see Chapter 5). Specific security needs will depend on the type of emergency and the security risks that can accompany it. A small staff may need to be supplemented to provide the needed level of security during and after an emergency.

The goal of any security program is risk reduction. The level of risk and, thus, the security needs of a property will vary with the size, design, and type of building, as well as with the property's occupancy and uses, its location and physical construction, and the value of the possessions on the premises. In mid- to high-rise office buildings, for example, a security program is primarily designed to control entry to the building. In a regional mall, on the other hand, the objective of the security program is a safe and pleasant shopping experience for tenants' customers. As part of emergency planning, it is a good idea for the property manager to determine what security measures are needed or need to be added.

A security system can take many forms. It may rely on humans or on technology or both. It can include some or all of the following:

- On-site guards
- Drive-by patrols
- Fences and gates around the grounds
- Landscaping
- Specific indoor and outdoor lighting
- Intrusion alarm systems
- Electronic (card or other devices) access controls
- Closed circuit television (CCTV)
- Biometric scanning (fingerprint/handprint, retina)
- Remote Internet video monitoring
- Community or neighborhood watch programs

Security is also a matter of perception. It is important to incorporate security consciousness in the training of maintenance personnel, and building occupants should be encouraged to assume responsibility for their personal security.

Evaluate Existing Security

Planning for security requires the property manager to identify existing security measures and evaluate their effectiveness, preferably in consultation with a security professional. If existing security is determined to be insufficient, other alternatives could be pursued.

As noted previously, security is partly perception. A survey of property staff, building occupants (residents, commercial tenants' employees), and others (retail customers, service contractors) can be used to determine in which areas of the property they feel most comfortable and in which areas they think there are gaps in security. For instance, users of the premises may feel less at ease in underground parking garages than in building lobbies. Efforts can be made to better secure areas perceived to pose a risk.

Establish or Enhance a Security Program

There are many steps a manager can take to safeguard a property. For instance, since lighting is one of the most important components of a good security system, common areas both inside and outside of a building should be checked regularly for inadequate lighting, no lighting at all, and overgrown landscaping that can create hiding places. Periodic inspections should be performed during the evening, which is the optimum time for identifying lighting deficiencies.

Managers of commercial properties may wish to consider landscaping as a deterrent. Barberry, holly, or other dense, prickly shrubs can inflict painful scratches on potential intruders.

Many newer buildings have state-of-the art lockup systems for all exterior access points along with closed-circuit television (CCTV) monitored by security staff. Electronic access control systems using cards or other devices can be an excellent deterrent to unwanted visitors gaining access to a property as well as unauthorized move-outs by occupants.

Identification (ID) cards that include pictures should be considered when there is a sizeable management staff and when the occupancy includes large numbers of people. While picture IDs might be required for management staff only at residential properties, in a commercial building they may be advisable for all tenants' employees. They may also be used for visitors to the property. In any emergency, but especially in a terrorist incident, picture IDs will quickly differentiate people who work in the building from those who do not.

Maintenance personnel, whether they are employees of the property management company or contracted, may be regarded as part of the building's security awareness program. They can be encouraged to report to management any trespassers and suspicious activities they observe on the premises.

The pages at the end of this chapter list a number of actions that can be taken to enhance property security. The property manager should review the list, determine which items are appropriate for the property, and implement them as needed. The following should also be considered in regard to premises security.

- Include security as part of regular inspections of both buildings and leased premises.
- Promptly repair or replace security devices that are inoperable.
- Visibility of staff, in particular maintenance personnel going about their work, can be a deterrent to trespassing and break-ins.
- Enforcement of the lease can control who is on the property and how leased premises are used.
- Address security issues in the property's rules and regulations.
- Encourage occupants (residents, commercial tenants' employees) to be alert to their surroundings and to report suspicious vehicles or persons to management.

Individuals who manage properties where government agencies lease space should be aware that the Government Services Administration (GSA) has established specific requirements for security in buildings occupied by federal entities, whether the space is government-owned or leased. *GSA Security Resource Guide: A Guide to Federal Security* lists the standards that apply and outlines the requirements for Occupant Emergency Organizations (OEOs), which each agency and facility must have. It also includes Internet locations for related documents. The *Guide* can be downloaded from the Internet at www.usda.gov/da/physicalsecurity/gsa.htm.

Conduct Security Audits

Once a security program is implemented, it should be evaluated regularly to ensure that it has evolved with the property's and the occupants' changing needs. It may be desirable to hire an independent consultant to conduct an analysis or audit of the security at a property, identify vulnerabilities, and suggest actions that can be taken or measures to be implemented to help minimize risk and liability.

Note: In-depth discussion of specific security measures is beyond the scope of this book. Information on security issues, strategies, and liabilities can be found in *Spotlight on Security for Real Estate Managers* published by the Institute of Real Estate Management.

Suggested Security Action Items

Landscaping
- Plan landscaping so that it does not provide hiding places for would-be thieves or assailants.
- Use prickly shrubs to discourage trespassers and would-be burglars.
- Never plant shrubs or foliage in front of windows such that the presence of a person or the actions of a potential criminal may be hidden from the view of passersby.
- Keep all shrubbery pruned and even.
- Keep grounds clear of ladders and other tools that could aid a thief.
- Keep property clear of debris.

Doors, Windows, and Other Openings
- Confirm that each door and window has working locks.
- Check door and window frames for looseness and rotting.
- Install burglar-resistant glass.
- Do not heavily screen or bar low windows unless an emergency release mechanism is also installed.
- If appropriate, install electrical devices that will set off an alarm if windows are broken or doors are forced open.
- If appropriate, have entrance doors made of shatterproof glass that is not frosted or obstructed by curtains.
- Install hinges on the inside of exterior doors.
- Secure all building openings such as air ducts, skylights, hatchways, and transoms.

Lighting
- Ensure that alleys, the rear of the property, garages and parking lots, loading docks, and other isolated exterior areas are well-lighted.
- Ensure that stairwells are well-lighted inside buildings and parking garages.
- Ensure that sufficient inventories of light bulbs and batteries are stocked and available for battery-powered lighting systems, flashlights, and radios.
- Establish an emergency generator or battery-powered lighting system in common areas as backup in case of power failure.
- Leave night lights on throughout the property.
- Protect light bulbs with shatterproof lenses or recess the lighting so that bulbs cannot be easily unscrewed or smashed.
- Have working flashlights available to distribute to each management team member.

Key Security
- Never label keys; use a code if necessary.
- Mark all keys "Do Not Duplicate" to avoid having copies made.
- To avoid unauthorized duplication, obliterate any numbers on keys that identify standard key blanks.
- Keep an accurate record of persons who have a copy of each key. Have only one person in charge of distributing, collecting, and keeping all keys.
- Collect keys from terminated or transferring employees.

Suggested Security Action Items *(continued)*
- Do not leave keys in filing cabinets once the cabinets are opened.
- Consider investing in a key control system and enforcing it.
- Change locks and combinations frequently.
- Install electronic (card or transponder activated) access systems.

Alarm, Intercom, and Closed-Circuit Television (CCTV) Systems
- Check all alarm systems regularly. Verify proper operation (audible tones or other sounds, visible flashing lights, etc.).
- Post prominent notices of alarm systems as a deterrent.
- Regularly test building intercom systems to ensure that the connection is clear and free from static.
- Furnish stairwell doors with alarms if appropriate.
- If appropriate, install visitor call phones, gate houses, and CCTV cameras with video-cassette recording devices (VCRs) in residential properties; install peepholes in unit doors.
- Monitor remote and little-used entryways and/or high-activity areas by CCTV cameras with VCRs when and where appropriate.
- Do not announce security measures that are not actually in use.
- Do not use "dummy" security devices (e.g., cameras).
- Consider wireless monitoring technology using the Internet or local area network (LAN) systems.

Elevators
- Program elevators to stop at the lobby level before going down to or after coming up from the basement or other lower levels of the building.
- Program elevators to bypass uninhabited floors.
- Connect elevator stop buttons to an alarm bell and a security or monitoring station.
- Install 24-hour monitored phones in elevators.
- If appropriate, install mirrored walls in elevator cars so a person can see the whole interior before entering.
- Keep all elevator lighting in working condition.

Employee and Visitor Identification
- Require that all visitors present identification.
- Require that all visitors check in with a security guard and state the nature of their business on the property.
- Establish a system of employee/visitor identification badges or building passes when lobby security is present.
- Establish a system of employee sign-in and sign-out sheets for after business hours when a lobby guard is present (e.g., after 6:30 p.m. and before 7:00 a.m. Monday through Friday and 24 hours a day on Saturdays, Sundays, and holidays).
- Consider using an electronic access system with cards that can control entry after hours as well as during regular business hours.
- Establish a system for identifying vehicles of occupants and visitors on the property.
- Establish an authorization system for removing property from the building.
- Consider including electronic (biometric) systems for personnel identification; this can reduce or eliminate paper records.

Suggested Security Action Items *(continued)*

Resident and Commercial Tenant Education

- Publish a newsletter for employees, residents, and commercial tenants updating security practices and procedures.
- Alert occupants to any new procedures as they are adopted. Seek occupants' advice regarding safety measures.
- Regularly conduct professional safety meetings, focusing on such topics as self-defense, evacuation of the building, and cardiopulmonary resuscitation (CPR).
- Distribute seasonal reminders regarding soliciting and protection of personal property against sneak thieves, pickpockets, and purse snatchers.
- Encourage occupants to be aware of normal patterns of activity and to report suspicious people and activities to management.

Safes, Vaults, and Cash Registers

- Place safes in well-lighted locations that are easily observed by security cameras.
- Anchor safes to the floor and cash registers to their stands.
- Leave empty cash drawers and safes open.

Miscellaneous

- Lock desks in offices and workstations where the capability exists.
- Encourage staff and occupants to report suspicious-looking persons.
- Control access to the building.
- Paint floor numbers boldly on the stair side of hall exit doors or on the wall next to the door.
- Keep inventory records of equipment and possessions, listing a description of each item, its serial number, and any identifying marks. Assign specific inventory numbers as appropriate.
- Paint the property in light colors.
- Post emergency phone numbers for staff and occupants.
- Do not keep large amounts of cash on the premises.
- Make daily bank deposits, but alter the time these trips are made so they are not predictable by observers.
- Prosecute all offenders and inform residents, commercial tenants, staff, and contractors that the offender was prosecuted.

4

Evacuation

Evacuation of a building needs to be carefully planned. Evacuation plans should be designed to quickly move occupants out of the building using stairwells rather than elevators. In a fire, the fire department may use elevators to move firefighters and their equipment or simply shut the elevators down. An exception to this might be to operate one elevator to accommodate disabled individuals, if this practice is feasible. Members of the Emergency Management Team should be familiar with the building elevator controls so they know which ones can be operated independently. In a power outage, the elevators will not work unless there is auxiliary power from a backup generator with sufficient capacity to operate the elevators along with other vital building systems A backup generator may only power one elevator. A system failure or an accident may preclude using some or all of the elevators in a building.

Property managers are likely to encounter the need to evacuate their properties at some time in their careers. The Emergency Management Team must be prepared to evacuate the premises at any time, whether this is done as a practice drill involving the building's occupants or in response to an actual emergency.

The evacuation procedures for a property will depend on such variables as the type of property, its size, the number of occupants, the occupant profile, and the number of visitors. As a rule, larger and more complex buildings require more detailed evacuation plans. For example, a four-story residential building will be easier to evacuate than a high-rise; an open-air shopping center will be easier to evacuate than an enclosed mall.

Although every property is unique, all evacuation plans must be prepared to address five significant issues:

1. When to evacuate
2. Communications/getting the word out
3. Initiating and managing the evacuation
4. Returning to the property
5. Drills

A primary consideration will be evacuation of the building in the event of a fire. Those who respond to a fire—firefighters, often including a fire chief—will usually assume authority and order a full or partial evacuation based on what they know. However, the property manager or a designated person on site may have to assume this responsibility until the fire department has arrived. The emergency plan should provide guidelines for deciding whether a partial or full evacuation is appropriate.

Work with local authorities—e.g., the fire department—to develop an appropriate fire evacuation plan. When the plan is finished, review it in light of non-fire emergencies. Some procedures may not apply in every situation. Also, you may need to add specific procedures or guidelines to address unique situations related to weather emergencies and other natural events (e.g., earthquakes).

When to Evacuate

Any number of emergencies may signal the need to evacuate a building. These include a fire, a flood, an explosion, a bomb threat, a hazardous materials spill, or an act of violence committed on the property. Even a violent storm may necessitate evacuation. Whatever the emergency, the decision to evacuate should not be made lightly or in a panic.

Many emergencies, of course, do not require evacuation of the property. For those that do, partial evacuation may be sufficient. For example, a fire in a janitor's closet on the second floor of an office building may require evacuation of only the first three floors. Also bear in mind that evacuation does not necessarily mean that occupants must vacate the building. In the preceding example, for instance, those occupants on the third floor and below might be asked to leave the building while those on the fourth floor might be moved up to the fifth floor until the fire has been extinguished.

The property manager should consult the local fire or police department to determine the correct delegation of authority during an evacuation. A fire on the premises may require the order to evacuate to be issued by a fire department representative on the site. A bomb threat or criminal activity may require guidance from the police department or bomb squad, respectively.

Note: Often, but not always, the bomb squad will be a part of the police department and any hazardous materials (hazmat) response team will be part of the fire department. Be sure you know which authority is responsible for these important roles and include that information in your emergency contacts list.

Communicating Evacuation Orders

The most important step in evacuation is communicating to the property's occupants and the management staff that they must evacuate the building. A communications program or system should be designed so it can be used to report emergencies to the proper authorities, warn personnel on site of danger, and keep building occupants and off-duty management personnel and tenants' employees informed of the progress and severity of the situation. A building-wide communications system is especially important in large properties to coordinate response actions and to keep in contact with all parties affected by an emergency situation (see Chapter 1).

How an evacuation order is communicated depends on the type of property and the type of emergency. For example, large shopping centers and modern office buildings often have PA systems that can be used to broadcast evacuation orders and instructions. If there is no PA system, however, it is important to have an equally effective means of delivering evacuation orders and other emergency instructions.

The following suggestions may be helpful in planning and implementing an effective emergency communications program:

- Consider the impact on a property and its occupants if standard communications systems became inoperable, and prioritize the alternative methods of

Evacuation Orders

Different types of emergencies may require evacuation of part or all of a building. A crime scene may involve the Federal Bureau of Investigation (FBI), the Bureau of Alcohol, Tobacco, and Firearms (BATF), or state police in addition to local law enforcement. In civil disturbances or weather disasters, the National Guard may be called on to provide additional security. These authorities may also be empowered to order evacuation of a property.

Local jurisdictions may suggest or require specific evacuation procedures. The type of property or its size and complexity may warrant a specific response pattern. For example, an alarm may be a signal to evacuate, or people may be asked to assemble in a specific place on a floor (e.g., in a corridor) to await instructions whether or not to leave the building. In some emergency situations, authorities may instruct against evacuation, asking instead for the population to shelter in place (see Chapter 23). Emergency procedures should provide for evacuation procedures to be modified according to the type of emergency. They should also provide instructions for staff and occupants to shelter in place when that is appropriate.

communication to be employed in an emergency. Procedures should be established for restoring communications systems that may become inoperable. Battery backup can cure some communications equipment problems. Communications equipment vendors can provide advice about their products' response and recovery capabilities. Potential backup communications systems include messenger services, wireless and/or cellular telephones, point-to-point private phone lines, amateur (short-wave or ham) radio operators, satellites, high-frequency radios, and even hand signals. Wireless text messaging devices, walkie-talkies (for short distances only), and PDAs may also have a role along with the Internet. Some choices may depend on what equipment and services are available and/or workable in your area.

- Determine which sources will be used for communications between emergency responders and the property manager as well as communications with property employees, building occupants, neighboring businesses, and the media and the public at large.

- Include plans for communicating with families of staff members and building occupants in an emergency, and encourage individuals to consider how they would communicate with their families and each other in case of separation. Some properties arrange for an out-of-town contact for everyone to call in case of an emergency. It may be possible to arrange in advance for a communications trailer containing banks of telephones to be brought to the site in an emergency if such service is available locally.

- Maintain an updated list of outside emergency contacts (telephone numbers, pager numbers if available, and addresses) such as the fire and police departments, a local hospital or trauma center, a private ambulance service, the American Red Cross, and the Salvation Army. Also include the Federal Emergency Management Agency (FEMA) office in your area. State and local governments may have their own emergency management departments or agencies, and these entities should be included as well. Notification must be made immediately to appropriate local government agencies when any emergency has the potential to affect public health and safety.

• Ensure that staff and occupants are familiar with the property's warning system. Have a distinct and recognizable audible signal to be used *only in emergencies requiring evacuations,* and test this warning system periodically. If necessary to make provision for hearing-impaired individuals, a flashing light or other visual cue should be added to the audible signal. (Note: Local fire codes may require alternatives to fire alarms when evacuation is for a non-fire emergency.)

• Include building occupants in the communications network by establishing a call system or "telephone tree." For example, using a "three-call" system, each person calls three people, who in turn call three others, and so on. In this way, all residents or all commercial tenants' employees can be notified in a very short time. It may be possible to program a computerized phone system to send an automated broadcast phone message to all the numbers simultaneously.

• Decide in advance the wording for each message to be communicated to building occupants. The wording of the evacuation announcement should be included in the emergency procedures manual and posted at your previously designated command station for easy reference. In many situations, the announcement will be simple and straightforward. In some situations, however, management may not want to disclose the reason for the evacuation (e.g., a bomb threat).

In an actual emergency, the decision to evacuate and the announcement of evacuation directions should be made by a professional emergency responder (e.g., fire chief, police officer) unless the outside response has been delayed. In that case, the property manager may have to use his or her judgment, deciding whether or not to order an evacuation based on the information available at the time.

Evacuating the Occupants

It is important to establish a nearby location where people evacuated from your building can gather. This might be outdoors, but an indoor location may be preferable. Managers of commercial properties may wish to plan with individual tenants where their employees will assemble after an evacuation to minimize confusion and avoid overcrowding of limited space.

Companies that manage more than one building in an area may prefer to use one of their managed properties as the place for evacuees of their other buildings to assemble. You might also check with management at adjacent buildings to find out if they have a large space that can be used for the purpose. It may be easier to arrange if you can offer a reciprocal arrangement whereby the neighboring building would evacuate to your property.

It is also a good idea to designate an alternate gathering place for an evacuation. This may mean having to check at two locations, but if the first or preferred site becomes unavailable or people are unable to get to it because of barricades or other obstacles, the alternate ensures having a specific location for evacuees to assemble. After an emergency, if people cannot get into your building, there should be a primary and an alternate place for people to report if they have not been advised to stay at home.

The orderly movement of people away from a building requires careful planning and the participation and cooperation of everyone involved. It also requires a clear chain of command that identifies personnel with the authority to order an evacuation. The property's trained floor monitors, who are members of the Emergency Management Team (i.e., property staff), will help coordinate the evacuation. At a large commercial property, they may be assisted by tenants' employees who are assigned specific roles in an evacuation. When that is the case, the floor monitor may fill the role of the fire warden or area captain as described in Chapter 2.

Floor monitors play a key role in ensuring safe evacuation. They monitor the evacuation, make sure all people leave their areas and reach the proper destination, and may be assigned to safeguard against building re-entry until the danger has passed. (Note: Some buildings now require floor monitors to sign in each day so that management knows if an area is covered for an emergency.) The following suggestions may be applied to a property's evacuation procedures:

- Have floor monitors and building occupants become familiar with evacuation routes and procedures. These routes and procedures should be explained in the emergency procedures manual, and evacuation routes should be posted in areas of high visibility. They may also be given to each building occupant. In multistory buildings, selected stairwells may be reserved for use by firefighters, police, and other emergency personnel while the remaining stairwells are used for evacuations. In most situations, however, stairwells are used by both emergency responders and evacuees—evacuees are asked to stay to one side going down so responders can more easily move up the stairs.

- Have floor monitors encourage occupants to move quickly and calmly during an evacuation. Make sure evacuation routes are unobstructed at all times. Evacuees should be informed that talking should be kept to a minimum and smoking is not allowed. Occupants should be reminded to close the doors to their apartments or offices as they leave to help prevent the spread of fire.

- If there are two stairwells available for evacuations, designate one for evacuation of disabled persons and one stairwell for evacuation of everyone else. However, this may not be possible or practical in an actual emergency. It may be necessary for disabled persons to assemble, preferably near or in one stairwell when there is more than one, to await assistance. Specific members of the Emergency Management Team should be assigned to assist disabled and non-English-speaking occupants. (Note: If tenants' employees have assigned roles, as noted in Chapter 2, the handicap aides would assist disabled coworkers. It may be desirable as well for tenants to arrange for assistance for their employees who are non-English-speakers.)

- Establish a system for accounting for all management staff and occupants. One or more persons should be assigned to take the names of evacuees to ensure that everyone has left the building. This can be done by matching evacuees names to an updated list of residents or commercial tenants' employees once everyone has gathered in the designated location. (Everyone should remain at that location until the appropriate authorities say they can leave.) In a small property, a head count may be sufficient. An alternate approach would be to have the floor monitors account for the occupants in their assigned areas.

- Have building occupants evacuate to the outdoors, moving to established waiting and debriefing areas away from danger and out of the way of emergency crews. Evacuees may need to be debriefed by law enforcement officials before leaving the premises in case they have information relevant to the emergency. An alternative to staying outdoors is to have an agreement with the management of a nearby building to accept your occupants during an evacuation. If an emergency should occur, that manager should be notified at the start of the evacuation so that he or she can prepare for the evacuees.

- Have evacuees congregate in one place when a building is evacuated, and then release them in small groups after their names have been checked against the occupant list. Often evacuees will go directly to their cars after exiting the building. This may cause congestion and impede the efforts of firefighters, police, and other emergency responders to deal with the emergency effectively and efficiently. It may also prevent a full accounting of all occupants, complicating the evacuation because of concerns that people may be trapped inside. If garage or parking lot attendants are employed on site, these personnel may be assigned to control traffic flow of exiting vehicles.

- Establish one or more pre-determined areas where injured evacuees can receive first aid in the event it is needed. Designated first aid stations and assigned personnel should be identified in the emergency procedures manual.

Personnel should be designated to shut down critical operations, such as gas supplies, during the evacuation. They must also be able to recognize when to abandon the operation and evacuate the area.

Returning to the Property

Re-entry of the facility for purposes of search and rescue should be done by the appropriate rescue or emergency professionals with assistance from the management staff if they are asked to participate. Here are some relevant suggestions:

- Do not allow occupants to re-enter the building until the person in charge of the emergency has confirmed that it is safe. Who gives the signal to re-enter the property may depend on the nature of the emergency. Authorization can come from police or fire department personnel, a structural engineer or city building department official, the property manager, or a member of the management staff. In a specific emergency, this person should be identified early.

- Depending on the extent of the property damage, and only if authorized to do so, the property manager and site staff may be required to assist emergency responders by escorting residents and commercial tenants' employees back into the building to identify goods, possessions, or equipment that need to be retrieved. Actual retrieval may have to be arranged for a later time.

- Require proof of identification before allowing a person to enter an apartment or commercial space. Proof of identification is required to re-enter secure buildings under the auspices of the General Services Administration (GSA) after evacuation drills as well as following emergency evacuations.

Note: If the damage is extensive, special care should be taken during such re-entry. Unfamiliar odors may indicate hazardous materials leaks. Unfamiliar noises may signal structural instability and further impending damage to the property. Initial re-entry should only be done by trained personnel. There is potential liability for the management company if occupants are exposed to hazardous situations.

Also, a damaged property presents an opportunity for looting. A guard service should be engaged to watch over the building once the occupants, staff, and emergency personnel have left the premises and any unnatural openings have been boarded up.

Drills

Evacuation drills are essential to a successful evacuation plan. They help familiarize occupants with evacuation procedures and routes, minimize panic during emergencies, and keep floor monitors and other members of the Emergency Management Team alert. Evacuation drills also allow the manager to review the performance of the staff and the building occupants and determine if the evacuation plan needs fine-tuning.

Some municipalities require evacuation drills—usually once or twice a year—for buildings over a certain height. These drills may be conducted on a floor-by-floor basis or the entire building may be evacuated. Occupants may be given advance notice, but occasional drills should be conducted with no warning.

Representatives of the local fire department may be invited to observe the drills and identify areas that need improvement. Some municipalities require fire department oversight of evacuation drills.

Finally, the property manager should meet with the Emergency Management Team, adjunct floor monitors, and police and fire department representatives periodically to review the evacuation plan. It may need updating as changes are made to the property or because of changes in the resident profile or commercial tenant mix.

5

Restoration and Resumption of Operations

After the emergency is over and control of the property has been released to the building owner and/or property manager, the next step is *restoration*. Restoring the property to normal operation after an emergency is one of the final steps in an emergency plan. While a fire will certainly result in property damage—not only from the fire itself, but also from water or other agents used to put it out—other types of emergencies (e.g., floods, windstorms, earthquakes) also cause damage that requires restoration. Planning what to do after an emergency is just as important as planning for and responding to an emergency.

Immediately after an emergency, the property manager should assemble those members of the Emergency Management Team who have been assigned responsibilities related to recovery—ensuring safety of personnel on the property, assessing remaining hazards, and identifying any potentially dangerous areas in the building. Property employees and building occupants should be briefed on recovery plans and cautioned about potentially hazardous areas. The following are among the first actions to be taken:

- Protect the property by closing building openings to prevent unauthorized entry, theft, and vandalism.
- Remove smoke, water, and debris to avoid injury and minimize hazards.
- Make temporary repairs to prevent further structural damage.
- Restore power and other utilities as soon as it is safe to do so (this may require assistance from the utility providers).
- Conduct an investigation into the cause of the emergency with your insurance representative, an appropriate government agency, or a restoration consultant.

While property staff may be qualified to perform some types of cleanup, a particular emergency may warrant having this work done by outside contractors. Not only can this expedite the restoration process, but a contractor is more likely to have the specialized training and equipment needed for some jobs. The manager can determine what restoration services will be available by consulting with local contractors before an emergency occurs. Arrangements for a wide range of services and prices may be negotiated with restoration firms, general contractors, and cleaning contractors *prior to* an emergency. The property's insurance carrier may also be contacted for recommendations. Working with vendors that have a prior service relationship with the insurer can save considerable time and effort in restoring the property after an emergency.

Contractors may provide a wide range of services, including:

- Securing the site against further damage.
- Estimating structural damage.
- Estimating the cost to repair or renew items of personal property.
- Repairing structural damage.
- Packing and transporting damaged or repaired property from and to the premises and storing it off site during construction.
- Cleaning or restoration of interior finishes and mechanical equipment.
- Cleaning or restoration of office furniture and office furniture systems (workstations).
- Cleaning or restoration of telephones, computers, and other electronic equipment.
- Restoration of documents.
- Smoke and odor removal.
- Cleanup of mold, asbestos, and other environmental hazards (this work should be done only by appropriately licensed companies).

A restoration contractor's objective is to return severely damaged property to its original or near-original condition. The contractor's employees are trained and educated in the specific strategies and technical applications required to restore property and contents after fires, floods, storms, and other major disasters.

The property's insurance carriers should be notified immediately that an emergency has occurred. It may also be advisable to consult with the owner's or the management company's attorney. In working with insurance companies, two approaches are possible: (1) work directly with the insurance company, using the expertise of the property's insurance adjuster to represent the property, or (2) hire a public insurance adjuster who evaluates the financial loss of property due to damage and acts as your "agent" in negotiating the settlement. (Note: The approach and costs of services are very different. There should be a specific plan.)

The objectives of restoration are to secure the area, prevent further loss, and return the building to normal operation. Throughout the restoration process, it is necessary to keep all interested parties informed.

Securing the Area

A disaster can make a building uninhabitable for an extended period. In such instances, one of management's most important tasks is to keep people out of the building. Potential looters and thieves would like an opportunity to plunder such a building. Representatives of the media, always eager to report on the damage to a building, could enter without permission, endangering their own physical safety and that of others. To help protect people and property, consider the following suggestions as supplements to your emergency procedures plan:

- In order to keep unwelcome visitors from entering the building, arrange for security personnel to patrol the property as needed. As an additional interim preventive measure, arrange for boardup of windows and doors and installation of fencing around the perimeter of the building or the property. Designate specific points of entry for use by contractors and others and barricade the remainder.

- When appropriate, ask a structural engineer or other suitable professional to declare the building safe before allowing property staff, vendors, or occupants to enter. Do not allow free access to the property until its safety have been verified.

- Make arrangements for occupants to retrieve their personal property. It is only natural that people will want to get back into the building as soon as possible to collect their belongings. Commercial tenants will want to retrieve files, computers, and other necessities to conduct business. Management staff or security personnel should accompany people to their office suites or residential units, making sure that they do not wander into potentially dangerous areas or enter another occupant's leased space.

- Require occupants (residents, commercial tenants' employees) to show identification before they are allowed into their units or work spaces in order to prevent theft and vandalism. Keep a record of who entered, when they entered, and how long they stayed.

Preventing Further Loss

A number of actions must be planned in order to prevent a property from experiencing additional losses beyond the damage caused by a fire or other emergency. In particular, an emergency plan should address debris removal; structural damage; cleaning, salvaging, and temporarily storing minimally damaged fixtures and equipment; and preservation of property records. It should also include procedures for documenting damage before restoration efforts begin.

Documenting Damage

Once it is safe to enter the building, and before beginning any cleanup, the property manager should enter the building with a camera—preferably a video camera—to document the extent of the damage to the building and its contents. This is important for insurance claims and may be helpful if an occupant brings a lawsuit against the management company or the owner as a result of the emergency. Make sure the videotape is dated and has a proper introduction before taping is started.

Removal of Debris

The first step in preventing further loss is to protect the property from debris and trespassers. (Specific steps for securing the area are presented later in this chapter.) The manager should call maintenance restoration contractors and utility companies immediately after the disaster to remove debris and broken glass, repair any damage to plumbing, gas, or electrical systems, and prevent any further damage. If property staff have the requisite skills, they may be assigned to perform some of the cleanup.

A word of caution: The emergency itself or the response to it may create environmental hazards. Asbestos-containing materials may become friable when insulation on piping or inside walls is damaged. Damage to walls or ceilings may expose toxic mold whose presence had not been detected previously. Hazardous chemicals may have been spilled. Not only is exposure to these types of environmental hazards potentially harmful to humans, in the aftermath of a disaster, asbestos fibers, mold spores, and other types of particles may be spread throughout a building by air currents from open doors and windows or when the HVAC system is turned on. As a result, salvageable items as well as debris and damaged goods may become contaminated. If environmental problems are suspected, a qualified professional should determine whether or not there is contamination and what should be done to mediate it before debris and salvageable items are removed.

What If the Worst Happens?

Emergency planning should also consider the worst-case scenario. Fire, earthquake, or a weather-related disaster can leave a building uninhabitable. Beyond a certain level of damage, it may not be feasible to make repairs. Construction costs may be only part of the equation. Building codes may require restoration to meet safety or other requirements that were not in place when the building was originally constructed, and these requirements may add substantially to the restoration costs. In such a situation, the property owner may decide not to restore the property.

The decision not to restore the property has consequences for the occupants. Leases may include language stating that if a certain percentage of the building is destroyed, the lease will be cancelled, relieving occupants of their financial obligations under the lease. However, not having a place to live or conduct one's business is a serious issue for residents and commercial tenants.

A management company may be able to relocate displaced commercial tenants to another property in its portfolio if there is space available and the size of the space and the terms of a new lease are agreeable to both parties. It may be possible to offer a similar relocation arrangement to residents who are displaced. Residents who need assistance finding temporary shelter can be directed to the Salvation Army or the American Red Cross—or to the Coordinated Assistance Network in which both agencies participate.

In any major emergency that is not a natural disaster, the cause or source of the incident must be determined. The affected area should be closed off pending an investigation by the appropriate authorities (police, fire department) and the insurance company. Cleanup should be deferred until the area has been thoroughly documented, photographically and otherwise, and the authorities have released it.

Protection from Further Structural Damage

Next, steps should be taken to secure the property from further damage resulting from any structural problems caused either by the emergency or by rescue efforts. Water should be extracted or pumped out. Prompt dehumidification may prevent thousands of dollars in additional damage to walls, carpets, and floors. (Molds thrive in moist environments.) Structural damage should be identified by a structural engineer although the building's engineer or a qualified contractor may make a preliminary assessment. It may be necessary to stabilize joists that have been weakened due to fire or the weight of water or to build a temporary roof to protect the building's interior. Temporary plumbing or electricity may need to be installed. These types of work usually require qualified professionals. In some areas, permits may be required before specific types of restoration work are started. Weather conditions in the aftermath of a disaster may also be a consideration. For example, extreme cold temperatures may freeze exposed water pipes, causing them to burst.

Cleaning and Salvaging Items from the Property

The next step is to secure and clean all *salvageable items* from the property. These are items that have survived with little or no actual damage—carpeting, appliances, hardware, fixtures, plumbing fixtures, light fixtures. These items should be held in storage until structural repairs have been completed.

If there was a fire, it may be appropriate to open windows for ventilation, clean and coat metals with petroleum jelly or oil to prevent corrosion, brush smoke particles (i.e., soot) from dry furnishings, draperies, and carpets, and dispose of canned goods exposed to excessive heat.

If there was a flood, the heat should not be turned up in an attempt to dry the property; this could accelerate the growth of mold. Neither should walls or other porous surfaces be washed, as further damage could ensue when caustic soap is applied to the surfaces.

Occupants should avoid using electronic equipment and appliances until they are cleaned and checked by experts, and under no circumstances should smoking be allowed in or near the building.

The property manager should make an inventory of *damaged goods* and segregate them until an insurance adjuster has visited the premises. This is usually performed with the adjuster or the adjustor's salvager. (Adjusters usually visit within 48–72 hours; they may arrive sooner if it is a large-scale emergency.) The damaged goods can be moved outside if they are in the way and the weather will not harm them. If you release goods to a salvager, be sure to obtain a signed inventory stating the quantity and type of goods removed.

Records Preservation

Preserving property-related records is necessary for expeditious restoration of operations. The property manager and staff should determine *in advance* which records should be given special protection. First, identify the minimum information that must be readily accessible to perform essential functions during and after an emergency. These would include important emergency telephone numbers and plan drawings of the property.

You may want to classify other information into functional categories, such as management records/reports, finance, insurance, and administration. Once classification is completed, identify the equipment and materials needed to access and use the information.

Next, establish a plan to protect and access these records. Options include backing up the computer system (software as well as data bases and working documents), making copies of paper records and storing them in a separate building or in fireproof cabinets, storing digital records (backup tapes and disks) in insulated containers, increasing security for computer facilities, arranging for evacuation of records to backup facilities, backing up systems handled by service bureaus, and arranging for backup power. Historical records that are accessed infrequently should also be considered for off-site storage, especially if on-site storage is using space that might be rentable.

If the information is considered crucial, some property managers send periodic backup tapes or disks to companies that maintain storage vaults (data centers). If a disaster should strike, the company forwards the tapes to a pre-contracted disaster recovery firm, which sets up a work site for the property management staff. There are also Internet-based systems for storing digital information (see discussion of Records Storage in Chapter 1) and dual operating systems in which computers off site are synchronized (run in real time) with those on site in the management office. It may be worthwhile to explore those possibilities as well.

Note: The property manager is responsible for business records related to the property and its operations. Commercial tenants should have their own plans for backing up and retrieving business records and for resuming operations after an emergency. Residents should store vital personal and financial records in a safe place off site (e.g., a safe deposit box).

Documenting the Restoration

The restoration process should also be documented. Photographs can be taken at different stages to show progress over time. Videotape can also be used. As with any construction project, it is important to keep track of construction plans, change orders, directions to contractors, information received from them, and costs. Separate accounting codes should be used to account for construction and other restoration costs. It is also important to keep track of employees' time spent working on restoration activities, including overtime. Accurate records of construction work and costs and of employee time are needed to receive reimbursement from the insurer.

Resuming Operations

The emergency procedures plan should establish a strategy for resuming normal operations at the property. This should include arrangements needed for continuing operation of critical business functions during an emergency and then recovery afterward. The plan should include provisions for technology-supported activities (e.g., e-mail, databases) as well as functions that are performed manually.

For those wishing to develop a formal Business Resumption Plan (BRP), there is information in an article by Dr. Paul Rosenthal published in *The Business Forum* online at www.bizforum.org. The article suggests a strategy and identifies some costs of business resumption planning. It also includes justification for investing in a BRP. Other publications on the subject are included in the list of Additional Resources at the back of this book. (A glossary of business continuity terminology has been published on the Internet by *Disaster Recovery Journal* at www.drj.com.)

The hallmark of a successful restoration effort is to have the building returned to normal operation as soon as possible. Otherwise, there is the risk of additional damage to the property and additional expense.

Keeping Others Informed

In order to assess the damage and the amount of financial loss, the insurance agent and the adjuster should be among the first people called to the scene before restoration efforts begin. The property manager should consult with the insurance company in the selection of an appropriate restoration contractor. This should be done prior to a loss occurring, and the contractor should have visited the property to determine how to approach restoration after different types of emergencies.

Following are additional suggestions regarding dissemination of information after an emergency:

- Keep occupants informed of the condition of the property and progress of the restoration. As soon as possible, occupants should be told what has happened, what is being done, and when they can enter the building to retrieve their property. They may also be told how long it is expected to take for the total restoration to be completed when that is known.

- Tell residents and employees of commercial tenants when they can move back into the building (if that is known). Periodic updates allow the property manager to provide occupants with progress reports and let them know if the restoration's scheduled completion is on target.

- Consider keeping the media informed of the restoration's progress, but make sure that you have control of what information is released. Media representatives can be valuable allies at this time. If the manager is prepared, he or she may want to invite the media to tour the property during restoration and encourage them to bring photographers. Regular news releases announcing the progress of the restoration may be issued; however, be careful of "creative" reporters who may distort the facts or misrepresent your property. (Public relations is the subject of Chapter 6.)

- Keep the public informed of progress of the restoration. Depending on the incident and the property type, a series of advertisements in local newspapers informing the public that the building is operational may benefit both the building and its occupants. This can be especially worthwhile when a shopping center or other service-oriented property has been put out of commission by an emergency situation.

The property manager may wish to establish a telephone message line that occupants can call for updated information on the restoration. Periodically, the manager would record a new message. Major progress or a setback may warrant changing a message daily or more often. This can save the time and hassle of having a person answer repetitive phone inquiries directly. It may be desirable to give the message phone number to others as well (e.g., vendors and the media).

If the property maintains a web site, updates may be posted there in addition to or instead of using a telephone message line. An advantage of the web posting is the opportunity to include photographs showing how the restoration is progressing. Web postings should also be updated as new information becomes available.

6

Public Relations

After a major disaster, the property manager will face a multitude of problems and decisions, all demanding immediate attention. The building occupants want to know how the emergency will affect them and when they will have access to their belongings and reoccupy their premises. The building owner is on the telephone asking questions and expecting immediate answers. One of the last things the manager wants or needs at this time is an inquisitive reporter, notebook in hand, asking lots of questions to which the manager does not yet have answers. What should the reporter be told? What if the reporter is accompanied by a film crew? How should one respond to the media?

Public relations is an important component of emergency planning. In some situations, it may be one of the most critical elements of an emergency management plan. Property managers in charge of large properties may spend millions of dollars promoting their properties and image, yet they sometimes fail in working with the media in crisis situations. Whatever the situation—a fire, a flood, a criminal incident, loss of human life, responding to the aftermath of an earthquake—a crisis of any kind, if mishandled, can quickly negate the positive image that years of good management and well-planned public relations efforts have created. Conversely, a negative impact can be reduced or even used advantageously after a disaster if the property manager plans and prepares for emergencies.

Having established relationships with local media representatives can also be helpful. A property manager who writes on real estate issues for a local newspaper or is available as an industry resource for print and broadcast reporters may receive more cooperation from the media in a crisis than one who is not known to them.

Just as the occupants of a building should be kept fully informed as much as possible during and after an emergency, the public as a whole should also be informed, not only to satisfy public curiosity, but because the public could be affected as well. An astute property manager will use the media to relay information and to instill public confidence in the property and its management. It is important to be prepared: The manager should have a specific public relations plan in place that outlines the steps for dealing with the public and the media during and after a crisis.

Never Avoid the Media

The first rule in any crisis communications plan is "never avoid the media." The manager must recognize that the media may choose to cover the story with or without his or her cooperation. It is far better to take an active role in the process, using the press to tell the right story at the time and the place it should be told. Working with the media can be difficult and frustrating, but with proper planning, the property manager may be able to use the opportunity to advantage. Some members of the press take great pride in their "objectivity," but the slant they give a story may be affected by the manner in which they are treated. Moreover, if the property does not provide a public relations representative, the media will seek statements from people who are less well informed about the incident or emergency.

The media should not be brushed aside with such statements as "I'll talk to you later," or "This isn't the time," or "We have no comment." The appearance of a cover-up will only create skepticism, maybe even animosity, on the part of the media and the public. It is best to deal with the media honestly and openly. An organized crisis communications plan prepares the manager to do so.

Prepare for Disaster

A crisis communications plan will include instructions on how to respond to the media, appointment of a spokesperson, and timing of the response to media inquiries.

This is not as easy as it might sound and is why some management companies solicit the services of public relations firms to handle their crisis communications. Since such firms are experienced in dealing with the media, they can help develop media statements and sharpen the property manager's speaking ability and other required skills. The property manager can either hire an advertising or public relations firm that specializes in "crisis public relations" or appoint someone on the staff who is capable and comfortable dealing with the media.

Because of the importance of accurate and timely written press statements in crisis situations, an emergency procedures manual should include sample statements in the form of generic news releases. These releases—or "fact sheets"—may incorporate specific information about the property. Then, when an emergency arises, only the particulars of the incident need to be inserted. The basic property information is already in place. Following are typical contents of a property "fact sheet."

- Building or property name
- Street address
- Property manager's name
- Building age—when it was built
- A general description of the building and its occupancy

The owner's name may also be included, but release of that information should be approved by the property owner. (A sample "fill-in-the-blank news release format is shown in the accompanying box followed by a filled-in example.)

Who Should Speak?

Media relations is a delicate skill. On the one hand, it demands openness and honesty and the ability to keep a calm demeanor in the face of probing questions; on the other hand, the owners' and occupants' confidentiality and privacy rights must be maintained. Only accurate information should be provided to the media at the appropriate time. Finding the right person for this job can be difficult.

Sample "Fill-in-the-Blank" Press Release Format

[Management Company Name]
[Management Company Address]
[City/State/Zip Code]

For Immediate Release

Contact:	[Designated spokesperson's name]
Phone Number(s):	[Number to call—business, home, and/or cell phone]
Date Prepared:	[Today's date]
What Happened:	[Brief description of emergency/incident; this may include which authorities—e.g., fire, police, hazmat team—responded]
Where:	[Describe location of incident]
When:	[Incident date and time]
Cause:	[If known, state a cause; if not, indicate what is being done to determine a cause.]
Injuries/Damage:	[Describe any injuries to people or damage to property to the extent known; if there were no injuries or damage, this should be stated specifically.]
What Is Being Done:	[Statement of actions that have been taken or will be taken to make repairs, restore property operations, return occupants to the building, etc.]

[Brief Property Description]

This type of format can be stored in a computer, with the first information items through a contact phone number(s) typed in place along with the concluding property description. (Information appearing in brackets here would be omitted from the final template.) When the need arises, specific information can easily be added to answer the who/what/when/where/how questions. The same format can be used for follow-up releases which may include more details—such as a final cause being determined or an estimate of economic loss.

Sample Filled-In News Release

XYZ Management Company
1234 Main Street
Detroit, Michigan 98741

For Immediate Release

Contact:	John Smith
Phone Number:	555-555-5555
Date Prepared:	June 20, 200X
What Happened:	A fire in one store.
Where:	In the kitchen of the Coffee Shop at the Cedar Plaza shopping center at 100 Cedar Avenue.
When:	At 10:00 a.m. June 20, 200X
Cause:	Fire department officials are presently investigating the cause of the fire.
Injuries/Damage:	There were no injuries. All restaurant customers and staff were safely evacuated.
What Is Being Done:	Restoration of the damaged kitchen is already under way. The Coffee Shop will be open for business by Saturday. None of the other businesses in the shopping center were damaged, and they are open for business.

The Cedar Plaza shopping center at 100 Cedar Avenue was built in 1976 and has been managed by XYZ Management Company since 1985.

To maintain consistency in communications with the media, one person should be designated to act as a spokesperson for the property. Only that person is permitted to speak to the media on behalf of the property. This may be the same person who is the property contact for police, fire, paramedics, and other outside responders—a person dedicated to communications regarding the emergency.

The manager must make it clear to the rest of the staff that only the spokesperson has the authority to interact with the media, and all media inquiries must be referred to that individual. This way, the spokesperson can establish a relationship with media representatives, the rest of the staff will not be burdened with calls at a time when other demands are greater, and the risk of giving out conflicting information is eliminated. To accommodate this procedure, the spokesperson's name and telephone numbers (both home and work, including a cell phone number if available) should appear on all news releases and other media communications as the sole point of contact.

A person from the property owner's or the property management company's public relations firm may be assigned the responsibility of serving as the property's spokesperson.

What Should Be Said?

Information given to the media—whether orally or in written statements—should be as complete as possible and answer all the questions a good reporter will ask:

- What happened?
- Where did it happen?
- When did it occur?
- Who was involved?
- Were there any injuries, and if so, how many?
- What caused the situation?
- What is being done for the building's occupants?
- Is the situation under control?
- When will the property be restored to normal operating conditions?
- Has there been a hazardous material leak as a result of the incident?

Provide as much *confirmed* information as you can (avoid speculation). Once a property's credibility has been established, the manager can more readily fulfill his or her responsibility to the building occupants and the public by allaying rumors, fear, and panic. In short, never lie or cover up.

More than likely, some information will not be available when questions are being asked. When you do not have all the answers yet, say so and avoid guessing or giving out unconfirmed reports. Statements given to the media must be accurate. Providing inaccurate information, which later must be corrected, can cause untold damage. When answers are not yet available, the manager who is in control will reassure the media that more information will be provided as soon as it is known. The manager should follow through on that promise. It should also be noted, however, that release of certain information may depend on the local authorities. If there is a police or fire department investigation, some questions may have to be referred to their representatives to preserve the integrity of the investigation.

As noted earlier in this chapter, when meeting with media representatives, property managers could provide news releases that not only explain what happened, but also provide facts about the property. These "fact sheets" can save valuable time for both reporters and the property manager.

To help safeguard the property against fraudulent claims or potential litigation, it is important for the property manager to maintain prudent records of all information released to the public.

When Should Information Be Given to the Media?

Public relations professionals agree that public perception is formed within the first 24 hours of an incident. This means that any delay in communications during this critical period—taking too long to meet with the media, appearing overwhelmed by the emergency, or avoiding the media altogether—is likely to result in a poor or negative public opinion. Once the public's respect is lost, a manager will miss the chance to show who is in command of the situation and assure the public that the property will be back in operation as soon as possible.

Communication with the media begins as soon as reasonably possible during or after an emergency. In highly sensitive situations, the spokesperson should first discuss the release of information with law enforcement officials so as not to jeopardize an investigation. He or she should maintain media contact at regular intervals. This may discourage the media from launching their own independent investigations.

Where Should the Media Be Met?

Reporters will want to see the property. They will want a firsthand look at the damage. Those who respect the media's needs will go far toward establishing good media rapport. Reporters should be allowed on the property, but only under close supervision by the property manager and only after officials have stated that the area is safe. It should be made clear that access to the property will be controlled in the interest of safety and that areas where police or fire officials are conducting an investigation will not be accessible until the investigation is concluded. Instead of letting reporters and camera crews wander freely around a property after an emergency, the property should be closed off and secured until management is ready to allow media representatives on the scene. The property manager should then conduct the tour, showing reporters samples of the damage and examples of cleanup efforts. Access to potentially dangerous areas, if allowed, should be limited.

If the media cannot be allowed on the property, arrangements should be made to meet with reporters at the command center set up for the emergency to review the status of the property. In some situations, news conferences may be appropriate. In such settings, many questions can be answered at one time.

If possible, reporters should be asked to submit their questions in writing, which provides an opportunity to research the answers and respond with more complete information. Many reporters, however, will refuse to do this; and if it is a fast-breaking story, they simply will not have time.

Following Up with the Media

Good media relations does not end when the crisis has passed. Even after the emergency is over, channels of communication with the media should be kept open. The media may be used to keep the general public informed of progress being made to repair the building, make it habitable, and make the occupants feel more secure. Media representatives should be invited back to the property to observe cleanup and repair efforts. Above all, the property manager should not pass up the opportunity to let the public know when the property is back in business. A media "open house" for a restored property can be especially worthwhile.

The manager with an eye toward the future realizes that a crisis can strike again. Having good rapport with the media as a result of a previous incident may make coverage more favorable in the future.

7

Documentation

As a safeguard for the property's reputation and as protection against legal liability and financial loss, a thorough and accurate system for recording the events surrounding an emergency should be in place and regarded as a central part of the emergency plan. The insurance company will want to know details about the emergency, and the property manager will need a complete report of what happened and what steps were taken in response. It is also important to maintain accurate records of costs incurred as a result of an emergency.

Emergency Report

Emergency reporting and documentation should begin with a form that allows anyone on the management staff to quickly report an emergency. During and after an emergency, management personnel will be busy and will not have time to prepare exhaustive reports. For this reason, the emergency report form should be designed so that accurate and necessary information can be provided simply by filling in blanks. This is preferable to requesting detailed descriptions of events. The emergency report should include:

- Name and address of the person reporting the incident
- Date and time the report is being made
- Name and address of any witness
- A brief description of what happened, when it happened, and where
- Name and address of person(s) involved
- What authorities were called and when
- When the authorities arrived
- Actions taken by the authorities

The description of what happened should include any observed injuries or property damage as well as the nature of the emergency or other incident. An example of an emergency incident report form is shown on the next page. An example of a log form for cumulative tracking of emergency incidents is included at the back of this book.

Emergency Incident Report

Reported by:
  Name _____
  Address _____
  Date _____
  Time _____

Witnessed by:
  Name _____
  Address _____

What happened: _____
_____
_____
_____
_____

Injuries (describe): _____
_____

Property damage (describe): _____
_____

When did it happen: _____
_____

Where did it happen: _____
_____
_____

Person(s) involved:
  Name _____
  Address _____

Authorities: _____
_____

Authorities called:
  Time called _____
  Time arrived _____

Actions taken by authorities: _____
_____
_____
_____
_____

Insurance Report

The adjuster will notify the property manager as to what level of detail the insurance company requires. Generally, the more comprehensive the information the property manager can gather before meeting with the insurance adjuster, the better the chances of receiving a rapid and equitable settlement. This information should include:

- A brief written description of the events that transpired prior to the loss,
- Appropriate police or fire department reports,
- A record of all emergency repairs and expenses, and
- A prepared inventory of property contents.

The inventory should include a description of each item, the brand name, the model number, serial number if applicable, age of the item, and the number of like items if more than one. Specifications for built-in components of the building should be available so that materials and equipment of like kind and quality will be used for restoration or replacement.

This information will be used in conjunction with a physical inspection by the adjuster, the restoration contractor, and the property manager to determine the scope and cost of the damage and loss. It can also serve as proof of loss for possible deductions from income taxes. To supplement the insurance report, photographs or video recordings can be extremely valuable in documenting the damage. Your insurance agent may be able to provide more specific reporting guidelines for inclusion in the emergency procedures manual.

It is a good idea to have on hand examples of claim forms from the various companies providing insurance coverage on the property. This can facilitate compilation of information as well as expedite submission of individual claims. The property manager should be familiar with the insurance coverages and requirements for deductibles because the amount of reimbursement usually will not equal actual costs.

Expense Report

It is important to maintain a record of all expenses resulting from emergency response and recovery. Separate accounting codes should be established for allocating the costs of repairs and replacement. Also, the manager will need to create a precise work authorization or purchase order that defines the scope of work for outside contractors so they can accurately estimate costs of labor and materials as well as replacement equipment. The following expenses are easy to overlook when accounting for emergency costs:

- Employees' time (including overtime worked)
- The property manager's time
- Contractors' invoices
- Materials and supplies purchased specifically for this purpose
- Materials and supplies taken from other properties in response to the emergency
- Materials and supplies already on site that were used for the emergency

There may also be incident-related costs incurred separately from construction and restoration contracting to be accounted. Boardup service, removal and storage of salvageable items, business relocation fees, and consulting fees (e.g., for environmental reports) are examples.

It may also be appropriate to include in the emergency plan specific procedures for providing written reports to the property owner. Also be aware that some documentation may be requested in the event of litigation regarding the emergency, so it may be desirable to check with the owner's or the management company's attorney before adopting any specific forms or formats for documenting emergencies.

8

The
Emergency Procedures Manual

After becoming familiar with the basics of an emergency plan as outlined in the preceding chapters, the emergency planning team should be better equipped to design an emergency procedures manual to meet the needs of individual managed properties. An emergency procedures manual should contain necessary information to safeguard people (management staff, residents, commercial tenants' employees, visitors) and property before, during, and after an emergency. The manual may address:

- How to make the property more secure and prevent emergencies or minimize their impact.
- How to prepare for an emergency.
- What to do during an emergency.
- How to save lives and protect victims of disasters.
- How to restore the property after an emergency.

The emergency procedures manual should include a list of the members of the Emergency Management Team and the specific roles each one has been assigned, along with a detailed list of the responsibilities for each team member and instructions for carrying them out. This should differentiate the role of the property manager or other designated individual as the team leader and identify a clear chain of command for members of the team plus an alternate chain of command if members are not available.

An emergency plan should provide for periodic review of the emergency procedures manual. Minimally, this might focus on two questions:

1. Have any changes been made to the building structure or mechanical systems/equipment that can affect the response to an emergency?
2. Has the occupant population changed in any way that can affect how we respond to emergencies (e.g., elderly or disabled individuals or children where there were none before)?

Emergency procedures should be updated to reflect these types of changes and to incorporate new requirements established through local, state, and federal regulations.

At a commercial property, interior modifications for tenant improvements may be a factor to consider. Changes in the neighborhood—increased criminal activity, new construction, adaptive use of commercial properties for residential uses or vice versa—may also warrant modification of emergency procedures.

Planning the Manual

Putting relevant emergency procedures information in a readable format to serve your property's specific needs requires thorough planning and research. It also requires a capable writing team. Specific responsibilities for developing and documenting emergency procedures may be delegated to members of the property staff who are part of the emergency planning team. These same people may be involved in implementing emergency procedures as members of the Emergency Management Team.

The Emergency Management Team that you assemble will play a vital role by sharing their experiences and expertise. Working in a group environment provides opportunities to develop a more objective perspective and allows members to brainstorm, creating more efficient plans and procedures suitable to the property's needs.

The following suggestions may assist the property manager and the emergency planning team in creating a custom-made emergency procedures manual:

- Schedule a series of meetings for designated staff to brainstorm ideas and begin to develop emergency procedures.

- Encourage team members to read through *Before Disaster Strikes* and be prepared to discuss how it applies to the property at a team meeting. The first meeting could focus on issues addressed in Chapter 1, The Scope of Emergency Planning, as discussed below.

- Ask team members to research and address topics in Chapter 1 of *Before Disaster Strikes* and develop a profile of the property and its immediate surroundings. They should be able to identify some particular emergency needs.

- Determine which chapters of *Before Disaster Strikes* apply to your particular property, recognizing that not all the suggestions pertain in all cases.

- Use the fill-in-the-blank forms at the back of this book (or the digital files on the accompanying CD) to begin to assemble information for the property's emergency procedures manual. Include other relevant information as necessary and appropriate (site plan and building layout, local building codes, etc.).

- Decide who will be on the Emergency Management Team. As members of this team are closely involved with the day-to-day operations of the property, they should be encouraged to supply input on the manual's contents.

- Appoint the individuals who will assist in writing the manual.

- Decide on a format for presenting the emergency procedures manual. Because the information will need to be updated periodically, it may be preferable to use three-ring looseleaf binders so that replacement pages can be distributed from time to time rather than redoing the entire manual.

- Consider using a page numbering system that is keyed to individual sections and allows for integration of replacement pages when more than one new page replaces a single page.

- Update and revise your manual as local codes or structural changes dictate, and inform manual users of the changes.

- Encourage periodic meetings on emergency procedures. Such meetings provide a forum to present emergency concerns and problems that need to be addressed and help to ensure that the Emergency Management Team is well prepared in times of crisis.

Developing an emergency procedures manual requires a commitment and a budget. Initially, there will be indirect costs—staff time for planning, writing the manual, and training them to respond appropriately. Ultimately, there will be direct costs for preparing multiple copies of the manual—photocopying or printing the contents, three-ring binders or other means of keeping the contents together. The advantage of a three-ring or other similar looseleaf binder is that material can be added and portions of the contents can be replaced with updated pages when necessary.

Contents of an Emergency Procedures Manual

Generally, an emergency procedures manual comprises three sections:

1. Reference information,
2. Directions for the management staff and the Emergency Management Team to follow for each possible emergency, and
3. Directions for building occupants.

Reference Information

The emergency procedures manual should contain information a property manager might need in the event of an emergency. Suggestions include, but are not limited to:

- An extensive, updated list of telephone numbers to reach team members, management personnel, the building owner, emergency assistance (fire and police departments, etc.), restoration companies, and other outside resources (see Chapter 1) in an emergency.
- An up-to-date list of telephone numbers and leased premises of all occupants (residents, commercial tenants' employees), including specialized equipment and need for assistance. This should include extensions at individual desks or workstations at commercial properties.
- A designated spokesperson to provide information to the media and examples of news release formats for this purpose.
- A general description of the building (age, construction materials, mechanical systems and equipment).
- A list of the building's current safety features and equipment (fire extinguishers, alarms, etc.), along with their locations and operating instructions.
- Building systems plans and specifications.
- Floor plans and as-built drawings showing all equipment, systems, and exits to which access may be needed during an emergency.
- Current local building codes and state and federal regulations that apply to the property.
- Insurance information (agent's name, business and after-hours telephone numbers, type of insurance coverage, policy number and name of carrier for each policy, current inventory of property possessions).
- A list of emergency equipment and supplies available on site, including quantities and where they are stored.
- Contents of the first aid kit or a list of medical supplies available on site, including quantities and where they are stored.
- A list of any hazardous materials on the property.

Reference information may also include potential staging areas for emergency responders if known.

Emergency Team Directions

The emergency procedures manual should cover emergencies that could happen on the property and procedures that should be followed in response to them. For each emergency, the manual may address specific areas such as the following:

- Detailed descriptions of the duties of the Emergency Management Team during the emergency.
- A flow chart of the chain of command during the emergency.
- The person or persons responsible for communications with the media and with emergency responders (police, fire department, paramedics, etc.).
- A copy of the emergency (PA) announcement for the particular emergency.
- Procedures to account for all management personnel, residents, and commercial tenants' employees.
- Procedures for notifying families of management employees about the status of personnel on the premises. (Commercial tenants should assume this responsibility for their employees.)
- Evacuation and re-entry procedures as they apply to each emergency, including specific instructions for guiding disabled individuals and elderly residents to safety.
- Reporting, documentation, and regulatory procedures as they apply to each emergency.
- Restoration procedures.

It may be appropriate to include information about administering first aid to injured persons as they wait for medical assistance to arrive. The manual should also include assignments for Emergency Management Team members in the recovery process (see Chapter 5.)

Directions for Building Occupants

The property manager should also consider how the property's occupants could prevent and respond to emergencies and educate them on basic emergency procedures and precautions. Information they need would include:

- How they will be notified of an emergency.
- How to identify members of the Emergency Management Team and its leadership.
- Directions for evacuating their residential units or work spaces and leaving the building.

Management staff can also help building occupants become aware of safeguards they can employ to protect themselves and others in the building. Recommendations include:

- Post emergency directions and safeguards on the premises in a conspicuous location where they will be visible to occupants (a laundry room or other common area of a residential property; common corridors, stairwells).
- Promote safety guidelines from police, fire officials, and others in a newsletter directed to occupants. These may include holiday safety tips and reminders to drive and walk carefully on icy surfaces in winter. Other frequent reminders include to keep doorways, corridors, and stairwells clear of obstacles.

Emergency procedures for building occupants are discussed in more detail later in this chapter.

Distribution of the Manual

The property manager, Emergency Management Team members, and on-site managers should each have a copy of the manual. Additional copies may be stored in a safe place, in case originals are misplaced or destroyed.

At least one copy of the manual should always be easily accessible at the property, with another stored off site. This off-site manual may be needed if an emergency prohibits entrance to the property and could also be of benefit if the owner, an Emergency Management Team member, or an emergency professional needs access to the manual but is far away from the premises.

When a team member leaves the property's or management company's employ, that employee's copy of the manual should be retrieved and reissued to his or her replacement. Whenever a manual is given to a new employee, the property manager should emphasize the confidential nature of the material in the manual, particularly the telephone numbers, security systems, and insurance information.

Emergency Procedures for Occupants

Whatever the property type, occupants should be educated in emergency procedures and safety precautions. One way this can be accomplished is by creating an emergency procedures handbook or guidebook for them. This will not be as detailed or complex as the emergency procedures manual for the management staff. The main concern is that building occupants follow the instructions of the Emergency Management Team and move themselves to safety as soon as possible.

Even a small building that does not have on-site management should have emergency procedures for the occupants. These should address:

- Directions to evacuate the building, especially not to use elevators.
- Recommended assembly areas.
- Guidelines for maintaining personal safety and security for residents and for commercial tenants' employees.
- Consideration for pets in residential buildings and for assistive animals at both residential and commercial properties.

When there is a minimum of information to be provided, the emergency procedures may be presented on a single sheet of paper. When the amount of information is large, it may be necessary to use several sheets of paper and staple them together. Sometimes it is appropriate to incorporate emergency procedures information into a Resident Guidebook or commercial Tenant Handbook along with other property rules and instructions so occupants have all such information in one place.

Contents of an Occupant Emergency Handbook

An emergency procedures handbook for occupants should include lists of safety precautions occupants can follow to avoid certain emergencies, including:

- Proper use of in-unit appliances
- Storage of potentially dangerous items
- Use of smoke and fire detectors
- Safe smoking practices
- Proper use of office equipment

Many times, a building's occupants will be the first to notice an emergency situation. Therefore, residents or commercial tenants should be given instructions on how to

Information Sources for Occupants

Government Publications
Floods: The Awesome Power (NOAA)
Hurricanes: Unleashing Nature's Fury (NOAA)
Thunderstorms . . . Tornadoes . . . Lightning: Nature's Most Violent Storms (NOAA)
Winter Storms: The Deceptive Killers (NOAA)
Surviving the Storm: A Guide to Hurricane Preparedness (FEMA)
Are You Ready: A Guide to Citizen Preparedness (FEMA)
Emergency Management Guide for Business and Industry (FEMA)
How to Plan for Workplace Emergencies and Evacuations (OSHA)

Most of these publications can be downloaded from the respective government agency web sites.

Web Sites
www.fema.gov
www.ready.gov
www.nws.noaa.gov
www.redcross.org

Details on these and other information sources that may be appropriate to share with occupants are included in the list of Additional Resources at the back of this book.

report emergencies such as fires, assaults, bomb threats, chemical spills, and explosions. Generally, occupants should contact the building manager, the fire department, and/or the police department.

Other potential contents of an occupant emergency handbook may include:

- An explanation of building-wide communications (e.g., PA system), if appropriate, and how they will be used in emergencies.
- Locations of all building entrances and exits.
- Diagrams of evacuation routes.
- Explanations of evacuation and safety procedures.
- Items to have immediately available to facilitate evacuation (e.g., flashlight and batteries).
- Tips for prevention of theft and assault.
- 24-hour phone numbers of management staff.
- Information on the building's safety features.
- Telephone numbers of police and fire departments and government, social, and charitable agencies.
- Lists of safety precautions or actions that could be taken during specific emergencies, including storms, earthquakes, fires, bomb threats, and medical emergencies on the premises.

Commercial tenants should be encouraged to develop additional emergency procedures for their staffs and their businesses as may be necessary or appropriate. Residents should be encouraged to develop emergency plans for themselves and their families. An occupant emergency handbook might include information sources to help them make such preparations. (Some suggestions are presented in the accompanying box.) Potential sources for disaster assistance may be listed as well. These could include the American Red Cross and the Salvation Army, both of which participate in the Coordinated Assistance Network (see Chapter 1), as well as state and local agencies that provide emergency assistance. There is also an Internet site (www.FirstGov.gov) that is the official web portal for contacting U.S. government agencies. The list of Additional Resources at the back of this book includes more information.

Distribution of the Handbook

In a residential property, each resident should be given a copy of the property's resident emergency procedures handbook at the time of move-in and a new copy or replacement inserts whenever revisions are made. Copies should always be available to residents upon request.

In commercial properties, each tenant is given one or more copies of the tenant emergency handbook. Copies may be provided for each of their employees if appropriate. The property manager may wish to emphasize to commercial tenants the need to incorporate emergency procedures training into the orientation program for all new employers. Commercial tenants should be asked to assign at least one employee to an emergency response leadership role to facilitate evacuation. Tenants with large staffs should have one or more employees assigned to monitor stairwells and elevators, ensure that everyone leaves their premises, and provide assistance to disabled co-workers.

It may also be appropriate to post occupant emergency procedures on the property's web site if it has one. Such a strategy allows the document to be corrected and/or replaced and may preclude the need to distribute updated paper copies when the changes are minor, especially if the document can be downloaded and printed by the occupant. Occupants can be encouraged to check emergency (and other) information on the property web site at regular intervals to ensure they have the most current information. Notices alerting them to specific updates can be sent via e-mail with a link to where the changes appear.

Every floor in every building could have the name of a designated individual posted as the emergency contact person. In a commercial property, there might be an emergency contact person designated by each tenant. In such cases, the management office is responsible to inform this person of procedural or policy changes affecting the building. That contact person is then responsible to inform the other occupants on the floor. A current master list of such contacts, with both day and evening phone numbers, should be available in the property manager's office. An example of a form for listing commercial tenant emergency contacts is shown on the next page.

COMMERCIAL TENANT EMERGENCY CONTACT LIST

Suite/Store Number	Tenant Name	Contact Person	Business Phone	Home Phone	E-mail Address

Emergency Planning for Specific Property Types

9

Residential Properties

Emergency planning is property-specific. This chapter focuses on residential properties. If a property uses a Resident Guidebook to communicate resident policies and property rules and regulations, this vehicle may also include safety tips and emergency procedures. Residents will need to know how to evacuate their units and the building, where to assemble after an evacuation, and which member(s) of the property staff to contact in an emergency. Periodic evacuation drills should be conducted, if feasible, and emergency equipment should be tested and maintained on a regular schedule.

The resident profile will determine how emergency evacuations will be conducted. A chain of command should be established to facilitate emergency responses on site. Specific communications with residents are needed to ensure their awareness of how to respond to an emergency.

The Resident Profile

Emergency procedures for a residential property must take into account the resident profile. Having answers to the following questions about your residents before the planning process is started should be helpful.

- What are their ages? The overall age range? How many are elderly?
- Are there small children—infants and toddlers? Teenagers? How many in each age group? Which units do they occupy? Are the children alone during the day or evening? Can their parents be reached in an emergency?
- Are any residents disabled? What is the type/extent of the disability? Do they have assistive animals?
- Do any residents have skills that may be helpful in an emergency situation? Are any residents trained firefighters, police officers, active in the military or the National Guard?

While it may be possible to create a resident profile from information in residents' leases and lease applications, the particulars needed to facilitate evacuation must be current. To collect information for a resident profile, you might use a form letter such as the sample Resident Emergency Information Request shown on the next page. A section asking whether anyone has had training in first aid, CPR (cardiopulmonary

Resident Emergency Information Request

Dear Resident:

[Management Company name or Manager name] is preparing to *[develop/update]* emergency procedures for the building at *[street address]*. In order to be certain that every occupant of the building is accounted for in the event of an emergency, we need to know the first and last names of every person living in your unit, whether they are male or female, and their age. If anyone has a disability or would require special assistance to evacuate the building, we need to know that as well.

This information will be used by management only in developing specific emergency procedures. It will be made available to fire department and other emergency services personnel in the event the building must be evacuated.

Please complete the form below and return it to the management office by ***[due date.]***

Apartment Number _____ Apartment Location _____

Name(s)	Emergency Phone No.	Gender	Age	Need Special Assistance*
_____	_____	M / F	_____	Yes / No
_____	_____	M / F	_____	Yes / No
_____	_____	M / F	_____	Yes / No
_____	_____	M / F	_____	Yes / No
_____	_____	M / F	_____	Yes / No
_____	_____	M / F	_____	Yes / No

*Please indicate type of disability and assistance required. If an assistive animal is used, please include the type of animal.

Do you have any skills that might be helpful in an emergency? May we call upon you to help us in an emergency?

Thank you for your assistance.

[signature]

[Management Company or Manager Name]

resuscitation), or use of an automatic external defibrillator (AED) could be added, along with a request to indicate whether the person would be willing to act in an emergency. If the letter is sent by mail (U.S. Postal Service), it may be appropriate to allow ten to fourteen days for a response. If distributed by hand on site, a week may be sufficient.

An alternate approach would be to compile the information and ask the residents to confirm or correct it. The information also has to be kept current to be useful. New residents might be asked to provide emergency information at the time of move-in. Established residents should be asked at least once a year to update their information.

The information requirement applies to any type of multiple-occupancy residential property. If the property is professionally managed, the property manager or site manager would likely have primary responsibility for compiling the resident information. Members of the board of directors of a self-managed condominium or homeowners' association should be familiar with the profile of their residents so that they can take appropriate action in the event of an emergency.

Emergency procedures for residential properties should include specific provisions for evacuating and caring for children, disabled persons, and the elderly.

Note: Resident profile information should be available for use by firefighters and other authorities who respond to an emergency so they can quickly determine where to assign personnel to provide needed evacuation assistance.

Children

Children require special attention during emergencies and should be included on resident profiles. In the event of an emergency, a list of units where children reside, including the children's ages, should be readily available to share with police and fire department personnel.

Children can become frightened in emergencies. Disruption of their daily routine can cause children to panic or become emotionally "paralyzed." Because of this, management should be prepared to comfort and care for resident children during an emergency. Parents can help by teaching their children how to respond to emergencies, including whom to call—dial 911 if that service is available locally—and how to get to safety. Property managers should encourage parents to practice the response with their children.

Making a property "child-safe" is one of the best ways of preventing emergencies at a residential property. Access to areas containing machinery, cleaning equipment and supplies, and swimming pool maintenance equipment and chemicals must be kept secure (i.e., doors locked) at all times. Playground equipment should be regularly inspected and maintained. In complexes with drive-through areas, speed limit signs or other traffic-control measures (e.g., speed bumps) may be appropriate installations. In addition, requiring children under a certain age to be supervised while using any of the property's facilities can be a positive preventive measure.

If a day care center is operated anywhere on the premises—an increasing possibility for large residential complexes—the property manager should require the center operator to develop an emergency plan for the center, including specific evacuation procedures. The center may be staffed by a small number of adults, each responsible for several children, and some of the children may not reside on the property. In an emergency, building management may have to provide additional supervision as well as evacuation assistance. If that is the case, the property emergency procedures manual should include this information and assign personnel to provide such assistance.

Note: Additional information may be found in the American Red Cross publication, *Helping Young Children Cope with Trauma,* which is available for download at www.redcross.org/pubs/dspubs/terrormat.html.

Disabled Residents

Temporary conditions of disability, such as broken bones or illness may impede an individual's ability to escape from or avoid an emergency situation. Although difficult to track, property managers should try to be aware of these conditions and record them in the resident profiles, especially in large complexes.

Other nonpermanent disabling conditions also may handicap a resident's ability to react to an emergency. Size and agility affect a person's ability to escape and avoid danger. Arthritic conditions often preclude rapid movement. Property managers should attempt to foresee any conditions that will hamper a smooth evacuation.

Long-term disabilities often require advanced emergency planning. Residents with visual, hearing, and mobility impairments may benefit from having a "buddy"—someone on their floor—to provide personal assistance. Minimally, each Emergency Management Team member should have a list of disabled residents whom they may need to assist.

It is also important to consider mental disabilities that can impair emergency response. The Fair Housing Amendments Act of 1988 extended fair housing protection to mentally ill individuals, rehabilitated alcoholics, and drug abusers. Such individuals may have difficulty understanding directions or the reason for evacuation.

Note: More specific information can be found in the American Red Cross publication, *Disaster Preparedness for People with Disabilities,* which is available for download from the Internet at www.redcross.org/pubs/dspubs/terrormat.html. Another source for planning information is *The National Organization on Disability's Emergency Preparedness Initiative Guide on the Special Needs of People with Disabilities.*

Elderly Residents

More and more people are "aging in place"—remaining in their traditional rental units rather than moving into so-called elderly housing. This poses additional challenges to the managers of conventional apartments. Older persons may have limited mobility, impaired vision or hearing, or difficulty understanding what is said to them (mental incapacity) simply due to age. Some may rely on medical equipment or devices, including such things as walkers, portable oxygen tanks, and motorized wheelchairs. Emergency procedures should include provision for evacuating the equipment along with the person. Residents should be encouraged to arrange for auxiliary or alternative power sources for electrical devices in the event of an emergency. Information on which units are occupied by elderly residents and the special needs of these individuals becomes invaluable in emergency evacuations and should be readily available to fire and police personnel.

During practice evacuations, elderly residents should be allowed to be as independent as possible, even if they are physically slower than younger residents. Such practices should be used to observe and evaluate their physical capabilities. If special assistance is needed, it should be indicated as part of the individual's resident profile. If there is more than one stairwell, it may be desirable to direct elderly residents to use a separate stairwell from the other residents to allow for their slower evacuation.

When assisting elderly people, it is important for personal communication with them to be clear and respectful. Although some older persons may have difficulty hearing, loud and domineering speech may discourage cooperation or be found offensive. The resident's pride and dignity should be considered at all times. When personal attention is required to assist an elderly individual, it should not appear to be an extra effort or even a slight inconvenience. Such behavior may discourage an older resident from asking for help when needed.

Note: Managers of housing designed for elderly residents primarily or exclusively—e.g., congregate care facilities—should seek planning assistance from appropriate sources to ensure safe evacuation of their residents. Additional information may be found in a publication from the American Red Cross titled *Disaster Preparedness for Seniors by Seniors,* which is available for download from the Internet at www.redcross.org/services/disaster/beprepared/seniors .html. There is also information on the web site of the American Association of Retired Persons at www.aarp.org.

Establishing an Emergency Chain of Command

Residential properties present a particular challenge to property managers because the property manager often will not be available to respond immediately to an emergency. Because of this, it is important to establish a chain of command.

Properties with Site Managers

In planning for emergencies at residential properties, it may be advantageous to alter the normal chain of command and appoint the site manager, rather than the property manager, as the "team leader." The site manager is more familiar with the residents, vendors, contractors, and others involved in the daily operation of the property and thus can be a more effective leader. The property manager's role should be one of oversight, allowing the site manager to direct the emergency response. If the site manager is to have primary responsibility for overseeing emergency procedures, he or she should be involved in developing those procedures and trained to implement them.

Properties without Site Managers

At smaller residential properties where there are no site managers, the residents often report emergencies, and emergency telephone lists become a priority. Residents thus become integral members of the Emergency Management Team.

In such situations, the property manager must work closely with the residents, letting them know that they are responsible for a good part of the emergency response and clearly explaining the potential dangers of neglect. Management should meet with residents to explain the property's emergency procedures and consider appointing residents as floor or building monitors (with alternates). These monitors would be responsible for directing residents to safety until management or fire or police personnel can arrive on the scene.

In established condominium and homeowners' associations, members of the board of directors are often long-term homeowners. The manager should work with them in communicating emergency procedures information to owner-residents and appointing monitors. In a new condominium, one of the key questions to ask of those running for office is: What experience have you had coping with emergencies? For condominium developments without on-site staff, the need for owners to be responsible for certain emergency duties must be clearly understood.

Communicating with Residents

Residents need to be made aware of emergency procedures planned for the property, in particular evacuation procedures. Suggested approaches to these kinds of specific communications are addressed in Chapters 1 and 4. In addition, emergency and safety procedures should be regularly reinforced with residents. A property's emergency procedures should be explained fully to every new resident. They may be included in a Resident Guidebook along with property rules and regulations. Otherwise, a handout listing emergency procedures for residents can be prepared.

Resident newsletters are ideal to communicate information about safety and security. A resident bulletin board can serve the same purpose, as can an occasional flyer distributed to each resident. Flyers may take the form of holiday safety reminders about the danger of fire from improperly used Christmas decorations, Halloween decorations, fireworks, and barbecues as well as occasional reminders about personal safety in parking lots and garages. Reminders to use door locks properly and not leave entrance doors unlocked are also appropriate.

Sources for safety information include your local police department, which can provide information and tips on security and crime prevention. Local fire departments usually have outreach programs covering smoke and fire alarms, fire prevention strategies, and life safety tips. The Baltimore County Volunteer Fire Association has published safety tips and other information on the Internet at www.missfireprevention.com. The National Fire Protection Association (NFPA) offers a variety of printed brochures promoting fire safety and awareness (check out their online catalog at www.nfpa.org). Residents who have computers can be directed to the public education section of the NFPA web site to download and print copies of fact sheets on fire safety. They can also find emergency preparedness guidelines for individuals and families on the American Red Cross web site at www.redcross.org. Information on emergencies related to gas leaks, plumbing, and electricity can be found online at www.contentisking.com. Additional sources of information are listed in Chapter 8.

Residents might be encouraged to participate in a community watch program sponsored by local police. Residents should certainly be encouraged to look out for their personal safety and the security of their dwellings and personal property. Depending on property size, management might consider scheduling "safety days" in which local authorities (fire, police) come to the property to answer residents' questions. Activities might also include safety games for children.

A Special Incident: Death in a Unit

Residential property managers may experience the death of a resident or other individual in a unit. The nature and circumstances of the death will determine what action is warranted. The death may be due to natural causes following a serious illness or result from unnatural causes such as an injury, an accident, suicide, or foul play.

Upon the discovery of a death, the foremost concern of a property manager should be to ensure that proper authorities have been contacted. The family of the deceased usually assumes this responsibility. However, a residential property manager may have to arrange to have the body properly removed if there are no other family members in the unit. In all instances, it is essential to contact the police, coroner, and next of kin and seek direction from the appropriate authorities on how to proceed.

Because many apartment dwellers live alone and may have no family nearby, the residential manager or another staff member may be the one who discovers or is notified of a death in a unit. When this occurs, it is essential that the body not be moved or touched until after the police and other authorities have examined it. If the identity of the deceased person is known, the next of kin should be notified. Depending on the circumstances surrounding the death, the property manager may want to contact the property's attorney and insurance agent.

The following are indications that something may be amiss:

- Accumulated mail, newspapers, etc.
- Unanswered telephone calls
- Lights, televisions, or radios left on day and night
- Pets left inside or outside
- Cars not moved
- Failure to attend events as expected
- Inquiries from family, friends, neighbors, employers, creditors, etc

Apart from arranging for removal of the body, the property manager will be faced with restoring the unit to use in the event that the death has had some adverse physical effect on the property. Odors and damage from exposure to bodily fluids associated with the presence of a dead body will have to be mitigated. Death following an illness may mean that infectious agents or other contaminants are present. These problems may not arise in all incidents but are likely if the death was violent or self-injurious or if the body was not discovered for an extended period. It may be appropriate to hire professionals to restore the unit interior to ensure that stains and contaminants are properly removed.

In any death, the property manager is likely to be asked many questions by other residents. The manager should be prepared to answer them tactfully and with respect for the deceased individual and his or her family. In cases that may involve suicide or homicide, the property manager may also have to respond to inquiries from the media. All such inquiries should be handled by a designated media contact person.

Note: If there are pets on the property, helpful information may be found in *Pets and Disasters: Get Prepared,* published by The Humane Society of the United States in cooperation with the American Red Cross and available for download on the Internet at www.disasterrelief.org/Library/Prepare/pets.html. See also Chapter 35 for information regarding qualification of rental applicants as a preventive measure.

10

Office Buildings

Emergency procedures for office buildings follow the same general principles as those for residential properties, with several obvious and notable distinctions. Office buildings typically accommodate different types of businesses as commercial tenants. The equipment on site is generally more sophisticated than that found in residential properties, ranging from complex computer systems and building-wide HVAC systems to special ventilation and cooking systems if the building contains a restaurant or other food service business. The amount of activity can be very heavy, with customers and clients coming and going all day. Office buildings are generally closed overnight although flexible work schedules have extended the business day to twelve hours—7:00 A.M. to 7:00 P.M.—or longer. Retail businesses, especially restaurants and parking garages, may be open into the evening. However, management personnel may only be on site from 8:00 A.M. to 6:00 P.M., meaning no one may be on site if an emergency arises after hours. All of these factors have a bearing on the emergency procedures for an office building.

The Tenant Profile

The property manager should have profiles of building occupants to ensure safety and proper emergency planning, response, and evacuation. An occupant profile may include:

- The number of tenants in the building, including the number of people each tenant employs.
- The work and home telephone numbers, and cell phone numbers if available, of key tenant personnel or a business owner contact.
- What type of equipment or materials the tenants use or store in the building and if any of these are hazardous (e.g., flammable, toxic).
- Whether the tenants have many visitors during the day.
- Whether the tenants keep a significant amount of cash on hand.
- Whether tenants that occupy a full floor have a specific access code to that floor. The property manager should be aware of all floor access codes for use in case of emergencies.
- Whether any tenants conduct business around the clock or operate outside of normal business hours.

The property manager also needs to know whether and when any outside contractors such as cleaning, security, or construction personnel are working in the building. Because these people are not part of the established population of the building, they may be required to sign in and sign out as a security precaution and wear identification name tags .

Sometimes an office building will include a day care center operated or sponsored by a major company as a benefit to its employees or sought out by management as an amenity tenant. These types of facilities require special planning as noted in Chapter 9. In particular, the day care center's procedures for evacuation and assembly should be coordinated with the building's procedures so that parents working in the building can be united with their children quickly. It may be desirable to have parents report to their company's point of assembly initially, so they can be accounted for, and then move to a designated area to which the children will be brought.

Increasing numbers of disabled workers are actively employed, and managers of office buildings need to know which tenants employ disabled workers, who those workers are, and what special needs the individuals have. *Emergency Procedures for Employees with Disabilities in Office Occupancies* from the U.S. Fire Administration provides specific guidance on planning, assistive equipment, and methods for providing assistance. It can be downloaded from the Internet at www.fire.nist.gov/bfrlpubs/fire95/PDF/f95043.pdf.

Often physicians and other medical professionals will lease space in office buildings that are not designed specifically for use as medical office buildings. When these professionals are among your tenants, emergency planning must account for their uses and special needs. Apart from disposal of hazardous medical wastes, there are potential problems from exposure to bloodborne pathogens. Steps for addressing these added considerations are outlined in Chapter 11.

Working with Office Tenants

The success of office building emergency procedures depends in large part on the cooperation of the property's occupants. Their attitude regarding emergency response and preparedness, and their willingness to cooperate during a disaster, can make the difference between a successful program and a catastrophe.

Regrettably, some businesspeople view emergency procedures and evacuation drills as a time-consuming inconvenience. It is the property manager's responsibility to convince them otherwise. Before a new tenant moves into the building, the property manager should meet with the commercial tenant's office manager or other designated representative to review the building's emergency procedures and emphasize their importance. All tenants should be informed of their responsibilities in this regard, including the responsibility to inform their employees about the building's emergency procedures. It would be wise to put these procedures in writing and include a provision in the lease agreement noting that the tenant's representative was made aware of the tenant's obligations regarding building emergency procedures.

After the tenant moves in, management could schedule a meeting with all of the tenant's managers and/or employees to review the building's emergency procedures. If possible, a representative from the local fire department may be invited to discuss the life- and property-saving benefits of emergency plans.

Arrangements also can be made with tenants to choose floor monitors to assist their employees in evacuating the building in both emergency situations and practice drills. They should be asked to choose employees who are both enthusiastic and respected by their co-workers. During an emergency, employees will listen to someone they trust. Once floor monitors have been designated, the property manager should meet with them and explain their duties, distribute the printed emergency procedures, and train them in their roles in evacuation drills.

Establishing an Emergency Chain of Command

The emergency plan will benefit the property only if a clear chain of command is established and understood between the property manager and the commercial tenants. The property manager should ask that a representative from each office be designated as part of the Emergency management Team and ensure that each person plays an active role in performing assigned duties. In addition to floor monitors (also called fire wardens or area captains), tenants' employees may serve as floor leaders, searchers, stairwell monitors, elevator monitors, or handicap aides. Some tenants may have several employees in each of these roles; those with only a few employees may only designate a floor monitor. (Tenant employee roles and duties are discussed in Chapter 2.)

It should be made clear that, although some offices may occupy one or more entire floors, they must still adhere to the directions of the property manager or designated team leader as head of the Emergency Management Team. The property manager should keep commercial tenants' representatives up-to-date regarding changes in the building structure, emergency equipment, planning, and policies. Commercial tenant representatives, in turn, should periodically keep the property manager abreast of changes to their business activities and personnel and steps they are taking to prevent emergencies.

Security in the Workplace

Violence in the workplace is a continuing problem that should be addressed in the context of emergency procedures. The U.S. Department of Justice, Bureau of Justice Statistics, compiles statistics on the numbers and types of incidents (on the Internet at www.ojp.usdoj.gov/bjs/). According to that source, simple assault is the most common workplace incident followed by aggravated assault, then robbery, rape or sexual assault, and homicide. (Definitions of these types of crimes are provided in the box on the next page. See also Chapter 20 for additional information about preventing violence in the workplace.) Because this is a possibility in any type of office building, property managers should encourage security staff to monitor stairwells, parking lots, and other areas that may be potential hiding places for intruders. As part of security awareness, maintenance personnel and other on-site management staff also may be asked to monitor interior areas of the building as they perform their duties (see Chapter 3).

A high percentage of the instances in which violence occurs in the workplace are actions of angry former employees who were fired or feel they had been mistreated by their former co-workers or the employer. Since a security guard will not be aware of employee turnover, all persons whose employment in the building is terminated voluntarily or involuntarily should return their office keys or access devices and employee identification to their former employer before they exit the building. Many companies have procedures for collecting these items as part of the documentation of an employee's departure. The employer should also collect any identification or access devices issued by the building.

Workplace violence is not the only security issue for office buildings. More and more office building managers are reaching out directly to tenants' employees as part of their tenant retention strategies. They may sponsor health fairs or other types of informational presentations. Many use periodic newsletters to announce activities in

Definitions of Crimes Committed in the Workplace

simple assault An attack without a weapon that results in either no injury, minor injury (bruises, cuts, scratches), or an undetermined injury requiring less than two days hospitalization; also includes attempted assaults without a weapon.

aggravated assault A completed or attempted attack with a weapon, regardless of whether or not an injury occurred, and an attack without a weapon in which the victim is seriously injured.

robbery A completed or attempted theft of property or cash directly from a person by force or threat of force, with or without a weapon and with or without an injury.

sexual assault A wide range of victimizations distinct from rape and attempted rape and including unwanted sexual contact between the victim and the offender. It may not involve force but it includes such things as grabbing or fondling and verbal threats.

homicide The willful unlawful killing of one human being by another.

Adapted from definitions published by the U.S. Department of Justice, Bureau of Justice Statistics.

the building and the local area. These newsletters are also a vehicle for disseminating safety tips—including safeguarding personal belongings in employees' work spaces, protecting themselves in parking lots and while driving, and family at-home safety during the holidays—and reminders regarding building evacuation procedures. Emergency procedures information and safety reminders may also be posted on a web site if one is maintained for the building.

Evacuating the Office Building

While the procedures and advice in Chapter 4 apply generally to all types of properties, evacuation procedures for office buildings can vary and may require additional planning. Evacuating a small building may be easier during an emergency than evacuating a large office building, but that does not negate the need to have an evacuation plan for small office buildings as well. Commercial tenants' employees must know where all of the building's exits are and the closest one to their workplaces. (Evacuation route maps should be prominently posted on each floor.) They also must know where they are to congregate once they leave the building—which is especially important during violent storms and earthquakes—and how they will be informed when it is safe to return to the building (see Chapter 8).

Property managers may conduct regular announced and unannounced evacuation drills to keep tenants of office buildings prepared for emergencies. In cities, fire drills are often mandatory, and some cities require a set number of drills each year. As office building tenants often experience a high turnover of employees, these periodic drills serve the dual purpose of introducing new employees to evacuation procedures and keeping long-term employees familiar with the routes.

11

Medical Office Buildings

Medical office buildings have unique features that are due largely to the diverse needs of the medical professionals and their patients as well as the drugs and sensitive medical equipment on the premises. Occupants of medical office buildings must adhere not only to basic building policies set by the property manager but also to strict sanitary and medical compliance guidelines prescribed by the medical profession and the U.S. Occupational Safety and Health Administration (OSHA).

Among the issues to be considered in emergency planning for medical office buildings are the tenant profile, medical waste disposal, and security, as well as evacuations. Bloodborne pathogens are a special consideration.

Tenant Profile

Tenants in a medical office building may include a variety of health care professionals. In addition to specific medical and dental specialties, there may be representatives of some of the following professions:

- Physical therapists employ exercise and other means to restore mobility.
- Podiatrists treat conditions of the feet.
- Optometrists test people's eyes and prescribe corrective lenses.
- Osteopathic physicians employ medicines, surgery, diet, and other therapies to restore the structural integrity of body tissues.
- Chiropractors specialize in manipulation of the spine to restore normal nerve function.
- Psychologists treat patients with psychological problems.

Leased premises may be used for consultation and/or to examine patients, collect specimens of body fluids and tissues (blood, urine), perform laboratory tests, administer treatments, or all of these. Often the work of health care professionals requires specialized equipment, some of which may be installed in their leased spaces. Other possible tenants include x-ray services, magnetic resonance imaging (MRI) centers, outpatient surgery centers, medical laboratories, and dispensing pharmacies.

Medical office building tenants often have employees who are trained to provide specific treatments as well as administrative support personnel. Patients who seek treatment may be seriously ill. Information for a medical office building tenant profile might include the following:

- The types of medical or other specialties being practiced.
- The types of specialized equipment used in their practices and any hazards they pose.
- The categories of medicines and materials that may be stored in practitioners' offices.
- The type of work that is done in the leased space—examination only, taking of specimens, application of treatments, outpatient surgery, etc.
- The types of patients treated by tenants—ambulatory, disabled in wheelchairs, young children, elderly people, potentially serious injuries or illnesses.
- Numbers of patients treated—on a daily or weekly basis.
- What days of the week and hours of the day tenants provide services in their premises, days of the week they are closed, and holidays they observe.
- How many staff they employ and whether that number varies from day to day.
- The amounts and types of medical wastes generated and how they are disposed.

The patient population is an especially important consideration. Medical office buildings tend to have smaller suites—in the range of 2,500–3,000 square feet—but larger numbers of people on the premises. While a typical 100,000-square-foot office building might have ten tenants, each occupying 10,000 square feet on average, a medical office building of the same size is likely to have 30–40 tenants. Also, while the ten tenants in a typical office building might each have an average of five visitors per day for a total of 50 visitors, each tenant in a medical office building may have 15–20 visitors per day for a total of 450–800 visitors. During an emergency, it is likely that many of these visitors will be indisposed and unable to evacuate quickly. The medical professional's staff must know how to handle this eventuality.

There are safety issues regarding professionals who operate x-ray and laser generating equipment. The presence of certain categories of drugs can be a security issue (burglary, theft). It is also appropriate to consider many of the general tenant profile issues suggested for office buildings regarding contact lists, cash on the premises, business hours, etc. (see Chapter 10).

Medical Waste Disposal

If not properly attended to, hazardous medical wastes can threaten the safety and health of the management staff as well as the professionals themselves, their staffs, and their patients. Syringes and used needles can contain infectious material that may cause serious illness in an unsuspecting staff member or janitor who comes in contact with them because they had not been disposed properly or the disposal container was not properly marked.

The disposal of medical wastes can involve detailed procedures, such as requiring specially marked containers for specific wastes. Occupational Safety and Health Standards require medical offices to segregate their medical waste into three general types—soft medical waste (gauze bandages, etc); "sharps," or needles and syringes; and other medical waste. In particular, needles and syringes are commonly disposed by insertion into a sealed receptacle that includes in the opening a device for destroying these items. The container is replaced when it has been filled. Other medical wastes are commonly disposed in heavy-duty red plastic bags. Managers of medical office buildings should ensure that occupants keep hazardous medical wastes separate from regular trash and use appropriate containers for disposing of them.

Tenants typically contract directly with a state-approved and licensed medical waste disposal service; usually this is required in their leases. These services commonly provide appropriate containers. If these are not supplied by the waste disposal service, medical professionals can usually obtain appropriate containers from medical supply vendors.

As most medical waste disposal companies provide only monthly pickups, medical office tenants should be encouraged to store their medical waste in proper containers in a locked closet or other secure area. Once retrieved by the contractor, the materials may be scanned for potential radioactive material before being incinerated. Janitors should be advised not to touch or retrieve medical waste containers.

If a property manager learns that a tenant is not disposing of medical waste properly, or if there is a spill or accident, such mishaps should not go unrecorded. The manager should document the information by sending a letter to the occupant and keeping a copy in the occupant's correspondence file. This will help safeguard the property manager against potential lawsuits. It may also be appropriate to notify the authorities.

Security

The discussion of security issues in Chapter 3 relates generally to all types of managed properties. However, the nature of the tenants of a medical office building and the clientele they serve pose other unique security concerns. In particular, drugs that physicians keep on their premises to treat their patients can be a temptation for burglars, trespassers, or intruders.

Property managers are encouraged to write into their leases a requirement that all medical facilities must maintain their prescription drugs in safe and secure areas. Another security consideration to address in the lease is the physician's after-hours access to the building for medical emergencies.

Evacuation

A major concern for the manager of a medical office building is how to evacuate it while a physician is performing surgery or a patient is receiving treatment using medical equipment such as a dialysis machine.

The property manager should meet with each tenant to review the specific services provided and to prepare an appropriate response plan that adapts to the occupants' and their patients' needs. Keep in mind that evacuations of medical office buildings may take longer than with other occupancies due to the physical disabilities of some patients. The property manager may wish to consult with a local hospital regarding evacuation plans for the building and make arrangements for patients who have not fully recovered from outpatient surgery or who otherwise need special attention to be transported to the hospital in the event of an emergency.

Following are typical questions a property manager may ask medical office building tenants to develop an emergency evacuation plan:

- Are you likely to have patients under anesthesia and how do you plan to evacuate them if necessary?
- Are you likely to have patients connected to equipment that would need to be transported along with the patient in an evacuation? If so, what type of equipment would be involved? Is it portable? Have you made provision for its removal in an emergency?
- What is the range of ages of your patients and their general medical profile?

- Do you have special Medicare or other formalized guidelines that impact your emergency requirements? Please provide a list.
- Do you have certain days defined as surgery days?
- How many members of building staff are required to assist patients who are unable to evacuate on their own?
- Do you need wheelchairs/gurneys for evacuating patients? If so, how many might you need, and how many do you have access to?
- Do you have staff members who are disabled, and, if so, what are their specific needs?

Tenants should also be asked to list the names of at least two key people from their office who will be the emergency contacts for the building evacuation plan.

It is also a good idea to have tenants identify hazardous materials they have in their premises and indicate how they are stored and whether they are labeled for easy identification. Of particular concern would be flammable and combustible materials.

A Special Issue: Bloodborne Pathogens

Bloodborne pathogens are pathogenic microorganisms that are present in human blood and can cause disease in humans. These pathogens include the hepatitis B virus (HBV), hepatitis C virus (HCV), and human immunodeficiency virus (HIV).

Risk of Exposure

Occupational exposure to bloodborne pathogens is a major employee safety issue. The industry with the greatest exposure to and risk from bloodborne pathogens is the medical profession. However, there is also potential risk of exposure for those who come into contact with medical wastes as part of their work, including janitorial and cleaning personnel in medical office buildings. Because of this exposure potential, professionals who manage medical office buildings need to be aware of ways to protect their employees.

To protect workers who may be potentially exposed to bloodborne pathogens, OSHA published a specific standard (29 CFR 1910-1030) that became effective March 6, 1992. The OSHA standard covers *all* employees who could be "reasonably anticipated" as the result of performing their job duties to face contact with blood and other potentially infectious materials. However, "good Samaritan" acts, such as assisting a co-worker with a nosebleed, would not be considered "occupational exposure."

The OSHA definition of occupational exposure to bloodborne pathogens is "reasonably anticipated skin, eye, mucous membrane, or parenteral contact with blood or other potentially infectious materials that may result from the performance of an employee's duties." In medical parlance, parenteral means by injection into muscles or veins or under the skin, including needlesticks. Potentially infectious materials includes body fluids and/or tissues other than blood.

Exposure to bloodborne pathogens may occur in many ways, but needlestick injuries are the most common. Bloodborne pathogens can also be transmitted through contact with non-intact human skin (e.g., cuts, abrasions). Cultures of body fluids and tissues or organs containing such pathogens may also be sources of exposure. (Specific requirements of the OSHA Bloodborne Pathogen Standard are outlined in Chapter 19, Medical Emergencies.)

The Property Manager's Responsibilities

Currently, only property management personnel who are assigned first aid duties in case of an accident or emergency would be covered by the OSHA standard. However, management employees responsible for any type of cleanup duties (e.g., maintenance and janitorial personnel) may be at risk of exposure, particularly in a medical office building. Requirements of the OSHA regulation that may apply include the following:

- Development of an exposure control plan.
- Taking precautions to protect workers from exposure.
- Providing medical evaluation and follow-up for exposed workers.
- Use of biohazard labeling to communicate the type of hazard.
- Provision of specific training regarding bloodborne pathogens.
- Maintaining records of exposure and training.

Although most property managers would not "reasonably anticipate" that they or their employees would face occupational exposure to blood, it is prudent for managers of medical office buildings to have a policy and procedures regarding cleanup of blood and other bodily fluids. Because there is potential for liability in the event of such exposure, property managers may wish to seek guidance from a qualified professional regarding development of policies and procedures related to bloodborne pathogens and compliance with the OSHA requirements. Also, it may be possible or preferable to contract for janitorial services with a company that specializes in medical office buildings or has specific experience with this type of property.

Preventing Employee Exposure Although only operators of medical facilities are required to provide vaccinations for hepatitis B virus to their employees who may become occupationally exposed, the property manager may encourage the same with any "at-risk" employees. In addition, occupationally exposed personnel should take the following steps to reduce their risk:

- Wear protective clothing and equipment when necessary. Personal protective equipment may include gloves, gowns, laboratory coats, face shields or masks, and eye protection. In particular, employees must wear appropriate gloves when contact with blood or infectious fluids or materials can be reasonably anticipated. They should wear appropriate eye and mouth protection (e.g., goggles, masks) when dealing with splashes.
- Remove protective clothing and equipment *before* leaving the work area or when it becomes contaminated.
- Place used protective equipment in appropriately designated areas or containers when being stored, washed, decontaminated, or discarded.
- Decontaminate utility gloves for reuse if their integrity is not compromised. Discard them when they show signs of cracking, peeling, tearing, etc.
- Never wash or decontaminate disposable gloves for reuse.
- Wash exposed skin with soap and water; flush eyes with water as soon as possible. Liquid antiseptic or moist antiseptic towelettes may be used if soap and water are not immediately available, followed by washing with soap and water as soon as possible.

It is the employer's responsibility to provide protective clothing and equipment and to launder and clean these items and repair or replace them as necessary.

Self-sheathing needles and puncture-resistant containers for disposing contaminated sharp instruments are examples of preventive controls that should be employed by medical tenants. Resuscitation bags and pocket masks used for administering CPR should be similarly disposed as contaminated wastes. Managers of medical office buildings may find it useful to address the OSHA standard requirements in tenants' leases.

Labeling   The OSHA standard also requires fluorescent orange or orange-red warning labels to be attached to containers of regulated waste, to refrigerators and freezers containing blood and other potentially infectious materials, and to containers used to store, transport, or ship blood or potentially infectious materials. (Red bags or containers may be used instead of the labels.) Janitorial workers, especially, should be aware of such labels and the potential hazards they warn against.

Housekeeping   Under the standard, each place of employment must be kept clean and sanitary. To comply, the employer must develop and implement a cleaning schedule that includes appropriate methods of decontamination based on location within the facility, type of surface to be cleaned, the type of contamination present, and the tasks or procedures being performed in the area.

Handling Exposure to Bloodborne Pathogens

The property manager, as well as the tenants of a medical office building, should consider developing a written exposure control plan based on the requirements stated in the OSHA bloodborne pathogens standard. These include providing specific training for employees that covers:

- The contents of the OSHA standard
- Bloodborne diseases and their transmission
- Response to emergencies involving blood
- Use of personal protective clothing and equipment
- Safe work practices
- What to do in the event of exposure
- Use of biohazard labeling

As an employer, the manager will be required to provide treatment and post-exposure medical evaluation to an employee who may have had an exposure incident. The employee should immediately follow special procedures to clean the exposed area of the body, report the incident to his or her supervisor, and seek medical treatment.

If the property manager introduces these programs, he or she should maintain training records that include dates of all employee training sessions on handling bloodborne pathogens, the names of employees who attended each session, the trainer's name and qualifications, the method of training, and the topics discussed. The employer is also required to maintain records of employees who are exposed to bloodborne pathogens.

Property managers can contact OSHA regarding regulations and educational materials. Information about the OSHA standard and related fact sheets can be downloaded from the Internet at www.osha.gov. It is also a good idea to check with the states where they manage properties—state regulations are often more stringent than those at the federal level. Information about bloodborne pathogens may also be available from insurance companies.

12

Shopping Centers and Other Retail Properties

There are several types of retail properties—free-standing stores, which may be independently owned and situated on their own property, strip centers with small numbers of retail tenants, open-air or enclosed shopping malls with large numbers of retail tenants, and retail space included in multistory mixed-use developments (MXDs). Although this chapter is focused on multitenant shopping centers and malls, much of what is stated here can also be applied to free-standing retail stores, retail space in an MXD, and ground-floor retail in an office building.

Safety

Because retail premises are workplaces, safety of workers is an important consideration. The issue has increased in importance with the rise of the warehouse superstores. As in industrial warehouses (see Chapter 13), items for sale are stacked or racked in multiple levels. Workers move pallets of goods around in aisles where consumers are looking at display items and selecting packaged items for purchase. Workers may be injured—or even killed—by falling objects or encounters with forklifts.

The presence of consumers complicates the situation. Shoppers in warehouse superstores have been injured and killed by falling merchandise. They have also been injured by forklifts and automatic doors. This is in addition to shopper injuries from slipping/tripping on debris and floor mats and cuts from sharp items on display (e.g., knives, glass), which can also happen in traditional retail stores.

Recommended practice from the American Society of Safety Engineers is for cartons to be stacked in an interlocking pattern only to a height that is stable. Shrink-wrapping or banding stacked goods provides additional stability. They also recommend racking pallets individually. Pallets stacked on top of each other, especially within shoppers' reach, pose a danger because unsuspecting shoppers often remove merchandise from the lower pallet, creating instability that can cause the stack of pallets to collapse. They may also tip over.

Security

Shopping centers and retail properties may be characterized by large amounts of ground-floor space and high levels of visitor traffic. Because of the public nature of these properties, it is virtually impossible to control access.

Conducting research on the incidence of crime in the surrounding area and evaluating a shopping center's security needs are the first steps in creating a sound security plan. Such research involves obtaining statistics on the types of crimes and the number of incidents from local police or other experts on crime in the vicinity.

Needed security may include special lighting systems, surveillance cameras for parking lots or garages, or conveniently located direct-line telephones so shoppers can easily contact the security office. Large open-air malls and their parking lots may be patrolled by security personnel in vehicles; enclosed malls may have uniformed security personnel patrol on foot. The manager of a strip center may arrange for a private security service to drive by the property on a regular schedule, or increased police patrols may be requested.

Property managers can provide retailers with information and tips on security issues while other programs (e.g., community relations) may provide shoppers with safety tips or escorts to their cars.

Responding to Crime and Violence

To avoid confusion, it is important to clearly differentiate management's security responsibilities from those of the retail tenants and the police. The mall manager is generally responsible for security in the public areas, such as the parking lot, the corridors, unoccupied lease space, and restrooms, while the retail tenants are responsible for security within their leased premises. Since a retailer's company policy dictates what action can be taken within a store, the store manager must decide how store employees will respond to criminal incidents or other offenses. A mall may employ a security force that retail tenants can call for assistance, but retail tenants must keep in mind that their stores are ultimately liable for property damaged at or stolen from their premises.

To increase shopper confidence, malls may offer some or all of the following services:

- A lost and found area (items may be kept in the security office for a maximum period of 30–90 days until claimed).
- A telecommunications device for the deaf (TDD)—a text-messaging machine that allows deaf or hearing-impaired people to communicate.
- Jump starts (visitors whose cars have stalled may call security for assistance or referrals).
- Escorts (a specially appointed roving security guard may be assigned to escort shoppers to their cars; a similar service may also be extended to employees of the retail tenants).
- Medical emergency services (security may assist with medical emergencies or may contact local authorities as needed).

Gangs

Although most malls do not have gang problems, gang activity is no longer limited to urban areas. Gangs also pose problems in some suburban areas.

Why should managers of shopping malls be concerned about gangs? Gangs are driven in part by a desire for profit, and shopping centers provide an outlet for profitable crimes. Shoplifting, robbery, drug transactions, and car theft are examples.

Fights (territorial disputes), assaults, and graffiti are likewise activities of gangs. These and other types of intimidating behaviors can chase shoppers away.

How can a mall manager know if gangs have infiltrated a shopping center? One of the obvious signs of overt gang activity is graffiti, especially if incidents are on the rise. (Graffiti should be photographed so police can identify the person or group responsible, then it should be washed off or painted over as soon as possible.) Another key indicator is a rising number of crimes of opportunity such as shoplifting, purse-snatching, and thefts in parking lots.

In general, any suspicious activity in the parking lot should raise a red flag. Gangs often use mall parking lots as drop zones for drugs. The usual clues are youths driving cars without license plates or a car that attracts a steady stream of teenagers.

The following are specific suggestions for minimizing the presence and activities of gangs at shopping centers:

- Cooperate with the police department and community organizations that work with youths and gangs.
- Hire security officers who reflect the demographics of the neighborhood to encourage a sense of community.
- In large open malls, a mobile security force can closely watch parking lots, mall plazas, or isolated restaurants.
- Provide seminars on shoplifting, credit card fraud, response tactics, and arrest procedures for retail tenants' employees. Proper training creates more awareness and confidence among retailers' employees that they can help combat gang-related activities.
- Try to place similar-content retail stores at different ends of the mall to discourage large gatherings of gangs.

Additional information on how to detect gang presence on managed properties and how to address gang activity is presented in Chapter 20.

Teens in Malls

According to ongoing research by Teenage Research Unlimited in Northbrook, Illinois, American teens spend more than $170 billion per year ($171 billion in 2001; $172 billion in 2002; $175 billion in 2003), and the amount continues to grow. Obviously, teens are responsible for a significant percentage of sales in shopping centers, and they must be handled with great care. Specific statistics on teen shoppers can be found on the Internet at www.teenresearch.com.

How can managers of shopping centers make a difference? Getting teens involved is a proactive answer to combat aimless loitering and encourage mutual respect. Some malls sponsor career education seminars in local high schools to help give teens direction and goals. Others allow high school clubs to meet in empty retail spaces or invite them to edit and publish a teen newsletter sponsored by the mall and distributed throughout the community. Still others participate in jobs programs for at-risk teens.

Police Substations in Malls

The presence of local police on the mall is always reassuring. Some mall managers provide local police with a specially designated substation on the mall premises. Such substations provide a sense of security for mall patrons and retail tenants and may serve as a meeting place for uniting parents with lost children. They also allow for a stronger security presence, which discourages civil disruption and criminal activity.

If you invite police to operate a substation in a mall you manage, be sure the mall's insurance and the substation's insurance provide adequate and appropriate coverages since the mall ownership is allowing a formal police presence on private property.

Customer Awareness Programs

To create and reinforce a sense of order on the premises, shopping center managers should clearly post mall security policies and standards of conduct in visible locations. These standards of conduct will apply to mall patrons and gang members alike. Security guards should wear uniforms that identify them as mall security. If the mall includes a police substation, the security posting should include directions to the substation for easy access.

Some mall managers encourage weekly family nights for patrons to build a strong sense of community. Others work hard to establish relationships with local high schools by offering special discounts to students who present satisfactory grade reports or allowing high school groups to stage fund-raising events at the mall. This helps build a sense of trust and mutual respect between patrons and mall staff.

Mall Watch   Retailers want more customers in their stores. Customers want to feel safe where they shop. However, the fears and negative perceptions generated as a result of actual or attempted criminal incidents drive customers away.

As another approach to security awareness, shopping center managers might consider starting a mall watch program. Mall watch is a proactive program that allows customers, mall merchants, mall security, and law enforcement agencies to work together to fight crime and control store losses. A mall watch can be effective in curtailing all kinds of undesirable activity at a retail site, including shoplifting, the passing of bad checks, and credit card fraud as well as car theft and personal assaults. The local police crime prevention unit may be willing to provide information and training to mall management personnel and retailer's employees.

Most mall watch programs are patterned after a neighborhood watch, combining awareness with educational seminars and a telephone alert network. Sometimes community groups volunteer to patrol the parking lot and exterior areas of a mall on bicycles or in cars, wearing colored caps or T-shirts that identify them as part of the mall watch.

Customers are also an important component of a mall watch. They can participate actively by reporting any suspicious behavior they might observe in the parking lot or inside the mall to the nearest mall security guard or store employee who can contact the appropriate persons in the mall watch network. By helping make the shopping mall property unfriendly to criminals, customers make their own shopping experiences more enjoyable and profitable and make the mall more inviting to other shoppers.

Evacuation of Malls

Evacuation procedures that apply generally for all types of properties are outlined in Chapter 4. There are also specific issues that should be considered in planning evacuation procedures for shopping centers and retail properties.

Shopping center evacuation is, at first glance, a heart-stopping thought. Moving large numbers of people—many of whom have no idea where to go or what to do during an emergency—is no easy task. Management must create an evacuation procedure that everyone can follow quickly with minimal questions.

The larger the center, the more complex the evacuation plan. Strip centers with stores that open directly onto a parking lot do not need sophisticated evacuation procedures. People generally will be able to find their own way to safety without difficulty.

Large multistory centers and enclosed malls, on the other hand, require well-thought-out evacuation procedures. Getting the word to merchants and their employees and customers that the property must be evacuated is more difficult. Management is dependent on the cooperation of retail tenants to make sure their customers know what to do during an emergency. If the center needs to be cleared, customers must be directed to the nearest safe exit. If the emergency is a violent storm or a tornado or an earthquake, retailers' staffs will need to know where to direct customers to gather in safety. However, training in emergency procedures and especially in evacuation procedures poses several challenges. Unlike apartment residents and employees of office building tenants who can be trained to evacuate their premises and the building by conducting drills, the majority of the people at a shopping center are retailers' customers who are only visiting the property. The potential for training is further limited because retailers often employ seasonal and part-time salespeople, and there is a high turnover among these workers.

There are a number of ways to notify retail tenants and customers of an emergency. A center-wide PA system, phone calls to merchants, and security vans with loudspeakers in the parking lots are popular alternatives. Whatever system is used, management should repeat the announcement on a continuous basis, telling customers what they should do and where they should go. Some managers prepare written scripts for different situations that require evacuation. This saves time and prevents errors and omissions during public announcements.

The shopping center manager determines whether or not the center should be evacuated. This decision should be made following a discussion with the police, fire department, or other appropriate authorities and an evaluation of what is known. In turn, the shopping center manager notifies security and maintenance staff. In some situations, such as the discovery of a bomb or suspicious object, the police may order an evacuation. It should be pointed out, however, that different situations require different tactics, and unnecessary delay evacuating a shopping center in the event of a fire, a hazardous material spill, or any other incident posing danger to people on the property could cost lives.

Shopping center management staff should be assigned specific duties for evacuating a mall. Have them start at the center of the mall on each level and move outward, instructing shoppers to move toward the exits and advising store managers to close immediately. Additional staff members should also be stationed at each end of the mall.

The evacuation announcement should be worded in a way that will avoid panicking customers. For example, if the shopping center receives a bomb threat and the manager decides to evacuate the mall, the announcement should be nonspecific. Customers may simply be told that the mall is being closed. If a reason is stated, it may be vague, but it should be plausible so that people will begin to evacuate the mall. Once the announcement has been made and the property is evacuated, retailers' employees should conduct storewide searches to make sure no customers are lingering. The mall staff would search common areas for customers.

Note: *Guide to Writing a Shopping Center Security Manual* and *Guide to Writing a Shopping Center Tenant Manual,* both published by the International Council of Shopping Centers (ICSC), include information on emergency procedures that may be helpful to property managers and retail tenants

Special Lease Provisions

For retailers recovering from a disaster, the damage lies not only in the physical destruction of the property, but also in the vulnerability of established consumer shopping habits. When a store closes for any length of time, customers will find new places to shop, and their allegiance to the damaged shopping center may be lost.

Rebuilding quickly is the key to protecting a mall's business and reputation after a catastrophe. Other than a sound insurance policy to allow the manager to rebuild the damaged property, no document may be more important than a shopping center lease. As part of emergency preparedness, consider including the following provisions in shopping center leases:

- *Continuation of rent.* In most situations, tenant payments and other lease obligations should remain in full force while damage is being repaired.
- *Responsibility for repairs.* The landlord is generally responsible for repairing damage to the building's structural elements, such as the roof, walls, and common areas, while retail tenants must restore leasehold improvements such as wallpaper and carpet.
- *Time frame for repairs.* The lease should specify a time frame in which the owner is obligated to complete repairs.
- *Escape clause.* This provision makes it possible to release tenants without penalty if the landlord fails to finish the building repairs within a required time period or if the damage exceeds a predetermined limit. This can be beneficial for retail tenants during unexpected repair delays.

The manager should make every effort to encourage positive relations among the shopping center ownership/management, the retail tenants, and the insurer. If all are committed to restoring the building as quickly as possible, the retailers can get back into business and the property manager can reestablish rapport with the consumers.

13

Industrial Properties

Industrial properties typically fall into five basic categories—owner-occupied plants or manufacturing facilities, single-use bulk warehouses, multitenant warehouse/light manufacturing facilities, research and development buildings and parks, and office service/showrooms. Industrial properties in older urban areas are likely to be multistory buildings. Industrial developments in suburban areas are more likely to be single-story structures with large areas allocated for parking. Sites that include several buildings are often landscaped to create a park-like setting. There may be less interaction between the property manager and the tenants than at other types of properties. Tenants have specific responsibilities to provide a safe work environment for their employees as mandated under the Occupational Safety and Health Act. They should also have emergency plans to respond to incidents that are likely to occur in their work places based on the nature of their activities. However, there is still a need for the property manager to develop an evacuation plan for the property as a whole.

Emergency planning for these types of properties must consider the type of activity in the leased space, the equipment being used, and the number of tenant employees. Actions being taken to prevent emergencies are especially important. Property managers should seek assurances that tenants provide a safe work environment for their employees.

Note: The safety information presented in this chapter relates primarily to responsibilities of individual industrial employers. However, many of the rules also apply to property management staff and Emergency Management Team members as these individuals have need to enter a tenant's premises, whether in response to an emergency or otherwise.

Emergency Planning Considerations

Due to the nature of industrial users, emergency plans may need to include securing the area to prevent trespassing and to protect vital records and products on the premises. This is necessary also to prevent anyone who does not belong on the premises from being exposed to danger.

Due to the greater likelihood of hazardous materials (e.g., flammable, combustible, corrosive, and toxic chemicals) being present on industrial sites, it is helpful to maintain a duplicate set of vital property records off the premises, as noted in Chapter 1.

Because many manufacturing employees work in large enclosed spaces with few exits, exit routes must be clearly marked. Alarms or PA systems need to be loud enough to be heard above machinery noise; alternatively, flashing lights can be used to attract attention. Floors should be skidproof, due to the constant foot traffic.

Special attention should be given to the storage and management of hazardous raw materials, finished products, and wastes. Tenants must adhere to occupational safety and health standards and other labor regulations to prevent human errors and mechanical accidents on the property.

The property manager should be aware of what types of hazardous materials are present on the property. Tenants should be required to provide the manager with copies of material safety data sheets (MSDSs) covering the types of hazardous materials used and/or stored in their leased premises. They should also advise management when new, potentially hazardous materials are introduced.

Special Considerations

Industrial uses present numerous challenges because of the size of the space and the materials and equipment used in tenants' operations. As stated previously, industrial tenants have primary responsibility for safety in their leased premises. However, managers of industrial properties may wish to become familiar with some of the requirements that apply to specific types of tenants. Such information may be helpful in planning for emergency responses.

Warehouses

Management concerns about warehouse space are clean areas, proper storage of chemicals, safety devices on loading dock doors, clearly marked exit routes, and proper clearances. In particular, stored materials should only be stacked to prescribed heights to allow sprinklers and fire suppression systems to work properly.

Tenants and their employees are responsible to keep work areas free of materials and debris that can cause slip or trip and fall accidents. OSHA regulations and standards provide guidelines for recognizing these types of hazards and preventing accidents. Pallets and forklifts in aisles can slow evacuation in emergencies.

Multistory Structures

Manufacturing processes rely on complex heavy equipment, often set up in production lines that include conveyor systems and/or complicated pipelines. Industrial tenants who overload floor slabs in multistory structures can unknowingly put excessive weight on a structural support so that it eventually collapses. Collapse of an upper story can affect supporting walls, collapsing them as well. Because industrial machinery can weigh more than floors in the building are capable of holding, the lease may stipulate the weight capacity for each floor level. This may be stated on a square foot basis.

Hazardous Materials Storage and Disposal

Since industrial tenants may have numerous chemicals and other hazardous materials in or on their leased premises, proper storage and disposal should be a priority. Public walkways and heated rooms should be kept clear of hazardous materials to avoid spills, accidents, or heat-related explosions. Property managers should encourage their commercial tenants to become familiar with storage guidelines for chemicals they use. Storage guidelines are provided on product labels and material safety data sheets (MSDSs) from the chemical source along with information on specific hazards and recommended protections. Specific information can also be found in the *NIOSH Pocket Guide to Chemical Hazards (NPG)*, Publication 97-140, available for download on the Internet at www.cdc.gov/niosh/npg/npg.html. Guidelines for first responders to hazardous materials incidents can be found in the *2000 Emergency Response Guidebook* from the U.S. Department of Transportation and available for download at http://hazmat.dot.gov/erg2000/erg2000.pdf.

Leaking containers or spilled chemicals can generate deadly fumes. If the chemicals are flammable or combustible, the fumes may cause fires or explosions. Such an occurrence in an enclosed space can be devastating. All chemicals should be clearly labeled with their chemical name and specific hazards, as required under the Toxic Substances Control Act (TSCA) administered by the U.S. EPA. (More information on hazardous materials incidents can be found in Chapter 23.)

Industrial tenants should also understand and comply with proper disposal guidelines for their chemicals and hazardous wastes. Disposal of such wastes is closely regulated by the EPA under the Resource Conservation and Recovery Act (RCRA), also called Solid Waste Disposal Act. Numerous lawsuits have been filed against tenants and owners of industrial sites for improper disposal of hazardous wastes. Industrial property managers should research local, state, and federal waste disposal laws and regulations and make sure industrial tenants are aware of their responsibilities and liabilities. This issue should also be addressed in the lease to safeguard the property's management and ownership against potential liability resulting from an industrial tenant's negligence.

Ventilation

In fully or partially enclosed buildings such as factories or industrial plants, the industrial employer must ensure that proper ventilation exists to accommodate a large group of workers. Improper ventilation can result in poor indoor air quality (IAQ), which can impair the health and performance of industrial employees, especially if chemicals release fumes in use.

The local OSHA office can be contacted for a free on-site consultation regarding the safety of the property. Congress has authorized a joint federal-state activity whereby a state consultant can visit the site and give practical advice on a property's job safety and potential health problems, without issuing citations, proposing penalties, or reporting workplace conditions to authorities. The program is explained in OSHA publication 3047, *Consultation Services for the Employer*, which is available for download from the Internet at www.osha.gov.

Confined Spaces

Some emergency situations may necessitate entering confined spaces to rescue workers overcome by lack of oxygen or toxic fumes. Such spaces may include tanks, pits, vaults, sewers, and pipelines. Entry into these spaces can expose the rescuer to toxic gases, explosive atmospheres, oxygen deficiency, and electrical hazards. A person should never enter a confined space unless the atmosphere has been tested for lack of oxygen, toxic substances, and potential combustibility. If there is a possibility that management personnel may be called upon to assist in a rescue from a confined space, the property manager may wish to seek out more specific guidelines. Such information may be found in *Criteria for a Recommended Standard: Working in Confined Spaces* (NIOSH publication 80-106), which can be downloaded from the Internet at www.cdc.gov/niosh.

Personal Protection

Reliable protective equipment and clothing is essential for employees exposed to workplace hazards from machinery and materials, which could include:

Respiratory Protection

Respiratory protection is necessary for toxic atmospheres including dusts, gases, mists, or vapors and oxygen-deficient atmospheres. There are four basic categories of respirators:

- Air-purifying devices (particulate filters, gas masks, and chemical cartridges): These devices remove contaminants from the air but cannot be used in oxygen-deficient environments.
- Air-supplied respirators (airline respirators, hose masks): These should not be used in atmospheres that are immediately dangerous to human health.
- Self-contained breathing apparatus (SCBA): Required for unknown atmospheres, oxygen-deficient atmospheres, or atmospheres immediately dangerous to life or health (positive-pressure type only). SCBAs should have a minimum service life of 30 minutes.
- Escape masks or respirators.

Before assigning or using respiratory equipment, it is up to the industrial employer to ensure that: each employee has a medical evaluation to determine if the employee is physically able to use a respirator; a fit test is performed to verify a secure match between the face piece and the wearer; written use guidelines are posted; a regular maintenance program is in place to keep equipment safe and sanitary; and distribution areas for equipment used in emergencies are readily accessible.

Some types of equipment may require specific training to ensure proper use. Professional consultation is necessary to ensure adequate respiratory protection for specific work environments. Information on different types of respirators and their applicability can be found in the *NIOSH Guide to Industrial Respiratory Protection* (NIOSH publication 87-116) available for download on the Internet at www.cdc.gov/niosh/87-116.html.

- Chemical splashes or contact with toxic materials
- Falling objects and flying particles
- Unfamiliar atmospheres that may contain toxic gases and vapors or insufficient oxygen to sustain life
- Fires and electrical hazards

OSHA mandates the use of special protective gear by industrial workers in compliance procedures that must be enforced on the premises during industrial operations. Manufacturing supervisors should check with their state and local OSHA offices to ensure that industrial procedures and safety rules and equipment meet state and local guidelines.

In an emergency situation at an industrial property, members of the management staff may encounter the same types of hazards if they are required to provide assistance in a tenant's premises. They will need the same types of personal protection as the tenant's employees use. Protective safety equipment may include:

- Safety glasses, goggles, or face shields for eye protection
- Hard hats and safety shoes for head and foot protection
- Proper respirators for breathing protection (see box)

- Whole-body coverings, gloves, boots, and hoods for body protection from hazardous chemicals
- Body protection for extreme hot and cold temperatures, respectively, in environments that include industrial furnaces or refrigeration

Chemical plants should have multiple eye-wash stations as well as basins for hand washing positioned so they are readily accessible by workers in the event of a spill or splash.

Industrial operations often generate noise at levels that can be harmful. Workers in noisy environments should be provided with earplugs, earmuffs, or other protective devices to prevent hearing loss. (See *Personal Hearing Protection Devices*, published by NIOSH on the Internet at www.cdc.gov/niosh/96-110l.html.)

Selected equipment should be approved jointly by the Mine Safety and Health Administration (MSHA) and the National Institute for Occupational Safety and Health (NIOSH), or comply with the standards set by the American National Standards Institute (ANSI). Consultation with health and safety professionals is encouraged before choosing specific protective equipment.

Communications

During a major emergency involving a fire or explosion, it may be necessary to evacuate tenants' offices in addition to their manufacturing areas. Normal water, telephone, and electricity services may be disrupted or nonexistent. Consequently, it may be necessary to establish an alternate meeting place for industrial workers and other employees to assemble and in order to communicate with the fire department and other local authorities.

Alarms should be audible above the machinery noise common on industrial sites, and the tenant plant manager should explain to employees the methods for reporting emergencies, such as PA systems, pull stations, and telephones.

Effective March 11, 1994, OSHA mandated that all employers are required to establish hazard communication programs to transmit information on the hazards of chemicals to their employees. This should be done by means of labels on containers, MSDSs, and training programs. (Information on a wide range of specific chemicals is also available in the *NIOSH Guide to Chemical Hazards* mentioned previously in this chapter.) Implementation of these hazard communication programs complies with employees' "right-to-know" the hazards and identities of the chemicals they work with and will reduce the incidence of chemical-related occupational illnesses and injuries.

Evacuation

Evacuation plans for industrial sites will be dictated by specific tenants' uses. Often the flow of a production line (from raw materials to finished product) will determine where aisles are positioned and where workers performing specific tasks will stand or sit. It is important for exit signs to be visible, especially since there may be only a limited number of exits for a very large space. Workers may have to travel a long route to reach exits. Additional directional signs may be needed to ensure that directions to exits can be seen from all areas of the plant.

Tenants should be advised to take care in laying out production lines and equipment so that there will be multiple clear paths to all exits. The same applies in warehouses where pallets are stacked in multiple layers, limiting sight lines.

It may be necessary or appropriate to include loading docks as evacuation exits if they open to the outside and include stairs or walkways that would allow for such egress. Practice evacuations are a must.

Preparing for
Specific Types of Emergencies

14

Fire

Seldom do fires in commercial buildings lead to fatalities. Fire deaths occur most frequently in multifamily residences and single-family homes when fires are out of control and occupants are unable to escape. These victims have been disproportionally children, elderly people, and those who were unable to flee from the home, even if a smoke detector sounded an alarm. It is perhaps surprising that the primary cause of fire deaths is not the fire itself, but smoke inhalation—the carbon monoxide in smoke can be lethal. Smoke can also impede escape by obscuring routes to safety.

The most effective tactic to minimize fire damage is to put out the fire while it is still small. A fire may smolder for hours before bursting into flame and then consume an entire room in two minutes. The best advice is to call the fire department immediately whenever there is a fire.

Properties at Risk

According to statistics compiled by the Fire Analysis and Research Division of the National Fire Protection Association (NFPA), 1,687,500 fires were attended by public fire departments in the United States in 2002. Of that total number of fires, 519,000 (30.75%) occurred in structures—401,000 of them in residential properties—and 329,500 occurred in vehicles. The remainder, some 839,000 fires, occurred in "outside properties" including brush and timber, farm crops, outside storage facilities, and Dumpsters. What these statistics mean is that a fire occurs in a structure every 61 seconds; in particular, a residential fire occurs every 79 seconds.

There were a total of 3,380 civilian fire deaths in 2002, 2,670 (79%) were in the home. There were 18,425 civilian fire injuries in 2002, 14,050 occurring in residential properties. Nationwide, there was a civilian fire death every 156 minutes and a civilian fire injury every 28 minutes

Property damage from fires was estimated at $10,337,000,000. Structure fires accounted for $8,742,000,000 of damage, $6,055,000,000 of which was in residential properties. The latter breaks down into $5,005,000,000 in one- and two-family residences and $926,000,000 in apartments or multifamily dwellings.

Very few high-rise fires expand beyond the floor or room of origin because many high-rises employ such preventive measures as heat and smoke detectors, sprinkler systems, and fire-resistive construction. When people die in high-rise resi-

Statistics on Fires and Fire Loss in 1999

The National Fire Protection Association (NFPA) reported the following statistics for 1999.

Building Type	No. of Fires	Civilian Deaths	Civilian Injuries	Property Damage
One- and Two-Family	275,000	2,359	10,688	$3,861,500,000
Multifamily Buildings	95,100	514	5,191	$993,700,000
Office Buildings	5,500	5	62	$147,100,000
Retail[1]	17,800	10	253	$858,800,000
Industrial[2]	13,300	6	447	$420,300,000

[1] This category includes all types of stores and mercantile properties, including gasoline service stations;

[2] This category encompasses food, chemical, textile, and other manufacturing and processing facilities.

Source: *The U.S. Fire Problem Overview Report: Leading Causes and Other Patterns and Trends* (Quincy, Mass.: National Fire Protection Association, 2003).

The NFPA also reported these specific statistics for fires in high-rise buildings seven or more stories tall in 1999.

Building Type	No. of Fires	Civilian Deaths	Civilian Injuries	Property Damage	High-Rise as % of Total[1]
Apartments	10,000	27	448	$47,200,000	10.5%
Office Buildings	600	0	14	$6,100,000	11.4%
All Structures[2]	15,300	39	708	$80,800,000	—

[1] Total refers to all buildings of that type—i.e., 10.5% of all apartment building fires occurred in high-rise structures; 11.4% of all office building fires occurred in high-rises.

[2] The 15,300 high-rise structure fires represented only 3% of all building fires and 1% of civilian deaths, 10% of civilian injuries, and 2% of direct property damage loss.

Source: *High-Rise Building Fires* (Quincy, Mass.: National Fire Protection Association, 2003).

dential fires, they are much more likely to have been in close proximity to the fire. (Statistics on high-rise fires are included in the accompanying box.)

Older structures are at great risk. This is due to a number of factors, but most notably, these properties tend to lack:

- Adequate heating systems
- Safe electrical appliances
- Construction in accordance with strict electrical and building codes
- Use of fire stops in walls
- Access for fire-fighting equipment
- Modern fire-resistant building materials

The 2003 edition of the NFPA *Life Safety Code* requires existing high-rise apartment buildings to have automatic sprinkler systems installed throughout. The U.S. Fire Administration advocates the use of automatic fire sprinklers in residential buildings. There is also a National Residential Fire Sprinkler Initiative to require residential sprinkler systems in new construction of manufactured homes, college dormitories, and residential units owned, leased, subsidized, or otherwise supported by the federal government. Work on this initiative began at a meeting in April 2003.

Because building and fire codes are subject to change, property managers should keep up-to-date with applicable requirements and be sure that their buildings are in compliance.

Preventive Measures

Every property is vulnerable to fires. To determine what these vulnerabilities are, a property manager can arrange a walk-through of the premises with fire department personnel to inspect fire and alarm systems. This type of inspection includes evaluating the adequacy of the current emergency annunciator system and the fire control panel. Each sprinkler head and fire hose should have a flow switch monitored at the fire control panel. The fire control panel should be monitored around the clock in case of any after-hour alarm emergencies and should be inspected annually (or as required) for any malfunction or required repairs.

Managers should work with fire officials when developing a fire safety plan. They should also ask whether the alarm system should be connected directly to the fire department. One should not be dependent on a single fire alarm system. If it fails, the building may be unprotected. It is best to evaluate a variety of alarm systems. The following are some fire safety systems that could be employed.

- A supervised automatic sprinkler system.
- A class I standpipe system.
- A fire alarm system with an approved emergency voice and alarm communication system.
- Emergency lighting standby power and a central control station.

Automatically activated fire alarm systems may have a direct line to the local fire department through a central station (in accordance with NFPA standards). It may be appropriate to consider retrofitting a building with sprinklers. This may have to be done if local fire codes require sprinklers in existing buildings. Standpipes are usually installed as part of new construction. The cost of installing fire sprinklers depends on several factors:

- Proximity to water supplies
- Building and space use
- Degree of compartmentalization
- Building size
- Building construction materials
- Building complexity
- Quickness of response

It is a good idea to consult a fire-prevention expert regarding complex buildings and situations. In complex or specialized buildings, it may be most appropriate to have a single integrated fire system that is monitored 24 hours a day. Property managers can develop a three-way approach to fire prevention that includes:

1. A detection system.
2. A way to compartmentalize the fire, using code-approved fire walls and floors, UL-labeled doors, or smoke-activated doors that are held open until they are released by fire or smoke alarms and still permit people to exit through them.
3. A method of extinguishing a fire using sprinklers and other extinguishers
   —Halon (halogenated hydrocarbon) for computer rooms
   —Water
   —Wet and dry foam

Fire Extinguishers

Class A   Water based; used to extinguish fires in wood, cloth, paper, etc.

Class B   Chemical based; used to extinguish fires involving gasoline, oil, solvents, and other flammable liquids.

Class C   Dry chemical; used to extinguish fires in electrical equipment, wiring, etc.

Class ABC   Multipurpose; can be used on all types of fires.

Other classes of fires require special extinguishing materials. Fire extinguishers are labeled to indicate the types of fires they can be used against.

—Carbon dioxide
—Dry chemical

Portable fire extinguishers should be installed within easy reach and near a door, for easy access and to ensure a safe escape route for the user. Here are some other fire and life safety measures to consider implementing:

- Paint floor numbers boldly on the stair side of hall exit doors or the adjacent wall.
- Install smoke detectors in corridors, common areas, and elevators.
- Install a speaker system to guide in evacuations.
- Form a fire brigade with help and training from fire officials. The brigade would be responsible for:
  —Extinguishing small fires,
  —Contacting the fire department in the event of a fire, and
  —Evacuating occupants, property employees, and others on the premises.
- Test fire equipment according to local fire codes. Equipment to be tested includes alarm systems, fire extinguishers, sprinklers, exit doors and exit lights, and smoke detectors.
- Consider inviting fire officials to the property for inspections so they become familiar with the property. This could be advantageous in the event of a fire.
- Provide fire-safety education and training for occupants as well as your employees.
- Post all fire regulations and instructions prominently.
- On each floor, prominently post a scale drawing of the floor showing exits and evacuation routes.
- Make sure occupants are always able to exit through designated fire doors and that none of the doors is locked or obstructed. All exits should be mapped and posted.
- Post signs warning people not to use the elevators in case of a fire.
- Learn which fire extinguishers are for what types of fires. Property managers, management employees, and occupants (residents, commercial tenants' employees) should know where they are located and how to work them.
- Designate nonsmoking areas in the building and enforce them.
- Take special care during the holiday seasons, when decorations could create fire hazards.

Some Fire Prevention and Safety Tips

- Keep storage areas clean; do not let files, empty cartons, waste, or rags collect.
- Keep heating appliances away from walls and combustible materials.
- Encourage occupants not to stack or store items close to fire sprinkler heads, where they may hinder the flow of water when the system is actuated.
- Inspect electrical equipment.
  —Does it work properly?
  —Does it give off an unusual odor?
  —Are cords frayed or cracked?
  —Are cords placed where they will be stepped on or chafed?
  —Is there more than one extension cord per outlet?
- Ensure that deadbolts and other locks work quickly and easily.
- Be sure that windows open and close easily.
- Specify/control how cooking appliances are to be used, including what types of appliances are permitted. (Typically, hot plates are prohibited, and microwave popcorn is specifically discouraged because it burns easily and sets off smoke alarms.) As a general rule, stoves and open-flame cooking are not permitted in office buildings other than in food service establishments.

There are also photoluminescent (glow-in-the-dark) exit signs with directional arrows and self-adhesive tapes that can be used to provide additional visual cues during an evacuation. The exit signs are often placed low on a wall (i.e., above the baseboard). The tape may be placed on the floor in stairwells or corridors or around stairwell door frames, preferably in areas that are normally lit 24 hours a day. If there is a smoky fire or a power outage, the glow-in-the-dark luminescence can help direct people to exits.

Aside from the obvious benefits of implementing fire prevention and safety precautions, having such a program can be a significant marketing tool. A sound fire safety program can encourage safety-conscious prospective residents and commercial tenants to locate in a given property.

Smoke Detectors

The best way to reduce fire deaths is to prevent fires, and fire experts agree that one of the most effective fire prevention tactics is an early-warning system to get people out as quickly as possible. The best way to provide the earliest warning is to install an adequate number of smoke detectors.

There are two types of smoke detectors—ionization detectors activate quicker for fast, flaming fires while photoelectric detectors are quicker for slow, smoldering fires. Either will provide sufficient warning. Smoke detectors emit a very loud audible signal when potentially dangerous levels of smoke are detected in the indoor air. If there are hearing-impaired people on the property, smoke alarms that flash a light or vibrate are also available.

Smoke detectors should be installed on each floor in residences and buildings. (Manufacturers' instructions for installation will often recommend specific locations; local ordinances may specify multiple locations for installation.) Smoke detectors may be powered by electrical current or batteries or a combination (hard wired with battery backup). Battery-powered detectors should be tested periodically to confirm that the battery has not expired. Many fires have raged out of control simply because the resident has neglected to replace a defunct smoke detector battery.

Carbon Monoxide Detectors

Carbon monoxide (CO) originates from faulty gas furnaces, gas stoves, automobile exhaust seeping in through attached garages, and fireplaces. Being odorless and colorless, CO cannot be easily detected, so victims experiencing symptoms of increasingly intense drowsiness may be unaware of the immediate danger. Due to the high number of deaths in homes resulting from carbon monoxide (CO) poisoning, many local building codes require CO alarms in residences that use gas or oil or have a fireplace. Like smoke detectors, CO detectors can be hard-wired, battery operated, or hardwired with battery backup. Batteries should be tested regularly and replaced as needed. The sensor element in CO alarms must also be replaced regularly. The property manager would be wise to inspect his or her property for potential pipe breaks or leaks and install carbon monoxide detectors where appropriate. The gas company may also be asked to send a representative to check for gas leaks.

Fire Command Stations

Fire command stations are another option for properties to use in fire prevention and response. The stations are equipped with fire command panels which display locations and floors where fire alarms and other emergency alarms are sounded. Many are also equipped with handheld microphones, which allow authorities with key access to make announcements buildingwide. This enables quick notification of evacuation for specific floors or the entire building. Telephone intercoms allow the person at the control panel to talk to floor monitors to assess fire conditions.

During a Fire

No matter how small a fire appears to be, the fire department should always be contacted. This should be emphasized as the first instruction in a fire response plan. Moreover, it should never be assumed that someone else has already called the fire department.

What else should the property manager and others on the premises do during a fire? These procedures should be included in the emergency procedures manual:

- Shut off power to the fire area. (Provide specific instructions and assign this task to a member of the Emergency Management Team.)
- Close as many doors as possible while escaping from a fire to prevent the fire from spreading; however, do not endanger yourself by doing so.
- Get down, and keep low. Smoke rises; clean air is nearest to the floor.

Instructions for leaving a building:
- Maintain contact with a wall.
- Use handrails while descending stairs.
- Take off high-heeled or awkward shoes.
- Test doors before opening by putting the back of your hand to them. If the door is hot, find another way out. If it is cool, open the door slowly and carefully, and be ready to close it quickly if heat or smoke pours in.
- Walk calmly; never panic or shove others.

- If clothing catches fire, stop, drop, and roll. Do not panic and run; this will only fan the flames.
- Cover your face with your hands.
- Drop gently to the ground.
- Never beat at the flames with your hands; rather, smother them with your body.
- After escaping the building and getting to the street, move away from the building. Do not block firefighters and equipment.
- Be careful of falling glass.

What to do if you cannot escape:

- Try to find a room with an exterior window, and stay there until help arrives.
- Use the telephone, if possible, to call the fire department and let personnel know exactly where you are.
- Open the window slightly to allow in fresh air and to create positive air pressure to help keep out smoke.
- Keep smoke out by sealing cracks and covering vents with clothing, newspapers, towels, etc.
- If possible, breathe through a wet cloth.
- Wave something brightly colored out the window to attract attention.
- Keep in mind that most fire department ladders do not reach above six floors, which means that other methods will be used for a rescue on higher floors.

Where appropriate, members of the Emergency Management Team and other specially trained personnel should administer first aid and tend to people who are injured. Use only water to soothe burns; never apply salve or butter. Professional medical attention is needed for serious injuries or burns. Those victims should be transported to a hospital or trauma center immediately. (See Chapter 19 for more information on medical emergencies.)

After a Fire

The fire department has jurisdiction until the fire is put out. They must release control or give permission to re-enter before anything can be done.

The property manager may be overwhelmed with responsibilities after a fire. There may not be time to think about exactly what must be done and in what order. That is why the duties in the aftermath of a fire should be detailed in the emergency procedures manual. Here are some suggestions:

- Notify the building owner, insurance company, and, if necessary, a disaster recovery contractor.
- For insurance purposes, be careful not to disturb anything at the fire site before arson investigators make a thorough search.
- Secure the property from the elements and looters.
  —Cover broken windows with plywood and plastic.
  —Fix all doors that have been burned or broken by firefighters.
- Call in all available employees and contractors to aid in the cleanup.
- Comply with all fire department requests.
- Restore power to damaged areas. This may require assistance from the utility.
- Arrange for an electrician to thoroughly check the electrical system.
- Inspect the property; appoint cleanup crews, and devise a schedule.
- Wear a hard hat while investigating the damage.

- Beware of hazardous materials such as friable or burned asbestos as well as burned or loosened lead-based paint.
- Clean common areas first so they can be used by the remainder of the building's occupants.
- Clean non-fire floors of debris, broken glass, water, and soot left by the fire and firefighters.
- Do the detail work last.
- Use encapsulated odor-absorbing particles to eliminate fire smells.
- Take prompt action to remove water, by extraction, dehumidification, or both.
- Do not attempt to wash walls, ceilings, or porous surfaces. This work should not be undertaken without supervision, as many cleaning techniques can actually worsen the damage.
- Have elevator mechanics check the operation of elevators.
- Have elevator systems cleaned; use deodorizing gels to prevent the pumping motion of the cars from redistributing soot and odors.
- Contract with a disaster restoration contractor, if appropriate, to evaluate the damage and provide specialized clean-up services.
- Seek outside help to evaluate potential for mold growth and/or remediate mold that occurs.
- Account for all expenses related to damage caused by the fire.
- Notify affected occupants of the damage and the status of restoration; it is important to keep residents or commercial tenants apprised of progress with the cleanup.

Fire with Other Disasters

Fire can accompany other disasters, as part of the event or in its aftermath. An earthquake can damage natural gas pipelines, propane containers, and gasoline tanks in vehicles causing leaks of materials that could explode or ignite. Alternative heating devices used during winter storms, tornadoes, hurricanes, or floods can pose fire hazards if they are not used properly. Unless they are properly used and maintained, generators used during power outages can be hazardous. Pools of water from floods or storms can be electrically charged, which can lead to an electrical fire. Fire safety should be a consideration in planning for other types of disasters. The U.S. Fire Administration has published a series of fact sheets on fire during and after different types of disasters. These can be accessed online at www.usfa.fema.gov/public/factsheets/safety.shtm.

15

Power Outages

Unforeseen power outages caused by faulty wiring, utility blackouts, thunderstorms, hurricanes, floods, or earthquakes can be devastating to both humans and real property. Property managers must pay attention to their buildings' power needs and be equipped to respond to power outages in emergency situations.

What to Expect

In the event of a power outage, all electrical systems in the building will shut down. The total darkness (except for perhaps a supply of flashlights) will greatly inhibit evacuation unless a backup lighting system is in place. Elevators may stop between floors, leaving inhabitants trapped. Electrically operated security doors, garage doors, and gates will not operate, impeding evacuation. Computer systems may lose their memories and files.

How to Prepare

The emergency procedures manual should include a plan to prepare for and respond to power outages. It is beneficial to have an up-to-date diagram showing where the building's power transformers, generators, circuit breakers, and standby electrical supply systems are located, which will enable the Emergency Management Team to track the source of partial or full power outages and restore service as soon as possible. A detailed diagram showing which switches serve which areas in the building and to what transformers they are connected allows a property manager to direct the contractor or repair person to the source of a localized outage. This preparation also reduces hourly contractor billing costs.

During an actual incident, the property manager should ask such questions as the following:

- How extensive is the power outage?
- Which floors and voltage loads are affected?
- Does the outage require an evacuation of the building?

The manager should also be familiar with municipal building and fire codes, which stipulate whether emergency power backup equipment is required on the premises.

Regularly check the property's backup equipment such as battery-powered lighting systems and emergency generators. Some municipal codes require periodic maintenance of emergency generators.

Become familiar with all equipment on the premises that could be affected by a power outage. The following two-step approach could be considered:

1. Identify all critical operations, including:
   —Utilities such as electric power, gas, water, hydraulics, compressed air, municipal and internal sewer systems, and wastewater treatment services.
   —Security and alarm systems, lighting, elevators, electrical distribution systems, and heating, ventilating, and air-conditioning (HVAC) systems.
   —Communications systems, both internal and external, data- and voice-controlled.
   —Business equipment necessary for business continuity (computers, fax machines, copiers).
   —Electronic access controls (exit doors, computer rooms, vaults).
2. Establish preventive maintenance schedules for all systems and equipment.

In California—and other parts of the United States—intentional power outages are activated by the utility on a predetermined schedule. Often called "rolling blackouts," a local utility may reduce electrical output in an area for a set period of time during peak usage hours to prevent large-scale grid failures. Because rolling blackouts are announced beforehand, you can post signs warning building occupants of impending outages. Before such an outage, sensitive electronic equipment that can be damaged by a power surge—such as computers, photocopiers, and faxes—should be shut off, and people in the building should be warned to stay out of elevators.

Install Backup Emergency Generators

Many buildings utilize an emergency generator to provide power to exit lights, stairwell lights, and emergency lighting in tenants' premises. In the event of a power outage, these generators provide critical voltage loads, which are connected to an automatic transfer switch. When the switches sense that voltage from a normal source has been interrupted for a predetermined time, they automatically transfer power to the emergency backup generator. The emergency generator, in turn, transmits the energy to transformers, which convert the power to a useable voltage.

Generators operate on diesel fuel or natural gas, so they must be located in safe, cool areas and maintained properly. Their location might be in or next to fire command panels, emergency lighting systems, communications boxes, elevators, or other easy-access locations. Sometimes large generators may be located outside the building, especially in suburban areas.

It is important to know how long the generators will provide backup power (30–90 minutes, for example). The Emergency Management Team will need to know how much time and light they will have to attempt to restore operations and safely evacuate building occupants if necessary.

Identify Other Power Sources

If your building does not have a backup emergency generator, determine if it is necessary to have alternative plans in case of power outages. A battery-operated backup PA system will facilitate smooth evacuation and help avoid panic. Additional emergency lighting with a battery backup system can be installed in each stairwell.

Floor wardens should have portable, battery-operated lamps or flashlights, and

Emergency Alert System

Created by the Federal Communications Commission (FCC), the national Emergency Alert System (EAS) uses digital technology to distribute messages so that state and local officials can quickly send out important local emergency information targeted to a specific area. The EAS uses the same digital signal as used by the National Weather Service and the Federal Emergency Management System. The signal is decoded by EAS equipment at broadcast stations and cable systems. Specially equipped consumer products (e.g., televisions, radios, pagers) can also decode EAS messages.

The EAS is tested weekly using an eight-second digital data signal. Monthly tests include a spoken message. This is the source of the "test" messages heard periodically on radio and television.

Because EAS messages may not be broadcast on all available airwaves, it is important to know which local radio and television stations make such broadcasts. Alternatively, one should have a transistor radio that can be tuned to NOAA Weather Radio (NWR).

the property manager should have a transistor radio to monitor local news updates in the event of an area-wide blackout. (Citizens are discouraged from calling 911 for information; the electric utility is usually the primary information source, providing announcements for broadcast to the public.)

Safeguard the Electrical System

Some additional actions a property manager may take to safeguard against electrical blackouts include the following:

- Ensure that all electrical panels, switches, and fuses are enclosed in metal cabinets that close securely.
- Ensure that all circuits are easily identifiable.
- Ensure that all fuses or circuit breakers are properly sized for equipment and lighting. (Maintain a supply of replacement fuses.)
- Ensure that the property does not have recurring problems with fuses or circuit breakers that are continually tripped.
- Ensure that all ground fault interrupters (GFIs) are safe to use—e.g., not in potentially damp areas.
- Protect/insulate power connections that are exposed to the elements. (These should be inspected periodically to ensure the integrity of the protective material.)
- Ensure that sound system, computer, and office equipment is protected by surge protectors. For some equipment, an uninterruptible power supply (UPS) may be more appropriate than a surge protector.
- Avoid using extension cords as permanent power sources in lieu of hard wiring or adding an electrical outlet.
- Ensure that adequate clearances or suitable protective layers are provided between recessed light fixtures and insulating materials.
- Inspect and test the emergency generator regularly.

Power Surges and Surge Protection

Power surges result when the electrical charge carried on power lines is boosted. Lightning is probably the most familiar source of power surges. A lightning strike can cause a surge that will overpower almost any system. A more common source is refrigerators, air conditioners, elevators, and other types of equipment that require substantial amounts of energy to switch motors on and off, creating sudden brief increases in demand for power. While not as intense as a lightning surge, these changes in demand can cause damage to sensitive equipment. Other sources of power surges include downed power lines, problems with the utility's equipment, and faulty wiring.

To protect electronic equipment from power surges, individual surge protectors are needed for each outlet. Surge protectors are available in varying levels of quality and capacity. The basic *power strip* is an extension cord with 5 or 6 grounded outlets. A better, more-expensive version will include an indicator light and separate switches for each individual outlet. (In a lightning storm, a surge protector may be inadequate; it is better to unplug the computer.)

Larger models, called *surge stations,* offer superior voltage protection and may include input and output phone lines to protect a modem and have built-in circuit breakers. Greater protection is provided by an *uninterruptible power supply (UPS)* unit, which converts alternating current (AC) to direct current (DC) stored in a battery. The UPS converts the DC power from the battery to AC power for the electronic components attached to it. While a UPS does give a high level of protection, a surge protector should be used along with it to protect the UPS from being damaged by a power surge.

Inventory Emergency Equipment

For insurance purposes and protection against liability, keep an up-to-date list of emergency equipment on hand. A backup generator may qualify the building for additional insurance benefits. Adhere to a periodic maintenance inspection schedule to ensure that all emergency backup systems and equipment are ready for immediate use.

Problems to Anticipate

While electrical blackouts or power failures are likely to occur during the course of other emergencies, they can also be emergencies themselves. In the event of a power failure, it is essential to determine its cause and extent. Even the smallest power outages should be investigated. The loss of power to a single apartment unit, office suite, or store space may indicate a potentially serious problem.

Loss of power affecting the entire building should be reported to the local electric utility immediately to ensure that electric company personnel know your property has no power and will begin efforts to restore electrical service if such work has not been started already. If the outage affects a larger area, utility personnel or an electric company hotline may provide information on the extent of the outage and when they expect service to be restored.

If power fails as part of another emergency, the emergency procedures for that type of event would likely be implemented. But when a power failure occurs apart from another emergency, it is wise to keep building occupants from moving around the building unnecessarily. In a residential property, an isolated electrical blackout is usually no reason to evacuate. Most residents could be encouraged to remain in their units and use flashlights during that type of power failure. (Use of candles and open flames should be discouraged.) At a commercial property, tenants' employees could be escorted from the building by Emergency Management Team members. It may be necessary to implement crowd control measures if there is an indication of panic among evacuees. If the power failure cannot be easily remedied (i.e., it is not related to blown fuses or tripped circuit breakers), the local electric utility should be called in to investigate and make repairs.

The property manager may inform residents and commercial tenants of the cause and extent of the loss of power, the recovery efforts under way, and the expected duration of the outage.

Stalled Elevators

Elevators that have stalled because of a power outage can usually be controlled manually by emergency personnel. (See Chapter 16 for specific information on elevator emergencies.)

Disrupted Sewage Lines

Because electricity powers pumps that move water and sewage in many areas, a power outage can disrupt sewage discharges. Include a backup alternative in case your sewage operations are disrupted. Keep an updated telephone number for a local portable toilet service or have plastic liner bags accessible for use in wastebaskets as temporary toilets. Advise occupants to tie the bag after each use to minimize odor, prevent spilling, and avoid spreading infection.

Other Types of Damage

Major equipment and sensitive electrical equipment such as computers that may be damaged by a power surge or that may cause damage when power is restored should be turned off until power has been restored. Tenants who have major computer network installations should have their own backup power for the network; however, individual computer terminals may be turned off as an added precaution.

Another concern during an electrical blackout is the spoilage of food in refrigerators and freezers that could result from a prolonged loss of power. Utilities usually recommend keeping refrigerator and freezer doors closed for the duration. Many retail tenants keep food and other perishable merchandise refrigerated. Some commercial refrigerators and freezers are open all the time. If a power outage is lengthy and risk of spoilage seems likely, property managers could encourage residents or commercial tenants to dispose of perishable items to avoid health risk.

Extended Power Outage

Power outages of long duration—24 hours or longer—require more extensive emergency planning, particularly if the outage is widespread. The 2003 blackout on the East Coast is one example. Also, a severe storm can cause heavy damage over a wide area, including downed power lines that take more than a day to repair. Because such events do occur, it may be wise to have plans in place that address these additional considerations:

- Evacuation will empty a building. Where do occupants go if it is night and there are no streetlights? Those who drive will have lights in their cars. What if public transportation is compromised by an outage? How do people get home? Do they go home?

- A power failure may trap people in one or more elevators. Do the elevators have emergency hatches or trap doors for rescuing people?

- Electronic door locks will not work without power. If backup generator power is exhausted, what provisions will be needed to secure the property? Will (additional) security personnel be needed? How will they be transported to the property?

- Essential building personnel may have to remain at the property. Are there stockpiles of food and water for such personnel? What about sanitation facilities? If personnel are off site and have to return to the building, what provisions will be needed for them to access the building during a power outage (e.g., identification passes)?

- Communications equipment may fail. While battery-operated radios and televisions will allow access to information from outside the property, how can people outside the property be reached? What if cell phone service is curtailed (e.g., because transmission equipment is knocked out or high traffic exceeds the capacity)? Are there hard-wired phone lines available for the property manager, building engineer, and security personnel? Are similar lines available for occupants' use?

- Emergency power generation equipment will only run till its fuel is exhausted. What provisions have been made to ensure a supply of fuel in an emergency? Has consideration been given to having multiple fuel sources in case a supplier is shut down?

- Extreme outdoor temperatures may cause damage inside a building. Do water pipes need protection from freezing? Is excessive heat and humidity likely to cause warping (e.g., of wood veneer finishes) or lead to mold growth?

Given the way U.S. and Canadian power grids are set up, it may be advisable to run an occasional test of the building power system to ensure that established emergency plans and procedures will work during a real power outage. The idea of such testing may raise concerns from commercial tenants about business interruptions. However, it makes more sense to test in advance than to wait for a real emergency to find out that a plan or procedure does not work.

An even more extensive plan may be necessary or appropriate. It may be desirable to install a gas-fired on-site generating system to provide power for the building. While this will require capital investment, the heat generated as a by-product can be used to heat and cool the property, and it may be possible to negotiate a favorable long-term contract with the gas supplier that protects the property against price fluctuations.

How to Respond

Once the emergency generator starts after a power outage, the source of the outage should be immediately located. This is where the diagram of power sources and connections is helpful. The property manager should then notify the utility company of the source and severity of the building's outage.

In addition, the property manager should instruct building staff to call all elevators to the ground floor to let out anyone who may be trapped. If it is safe, all stairwell doors should be unlocked to allow people free access from floor to floor. The freight elevator will be used to give emergency personnel access to the building and to transport those who may be unable to use the stairwells because they have a physical disability or other medical condition. It is also wise to activate one elevator in any parking garage that is part of the premises.

Building occupants should turn off all electrical equipment in their leased premises to prevent equipment damage from an electrical surge when power is restored. Even short lapses in power quality or a few seconds of electrical deprivation could inhibit use of electrical elevators as well as cause permanent loss of computer data files and programming. Emergency generators may only be programmed to route energy to more critical voltage requirements such as elevators, electric doors, and lighting.

Property managers may recommend that a building's occupants have a backup power system for their computers to maintain an uninterrupted power supply. A battery backup power system keeps computers from being affected by power surges. Depending on the product, the backup system can provide constant power from three minutes to several hours. These products can be purchased from a local computer supplier. (See discussion of Power Surges and Surge Protection earlier in this chapter.)

For general information on the status of a blackout, occupants can send one individual to the property manager or on-site security desk (if available). Post a staff person (or a guard, if there is one) at the main entrances and exits to ensure that no intruders enter the building and to monitor removal of equipment from the premises.

Partial Outages

A partial outage can occur when a fuse is blown or a circuit breaker is tripped or when excessive voltage is drawn from the power system—for example, when too many pieces of electrical equipment are drawing energy from one extension cord or electrical outlet. When this occurs, simply switch the appropriate circuit breaker off, then unplug some of the electrical equipment. When you switch the circuit breaker on again, the power should return. If it does not, unplug more equipment until the outlet matches the voltage demand.

Shutting Down Operations

Shutting down a facility is generally a last resort, but it may be necessary in extreme situations such as a natural disaster or a major threat to a property's occupants. Some facilities require only simple actions such as turning off equipment, locking doors, and activating alarms. Others may require intricate shutdown plans. The property manager should work with the Emergency Management Team in preparing shutdown plans for the emergency procedures manual. The procedures should address:

- When and how to shut off each utility.
- Who can order a shutdown.
- Conditions that could necessitate a shutdown.
- Who will carry out shutdown procedures.
- How a partial shutdown would affect other facility operations.
- The length of time required to complete a shutdown—and for restarting.

The Emergency Management Team should be trained in shutdown procedures. Posting shutdown procedures next to the respective equipment/system controls will allow for easy reference.

Restoring Power

If there is a power outage and a property is equipped with a backup power generator, the power will go off for approximately two or three seconds before the emergency system starts to supply electricity to corridors, emergency stairwells, exit lights, elevator communications systems, fire pumps, freight elevators, or wherever it is programmed to supply power.

When full power is restored, all emergency electrical systems will go off for approximately two or three seconds, and then they will draw full power from the utility source. After this occurs, advise your staff to restore permanent elevator service to the building as well as HVAC service. Remember that the air-conditioning system will take time to cool the building, especially if the blackout lasted several hours.

The amount of power passing through the building when power is restored may trip circuit breakers. An occupant whose total electrical supply is not restored should be advised to notify the management office. Care must be taken to restore power systematically and not cause additional damage.

16

Elevator Emergencies

An elevator car may stop between floors because of a power failure, activation of the car safety device, or a malfunction of the elevator equipment, or it may be stopped because of a fire or other emergency situation. Stalled elevators are a major concern for managers of multilevel buildings.

Being trapped in an elevator makes even the bravest person feel vulnerable. People trapped in a stalled elevator are often afraid that it will fall unchecked. However, this is unlikely to happen because built-in safety mechanisms activate immediately in most situations to prevent elevators from falling, even if an elevator cable is cut.

If an elevator breakdown occurs during an emergency and the incident is accompanied by property damage, the situation can be life-endangering. This is why occupants concerned about such malfunctions will take comfort in knowing that the property in which they live or work has a plan for responding to an elevator emergency.

Areas and Properties at Risk

Obviously, any building with an elevator is at risk of an elevator emergency. The taller the building, the greater the risk of an emergency arising if an elevator malfunctions.

Areas of the United States that are earthquake-prone present special risks, and it is appropriate to adopt preventive measures for buildings in such areas (see Chapter 30). Any disaster that disrupts electrical power can also impact elevator operation, so it is appropriate to implement some general measures to prevent elevator emergencies or, at least, minimize their impact.

- Develop a comprehensive plan of action in case of fire, earthquake, or other major disaster.
- Appoint an individual and an alternate to oversee implementation of the plan of action.
- Install a separate communication system for elevators that includes emergency signals for passenger use. Have a backup power source for these systems in case normal power is disrupted.
- Install emergency car lighting that will turn on automatically in the event of a power failure.

Elevator Safety Tips

- Do not attempt to enter or exit an elevator while the doors are closing.
- Stand aside for exiting passengers.
- Watch your step while entering or exiting elevators. Look down to make sure the elevator cab is even with the floor.
- Once inside, press the button for your floor and move to the rear of the car.
- Stand next to a wall in the elevator. If there is a handrail, hold onto it. Do not lean on elevator doors.
- When the elevator stops, stand clear so that passengers can exit and enter.
- If the doors do not open when the elevator stops, press the "door open" button. If that does not open the doors, use the built-in alarm, intercom, or telephone to signal for help.

In the event of an elevator emergency, passengers should:

- Stay calm.
- Use the alarm, intercom, or telephone in the elevator to signal trouble.
- Stay put. Never try to pry open elevator doors or climb out of the opening on the roof of the car unless assisted by trained emergency personnel.
- Always use stairways (not elevators) to exit a building in an emergency.

Note: These tips can be shared with residents and commercial tenants' employees in their respective tenant manuals or via a property newsletter.

- Make sure there are emergency work lights in the elevator machine room.
- Train management staff, especially maintenance and security personnel, on what to do in the event of an elevator emergency.

Elevator manufacturers and companies that provide contract elevator maintenance services are the best sources of specific information on elevators and elevator emergencies. In most situations, there will be little that on-site personnel can do, but they should know what can be done while they wait for the elevator service contractor's personnel to arrive.

Modern elevators often have emergency communications and lighting systems built in. If these features are not present in the elevators in an older building, the property manager may want to explore the practicality and costs of retrofitting them.

Preventive Measures

Elevator specifications are highly regulated. They cover construction, operation, and maintenance. At the very minimum, the property manager should know what federal, state, and municipal codes apply and follow them precisely.

The equipment is complex and specialized. Elevators integrate electrical, mechanical, and hydraulic subsystems or solid-state components to transport millions of passengers every day. Preventive maintenance is particularly important for elevator systems because 60 to 70 percent of an elevator's parts are subject to wear. Elevator cables, in particular, should be inspected regularly for wear.

Loss can be minimized or prevented by ensuring that elevators have emergency controls. Though many elevators come equipped with these controls, some of the features can be added later. Basic controls include:

- Smoke detectors that, when set off, signal the elevator to return to the ground floor and shut down.
- A switch that, when triggered manually, returns the elevator to the ground floor and shuts it down.
- A direct-dial telephone system that is connected to an answering service, the elevator service company, or a 24-hour security station.
- A button that triggers an audible alarm. (This may not be effective after hours because it does not allow two-way communication.)

Elevators may also be equipped for firefighter's service. This is a device that can signal for immediate recall to a specified landing (usually the lobby) to remove cars from normal use and permit controlled operation by firefighters or other authorized emergency personnel.

To help ensure personal safety of elevator passengers, the property manager can also implement the following precautionary measures:

- Program elevators to stop at the lobby level before going down to or after coming up from the basement.
- Program elevators to bypass vacant floors.
- Connect elevator stop buttons to an alarm bell and a security station.
- Investigate the appropriateness of installing mirrored walls in elevator cars so a person can see the whole interior before entering;

Areas prone to earthquakes increase the likelihood of elevator emergencies. Some additional preventive measures should be implemented in those locations. Here are some suggestions:

- Bolt down elevator machine room equipment to prevent "migration" due to vibration.
- Fasten control room panels securely to the building.
- Use collision switches to trigger the interlock mechanism to prevent car-to-counterweight collision.
- Use additional reinforcing brackets between normal mountings so guide rails are held in place.
- Install a guide on top of hoist motors to hold elevator cables in place on their sheaves.

During an Elevator Emergency

Every building with an elevator should be prepared to respond to an elevator emergency. Emergency procedures should address elevator malfunctions as well as elevator operation (or shutdown) in the context of other types of emergencies such as a fire.

If elevator service is disrupted, the first step to be taken is to contact the elevator service company. As this is highly specialized work, only qualified personnel—for example, elevator service company personnel, fire department personnel, and specially trained building employees—should be permitted to correct elevator malfunctions.

If occupants are stranded in an elevator during a malfunction, they should not be evacuated unless the situation is life-threatening. Sudden movements can be dangerous, and evacuating the elevator can actually increase the likelihood of harm. When evacuation from an elevator is necessary, first check for slack in the hoistway ropes; a quick movement of the car could be dangerous with slack or broken suspension. Remember, machines do not think; they respond to mechanical impulses.

With the best of intentions, untrained people may wish to remove a person from a stalled elevator. However, this could result in injury of loss of life if the elevator moves suddenly. Educating occupants and staff on these dangers could prevent a misguided rescue attempt.

At the same time, management should communicate with passengers trapped in an elevator—installed elevator phone systems are especially useful here. The communicator should assure the passengers that they are safe, caution them not to panic, warn them not to try to force the elevator doors open, and let them know what steps are being taken to free them. Management could ask if they can contact anyone on behalf of the trapped passengers. Communication should be maintained with stranded passengers until they are safely evacuated from the elevator.

It is a good idea to have emergency medical service phone numbers handy in case trapped passengers need assistance. Injuries are not the only concern. Some people may experience panic or anxiety attacks in enclosed spaces. The stress of the incident might cause a heart attack.

After an Elevator Emergency

Immediately after an elevator emergency, appropriate personnel should conduct a thorough investigation of the cause of the mishap and corrective steps should be taken.

If elevator service was disrupted because of an earthquake, or there has been damage to the elevator system, elevators should not be operated until the hoistway and machine room equipment have been thoroughly inspected and all necessary repairs have been made.

17

Water Leaks and Frozen Pipes

Water leaks may be the result of ruptured pipes, malfunctioning valves, or broken plumbing seals. The potential for damage will depend on the source and extent of the leak. Plumbing may also fail in extreme cold conditions because of water freezing inside the pipes. Water expands as it freezes and can rupture plumbing pipes and/or connections.

Water leaks are not always easily detected. There may be the presence of water but no clear indication of where it originated. There are alarm devices that can be positioned in areas that are likely to experience leaks (e.g., basement areas near water pipes and around appliances that use water). The alarm will sound when water contacts it. There are also firms that specialize in leak detection. It may be appropriate to include such a company as a resource to be cited in the emergency procedures manual. Contact information for the local water department would also be appropriate in the event the water supply has to be turned off and on at the source outside the building.

Turning Off the Water Supply

When a leak is encountered, it may be necessary to turn off the water supply and possibly to shut off electricity, depending on the location of the leak. If the problem is in an occupant's space, non-service personnel should be kept away from the area until repairs are made, the water is cleaned up, and water service has been restored. Only rarely might there be a need for partial or full evacuation of the building—e.g., if water service must be turned off buildingwide for an extended period.

Water shutoffs should be located at the water meter and near washer, sink, shower, and toilet hookups. A water shutoff is usually positioned in the tank section of a toilet (the type found in residences). The water supply that leads to a kitchen or bathroom sink is usually controlled by a shutoff located underneath the sink. There are also shutoff valves located at the inlets of water heaters.

Shutting off a valve will only stop water flowing to the areas beyond the shut-off point. It is important to locate the valve that will stop the flow to the area of the leak. When in doubt, or when it is difficult to locate the proper shutoff, the main valve should be closed. Once the correct shutoff is located and closed, water service can be restored to the remaining areas. In large buildings, there may be a shutoff on each floor or building tier which allows water service to remain uninterrupted on other floors or in other areas.

Care must be taken when attempting to shut off water in a fire sprinkler system. A trained technician may be consulted if it is necessary to shut off a portion of a sprinkler system, and the system water supply should be restored a soon as possible.

Some businesses, such as Laundromats and hair salons, are dependent on a continued flow of water. The property manager should notify these occupants when the water is to be shut off and when it is expected to be turned on again.

Restoring Water Service

When water service is restored to the building, it may be advisable to turn on faucets and let water flow for a period to clear out any sediment that may have settled in the pipes while the water was off. Also, repair work may have loosened sediment or introduced contaminants.

It is important to take precautions when restoring water service. A difference in water pressure can cause water pipes to blow out when water flow is restarted. A building's water system may need to be cleaned or decontaminated. The water supply (source) should also be checked to see if incoming water needs additional treatment.

Cleaning Up after a Water Leak

Sometimes a leak will introduce water where it does not belong. A leak that had been undetected for some time may have introduced water between walls. Even a small leak or breach can release a large amount of water over a period of time. It is important that anyone repairing a water leak avoids contact with electrical outlets or appliances, especially if the person is standing in water. Once the leak has been repaired, it is important to clean up the area where water caused damage.

Standing water can be removed with a wet/dry vacuum. This is especially useful for water spread out over a large area. (When there is an extremely large amount of water—e.g., measurable depth—it may be necessary to use a pump.) Any water remaining can be cleaned up with a mop. Floors should be thoroughly dried. This can be expedited using fans and directing the airflow over the wet surface. A dehumidifier may also be helpful. Plaster or drywall should be dried out similarly. Once it is dry, it should be inspected to determine its condition and the extent of any damage. Extensive damage may necessitate repairs (e.g., patching) or replacement. Wallboard that has been damp for an extended period may harbor mold. Mold may also grow on other surfaces, including equipment. In such situations, a mold specialist may be consulted.

Frozen Pipes

Extremely cold winter temperatures may cause pipes to freeze on some properties. Frozen pipes could deprive residents and commercial tenants' employees of water for drinking and personal hygiene. They can also limit the availability of water to help put out fires. Frozen pipes may cause water to back up, which could result in burst pipes and possible flooding of interiors. Plumbing pipes located on or within outside walls are the ones most likely to freeze, especially if they are not insulated.

Because pipes may not always be insulated as part of building construction, it may be prudent, especially in residential properties, to check potentially vulnerable piping and install or add insulation as appropriate. Sealing around pipes where they enter the building from outside (e.g., through the foundation or walls) may also be advisable.

Frozen pipes may be suspected if there are one or more reports of low or no water pressure in the building. If the report came from a resident or commercial tenant, a check with other building occupants should help determine whether the problem is building-wide or an isolated incident. If the problem is building-wide, it may be a good idea to check with neighboring buildings. If they have water, but your property does not, the problem may be a frozen pipe or meter. The following additional actions are suggested:

- Examine the water meter. Check it for leaks.
- Check the frost plate (bottom portion) of the meter. Is it cracked? If so, the meter is probably frozen. Do *not* attempt to thaw the water meter.
- If the water meter is frozen, contact the local water department or other appropriate authority to report the frozen meter and seek instructions.
- In some instances, the property manager may be instructed to remove the meter. If a maintenance technician on the premises knows how to disconnect the meter from the water line, the meter may be taken to the water department or other authority for replacement.
- If the meter is *not* frozen, proceed to check around the building perimeter, in the basement, or in the crawl space for one or more frozen water pipes.

The University of Wisconsin Cooperative Extension suggests the following measures for dealing with frozen pipes.

- Shut off the water supply and open faucets to the frozen pipes.
- Warm frozen pipes with a heat lamp, blow dryer, or portable heater. (Boiling water, propane torches, or anything with an open flame should *not* be used.)
- Be patient. Thawing pipes can take hours.
- If a pipe bursts before preventive action can be taken, turn off the main water supply to the pipe immediately and leave the faucet open until repairs are completed.

Frozen water pipes may also be thawed using special heating tape. This should be done with extreme care. Heating tape may be installed as a preventive measure and activated when extreme cold outdoor temperatures are forecast. Automatic tapes include sensors that respond to a preset cold temperature setting and compensate by warming the pipes they are wrapped around. Pipes can also be prevented from freezing by turning on a faucet and letting it drip slowly, keeping water moving within the pipes.

A booklet on winter storms published online by the University of Wisconsin can be downloaded at www.cft.uwex.edu/ces/news/info/winter.pdf. The long-term solution is to prevent frozen pipes by providing adequate insulation and heat.

Clean up after a frozen pipe bursts would be similar to cleaning up after a water leak.

Other Causes of Water Damage

In addition to plumbing failures and frozen pipes, water damage may occur as a result of leaking from aquariums or waterbeds, a stopped up toilet that overflows, or forgetting to turn off running water. Occupants, especially in residential properties, need to be made aware of the damage that can be caused by water from their personal furnishings. It may be appropriate to include reminders in resident newsletters and other communications about proper use of plumbing fixtures.

Water may also enter a building as seepage through foundation cracks or chinks in the mortar between bricks or stones of exterior walls. If the source of a leak is not readily found in the water distribution system, seepage may be a likely cause. Regular inspection of the building interior and exterior should reveal where such breaches are beginning to develop so they can be repaired.

As with any emergency incident, it may be advisable to take photographs of the water damage to personal property or to building interior finishes, systems, or equipment before repairs are made or items are replaced. This will assist in cataloging damage for insurance purposes if property policies include coverage for the type of incident.

18

Natural Gas Leaks

Natural gas is used for cooking, water heating, clothes drying, and residential heating. It may also be used to operate swimming pool and spa heaters. In commercial buildings, natural gas may be used for cooking in restaurants and for heating. It may also be used to operate backup power-generating equipment. Natural gas itself is not combustible; it requires air to burn. The optimum air-gas mixture is 85–95 percent air to 5–15 percent gas. Because natural gas is odorless, an odorant—the typical rotten-eggs smell—is added to it.

Natural gas is moved from its point of origin (an underground natural gas field) to urban and rural buildings via pipelines. There are more than one million miles of natural gas pipelines in the United States. They vary in size from small diameter pipes (approximately 1–1½ inches) entering buildings to very large diameter (24 inches or more) pipes used for transportation over long distances to the local distribution gas mains. The gas is under pressure; in large pipelines, the pressure may be 500 pounds per square inch (psi) or more. Transportation pipelines buried in rural areas—i.e., farmlands—are generally marked with a gas company name and an emergency telephone number. Distribution mains in towns and cities are not marked although they can be precisely located. Most gas utilities participate in a local one-call system that sends locating representatives to mark gas (and other utilities such as electricity and telephone) lines before any excavation is initiated. The party planning to dig must call for this service 48 hours beforehand.

Responding to a Natural Gas Leak

Natural gas leaks are potential fire and explosion hazards. Indoor leaks are recognizable by the smell. There may also be a hissing sound. A faint odor may be an indication that a pilot light is out, and relighting the pilot may solve the problem. However, a strong, persistent odor requires immediate action including evacuation of the building. Gas utilities recommend the following to prevent injuries:

- Leave the door open after leaving the building to minimize gas buildup in an enclosed space. If possible, ventilate the building by opening doors and windows, beginning where the odor is strongest, but do *not* re-enter the building to do this.
- Use a cell phone or other telephone outside the building to report the leak to the gas utility.

- Close the cutoff valve near the gas meter and do *not* turn it on again. The utility company should turn the gas on.

They also recommend *not* operating appliance controls or electrical switches or removing any plugs from electrical outlets, which could create a spark and ignite the gas. One should not light any matches either.

If leaking gas catches fire, the area should be evacuated. The supply of gas must be shut off before the fire can be put out. The utility company and the fire department should be notified immediately.

Natural gas leaks out of doors—i.e., from buried pipelines—may be indicated by an odor of rotten eggs or a hissing or blowing sound. Visible indications include dead or brown vegetation, dirt blowing into the air, fire at or near exposed piping or apparently coming from the ground, bubbling of surface water, and/or water blowing into the air at a river, creek, or pond. The gas utility should be notified if any of these signs are observed.

Gas leaks out of doors may also result when excavation is done too close to a gas main. A ruptured main can easily be ignited, and the resulting fire can cause a great deal of damage. There may also be an explosion or explosions with such incidents. Gas service to nearby buildings will be disrupted until the main has been repaired. The service disruption may only be hours, but it could be days. Usually utility representatives will relight appliance pilot lights when gas service is restored.

Natural gas leaks and their potential hazards should be addressed in a property's emergency procedures manual. Property staff should be able to recognize signs of a gas leak and act accordingly. They may be referred to emergency procedures for fire and/or explosion as appropriate. The fire department or other rescue squad may have to be called in if someone is overcome by carbon monoxide. Building occupants also need to be informed about the signs of leaking gas and directed to contact the utility company if they suspect a gas leak.

Preventive Measures

Gas-operated appliances and equipment should be inspected periodically to ensure that they are operating properly and not releasing carbon monoxide. Carbon monoxide is created when natural gas is burned without sufficient air. It can be produced when gas appliances are not properly installed, vented, maintained, or used or when vent pipes have gaps or leaks or are plugged with debris. (Carbon monoxide detectors are discussed in Chapter 14.)

Gas lines downstream of the gas meter (the building side) belong to the gas customer—the building owner. The customer is responsible for maintenance and repair of this portion of the distribution system. Buried gas piping needs to be inspected for leaks and, if the pipe is metallic, for corrosion. It may also be appropriate to test the level of gas pressure.

The local gas utility may conduct inspections of gas piping, valves, and connections on request. Alternatively, a private contractor may be hired to conduct such inspections as part of a regular preventive maintenance program. Otherwise, a commercial plumbing or heating contractor may be consulted when gas lines need attention.

19

Medical Emergencies

Medical emergencies can occur any time and any place, so property managers should equip themselves with guidelines for treating injured or medically endangered people on their premises. A medical emergency can range from a sprained ankle or broken bones, to burns, internal bleeding, a heart attack, or even death. Medical emergencies can be the result of a person's poor health, human actions, disasters of natural or human origin, or unexpected physical injuries (i.e., an accident). The property manager and the Emergency Management Team should be prepared to respond quickly and effectively to a medical emergency.

Areas and Properties at Risk

All properties in every area run a risk of medical emergencies. However, medical emergencies may be more likely to occur in certain types of properties. These include properties that house a large number of elderly people, commercial properties where heavy equipment or hazardous chemicals are used, and light industrial properties.

Managers of properties located in areas that are subject to temperature extremes may encounter weather-related medical emergencies. During extended periods of extreme cold temperatures, persons working out of doors for long periods may develop hypothermia. Areas of skin that are not adequately protected with clothing may develop frostbite. During extended periods of extreme heat, there may be incidents of heat exhaustion or even heat stroke. These conditions generally require professional medical attention. Problems from exposure to extreme cold require careful warming to thaw frozen tissues or restore normal body temperature. Those resulting from exposure to extreme heat may require intravenous administation of fluids and electrolytes to compensate for those lost through extensive sweating.

Preventing Human Loss and Liability

In developing a plan for responding to medical emergencies, the property manager should designate members of the Emergency Management Team to be trained in life-saving and medical treatment techniques. The best people to select are those who have a reputation for being calm, quick-thinking, and level-headed; who perform well in emergency situations, and who are often on the property. Certainly, anyone with interest, background, or experience in medical emergency procedures should be considered.

The emergency procedures manual should include medical and first aid procedures. The property manager should create and keep current lists of:

- Organizations and phone numbers to call for emergency medical services. A local hospital or trauma center and a private ambulance service should be considered along with fire/rescue services, which usually include paramedics and public ambulance services.
- Names and phone numbers of property staff and occupants (residents, commercial tenants' employees) who have received accredited training in life-saving techniques, first aid, cardiopulmonary resuscitation (CPR), and/or use of an automatic external defibrillator (AED).

The emergency procedures manual should also address the following medical emergency information, guidelines, and procedures.

- The first aid kit
- First aid, CPR, and AED procedures
- Avoiding disease transmission
- Preventing occupational exposure to bloodborne pathogens
- Calling for emergency assistance (e.g., 911 service)
- Treating elderly and physically disabled persons and children

The property manager should also ensure that management personnel and the Emergency Management Team receive up-to-date training on these subjects.

The First Aid Kit

The first aid kit allows the Emergency Management Team member or other involved person to provide anyone who is physically injured with essential medical treatment. The availability and proper use of first aid kit contents can often be sufficient in treating minor injuries or help sustain an injured person until necessary professional emergency care arrives.

First aid kits come in many sizes and can be purchased from a drug store, a medical supply company, or the local chapter of the American Red Cross. Retailers that cater to campers, boaters, and outdoor enthusiasts often sell first aid kits. For a large property, an industrial first aid kit or cabinet may be most appropriate. As an alternative, a property manager can purchase the items needed to make up a first aid kit. Be sure the kit contains all the items needed, and check expiration dates of medicines and previously opened disinfectants. It is important to restock as needed.

In anticipation of medical emergencies, every property should have on hand a basic first aid kit that includes an assortment of bandages in different types and sizes, disinfectant solution, pain medication, a tourniquet, soap (to clean the assistant's hands, not the injured person's wounds), and disposable gloves. A more comprehensive list of first aid kit contents is presented in Chapter 1. Other specific recommendations can be found on the American Red Cross and FEMA web sites.

First Aid Procedures

Knowledge and timely implementation of first aid and CPR, when applied correctly, may make the difference between life and death for an injured person. When there is a major injury, first aid should be administered to the injured person until paramedics arrive on the scene. If the injured party is not breathing or the person's heart has stopped, CPR should be administered immediately in an effort to restore heart functioning and respiration. An AED machine is another tool to restore heartbeat. Such machines are often installed in commercial buildings and public spaces. Specific training in AED may be needed, but the procedures are easy to learn. Some equipment provides instructions that include audible prompts for what to do and when to do it.

Application of first aid will depend on the type of injury. Minor cuts and scrapes can be cleaned and bandaged to protect them from infection. Heavy bleeding can be stopped with a tourniquet, but it may be preferable simply to apply pressure to the wound. The Heimlich maneuver may be used to dislodge an obstruction in the throat. More serious injuries—open wounds, internal or severe bleeding, burns—should be treated only by persons properly trained to administer the first aid that is required.

Specific first aid procedures are beyond the scope of this book. There are books on first aid, and the American Red Cross offers certification and training classes in first aid, CPR, and AED, along with informative pamphlets on responding to medical emergencies. Some classes and publications are available free of charge. Training can also be provided through specially contracted services.

Good Samaritan Laws

Are you risking a potential lawsuit when you assist someone in an emergency situation? Most states have enacted Good Samaritan laws, which protect people who assist victims in medical emergency situations from liability. Property managers should contact their local municipality or a legal professional, or check with their local library to determine if their state has a Good Samaritan law. The insurance company that underwrites liability coverage for the property may also be a good source of information in this regard.

According to the American Red Cross, when citizens respond to an emergency and act as a reasonable and prudent person would under the same conditions, Good Samaritan immunity generally prevails. This legal immunity protects the rescuer from being sued and found financially liable for the victim's injury. Keep in mind, however, that states with this law have had lawsuits enforced in which the judge ruled that the rescuer was grossly or willfully negligent or reckless in his or her medical assistance efforts. This underlines the necessity for the Emergency Management Team to be properly trained in first aid and CPR procedures.

What would be a reasonable and prudent emergency medical assistance effort by a rescuer? Examples include:

- Summoning professional help to the scene by calling 911 or other emergency assistance.
- Asking a conscious victim for permission before giving care.
- Checking the victim for life-threatening injuries before providing further care.
- Moving a victim only if the victim's life is endangered.
- Continuing to provide care until a medical professional arrives.

As a safeguard, property managers should keep accurate records of injuries and fatalities occurring on the property, and if possible, take a photograph of the scene. Personal injury reports should include information such as who was injured; when, where, why, and how the injury occurred; names and contact information of any witnesses present; time and date of the incident; and which medical assistance service responded to the call for help. Recording other details—the weather, lighting, condition of the surface, the victim's apparel—may also be helpful. (An example of an emergency incident report form is included in Chapter 7.)

Avoiding Transmission of Disease

A person injured on your property is bleeding. You want to help but are afraid of catching an infection or disease from the open wound. It is important to know how diseases are transmitted and how to protect oneself when providing first aid.

Infectious diseases can pass from one person to another through transmission of bacteria or viruses from contact with blood (bloodborne pathogens) and other body fluids. In administering first aid, such transmission can take place through touching, breathing, and biting, through contact of one person's body fluids with those of the other person. Germs can be transmitted through breaks or cuts in the skin or through the mucous membranes lining the eyes, nose, and mouth. A primary concern is the transmission of HIV, which causes AIDS, and the hepatitis B virus. The following basic guidelines can help you reduce disease transmission while administering first aid:

- Avoid contact with body fluids when possible.
- Place barriers, such as disposable gloves or a clean dry cloth, between the injured party's body fluids and yourself.
- Wash your hands with soap and water immediately after giving care.
- Do not drink or eat or touch your mouth, eyes, or nose when giving first aid.
- Do not touch objects that may be soiled with blood or bodily fluids.

Remember that the likelihood of HIV transmission during first aid is very low. Always try to give first aid in ways that protect you and the victim from disease transmission.

Occupational Exposure to Bloodborne Pathogens: The OSHA Standard

Property managers should be aware of the OSHA standard on occupational exposure to bloodborne pathogens (disease-causing viruses and bacteria). The standard covers *all* employees who could be "reasonably anticipated," as a result of performing their job duties, to face contact with blood and other potentially infectious materials. This means that the standard is not limited to workers in the health care industry. Indeed, property management staff such as security, general maintenance, and engineering personnel who are assigned to apply basic first aid techniques in case of an accident are at potential risk of exposure—especially during a medical emergency. OSHA regulations outline the following employer requirements.

- *Exposure control plan*—Requires employers to identify, in writing, tasks and procedures as well as job classifications where occupational exposure to blood occurs—without regard to personal protective clothing and equipment. The plan should include procedures for evaluating the circumstances surrounding exposure incidents along with a schedule and method for implementing other provisions of the standard. The plan must be accessible to employees and available to OSHA for examination. Employers must review and update it at least once a year—more often if necessary to accommodate workplace changes.

- *Methods of compliance*—Mandates universal precautions, treating body fluids/materials as if infectious. It stresses hand washing, requiring employers to provide facilities and ensure that employees use them after exposure to blood. It requires employers to provide protective equipment such as gloves. It requires a written schedule for cleaning and decontamination as well as handling of contaminated laundry.

- *Post-exposure evaluation and follow-up*—Requires employers to make available confidential medical evaluation and follow-up, documenting the circumstances of exposure, identifying and testing the source individual if feasible, testing the exposed employee's blood if he or she consents, post-exposure prophylactic treatment, counseling, and evaluation of reported illnesses.

- *Hazard communication*—Requires warning labels including the fluorescent orange or orange-red biohazard symbol affixed to waste containers and to refrigerators, freezers, and other containers used to store or transport blood or other infectious materials. Red bags or containers may be used instead of the labels. (Janitorial workers, especially, should be aware of such labels and the potential hazards they warn against.)

- *Information and training*—Mandates training, initially upon assignment and annually thereafter, that includes the text and an explanation of the OSHA regulation, a general discussion of bloodborne diseases and their transmission, the company's exposure control plan, engineering and workplace practices, use of personal protective equipment, HBV vaccine, responding to emergencies involving blood, handling exposure incidents, post-exposure evaluation and follow-up, and the requisite hazard labeling or color-coding. (The American Red Cross offers specific training in preventing disease transmission from bloodborne pathogens that complies with the OSHA regulation.)

- *Record keeping*—Calls for confidential medical records to be kept for each employee with occupational exposure for the duration of employment plus 30 years. Training records must be maintained for three years and must include dates, contents of the training program, the trainer's name and qualifications, and the names and job titles of all persons attending the sessions. Medical records must be made available to the subject employee, anyone to whom the employee gives written consent, OSHA, and the National Institute of Safety and Health (NIOSH). They are *not* available to the employer.

In order to safeguard employees from exposure to bloodborne pathogens and to ensure compliance with OSHA regulations, property managers should contact their regional OSHA office or corresponding state agency to request a professional safety consultation.

Most property managers would not "reasonably anticipate" that they or their employees would face occupational exposure to bloodborne pathogens, and they should not be inhibited from doing all they can safely do to assist injured victims.

Property Maintenance

Also important in preventing human injury or liability is for the property manager to ensure that the property is safe and in good physical condition. Management personnel should remove from public areas all potentially dangerous items and obstacles that might lead to trip and fall incidents and injuries. Maintenance work that creates slippery floors should be announced with appropriate signage. Crevices and cracks in sidewalks and paved areas should be filled, and overgrown hedges should be trimmed to avoid interference on walkways. Air-conditioning and heating systems should be checked and cleaned regularly to avoid illness from air contamination. Accommodations for disabled people should comply with guidelines of the Americans with Disabilities Act (ADA).

The property manager can evaluate his or her property to identify potential accidents that are waiting to happen on the premises and correct them up front through preventive maintenance and preservation of safe building conditions.

During a Medical Emergency

The emergency procedures manual should state specifically who should be contacted in the event of a medical emergency after 911 has been called. Unless trained and educated in specific medical procedures, the property manager and other members of the Emergency Management Team are best advised to leave medical treatment, beyond first aid and CPR, to medical technicians, nurses, and doctors. Given the litigious nature of our society, prudence is advised.

If first aid and CPR can be helpful, however, those educated and trained in these procedures should administer them immediately to the injured party.

Calling for Emergency Assistance

Calling for help is often the most important step in aiding a victim. A member of the Emergency Management Team or anyone present at the scene should call the local emergency assistance number as soon as possible, without leaving the injured party unassisted. Most communities have 911 service that dispatches police, firefighters, and paramedics to respond to emergencies. Communities that do not have 911 service may have separate emergency phone numbers for police and fire services; it is important to have the correct number to call. Where programmable telephones are in use, the different emergency numbers can be entered so they can be called by touching a single button. It may be possible to simply dial O for operator assistance if the number is not known.

What situations warrant a 911 call? If the victim is unconscious, call 911 immediately. At times, a conscious victim may tell you he or she is "OK," but the 911 number should be called regardless if any of the following symptoms, which may be warning signs of serious injury, are recognized by the person rendering aid or related by the victim:

- Current or impending unconsciousness
- Inability to breath or labored breathing
- Pain or pressure in the chest or abdomen
- Severe bleeding
- Vomiting or passing of blood from nose, mouth, or other body openings
- Seizures, severe headaches, or slurred speech
- Head, neck, or back injuries
- Possible internal poisoning
- Possible broken bones
- The victim cannot be moved easily

Be prepared to provide the following information to the 911 or emergency assistance dispatcher:

- The exact location or address of the emergency, including the name of the city or town and nearby intersections or landmarks.
- The telephone number you are calling from.
- The caller's name.
- What happened to the injured party and his or her physical condition.
- How many people are involved.
- What medical treatment/first aid is currently being given.

The information you provide is vital in allowing the dispatcher to send to the scene the specific medical help that is needed. The dispatcher may also be able to tell you how to best care for the injured party until the ambulance arrives. Once the dispatcher hangs up, return and continue to care for the injured party. Do not hang up first because the dispatcher may need additional information. If possible, assign someone to watch for the arrival of emergency medical personnel and guide them to the person or persons needing assistance.

Treating People with Special Needs

Particular groups of people are more susceptible to injuries, and therefore, special precautions should be taken. These include children, people with disabilities, and the elderly.

Children Accidents are the leading cause of death among children and teen-agers. Because of this, managers of properties where children reside or spend time in day care need to be prepared to prevent accidents and attendant injuries. They must also be prepared to address injuries to children resulting from accidents, most prominently those involving motor vehicles, falls, poisonings, drownings, and fires.

Checking an ill or injured child can be difficult. An injured child may be frightened as well as hurt. Younger children may not be able to communicate about an accident or their injuries. The American Red Cross makes the following recommendations:

- Observe the physical condition before touching an injured child. Children's condition may change when they are touched because they can become anxious or upset, especially with strangers.
- Remain calm. Caring for injured children can be stressful. Showing the child you are relaxed and confident will help keep child and parent calm.
- Communicate clearly with the parent or guardian and the child. When you can help the adults relax, the child will relax, too. Talk slowly and use simple words. Calmly telling the child what you are going to do to help treat the injury will earn his or her trust.
- Do not separate the loved ones from the child unless necessary. The child will need their emotional support.

Disabled Persons People who are physically disabled can be just as seriously injured as any other injured person, but if they are paralyzed to any extent, they may not be able to detect their injury. Attempts should be made to observe the victim's external physical condition before administering first aid; in any event, the victim's limbs and torso should be moved as little as possible.

A wheelchair-bound victim who is not paralyzed, and who does not have any major injuries, could be seated in a spare wheelchair from the premises if his or her wheelchair was damaged in the incident.

Elderly People As people age, they experience a general decline in body functions. The heart rate slows and blood vessels harden, causing the heart to work harder. As a result of weakening bones and slower reflexes and sensory perceptions, elderly individuals have a higher chance of falling and injuring themselves.

Because the size of the human brain decreases with age, there is more space between the brain and the skull in older persons, increasing the possibility of head injury. Because of this, elderly victims should always be checked for head injuries.

Elderly individuals are also at increased risk for strokes, confusion, and diseases as their nervous systems weaken. If care is being provided for an elderly victim who appears confused, the rescuer should try to talk loudly and clearly at eye level in an attempt to determine whether the victim's confusion is due to the injury or to a prior condition. The elderly victim may simply not be able to hear speech from some distances. Bear in mind also that a victim may not recognize a serious physical condition, and may even downplay his or her physical state out of fear of the loss of independence.

At all times, elderly victims—indeed, victims of any age—should be treated with respect and concern. It is helpful to check the victim's medications, if possible, and inform the professional medical assistance team of their identity. The medical team should also be informed of any first aid or assistance that was administered to the victim before their arrival.

After a Medical Emergency

When a medical emergency is the result of an accident on the property, the area where the accident occurred should be inspected. There may be debris and residual body fluids to be cleaned up. A vehicular accident may have caused damage to the building that needs repair. This is also an opportunity to identify maintenance and safety issues that need attention.

20

Crime

Property managers are justifiably concerned when it comes to crime on the properties they manage. Crime not only endangers a property's residents and/or commercial tenants and damages physical premises, it also threatens a property's value, reputation, and income.

A high crime rate will cause a property to suffer from a poor reputation in the community, can lower morale among employees and occupants, and can have a detrimental effect on prospective residents, commercial tenants, customers, and employees.

Criminal activity comes in many forms, among them:

- Burglary
- Robbery
- Vandalism
- Assault
- Rape
- Murder
- Child or spouse abuse
- Fights
- Drug activity
- Gang violence
- Gunfire
- Hostage situations
- Disorderly demonstrations
- Riots
- Acts of emotionally or mentally disturbed individuals

Crime Prevention Measures

A property manager can implement any number of preventive measures to combat crime. To help thwart *thefts,* be aware of the two types of perpetrators and the suggested measures to be taken:

Outsiders
- Casual or professional thieves—ask to assist unfamiliar persons on the property.

- Service or maintenance persons—ask to see identification.
- Delivery persons or messengers—escort them to their destinations.
- Food vendors—ask for identification.
- Repair persons—ask for identification.

Insiders
- Employees—check references and background information before hiring; work to educate employees and change negative attitudes.
- Security personnel—screen all employees according to an appropriate list of criteria.
- Maintenance personnel—provide uniforms with property identification and the person's name or require them to carry and show property-specific identification.
- Clients of property management or commercial tenants—institute a sign-in/sign-out program or ask the business they are visiting to provide an escort.
- Residents—establish and enforce strict screening procedures.
- Friends or relatives of residents—require visitors in high-rise buildings either to sign in and out at a main desk or to wear visitor badges while on the property.

Other Preventive Measures
- Inspect the property for the following and, if found, make appropriate repairs/replacements.
  —Flickering, broken, and burned-out lights
  —Dimly lit corridors, stairwells, staircases, restrooms, and other secluded areas
  —Doors that do not lock properly
  —Broken windows
  —Broken pay telephones
- Inspect the outside areas of the property to ensure safety of residents and commercial tenants' employees.
  —Is there overgrown landscaping (bushes, trees, shrubs)?
  —Is entry and walkway lighting dim, thus encouraging crime?
  —Do security guards patrol the property regularly as instructed?
- At properties that have security patrols, provide a guard to escort occupants and visitors to their cars after sunset.
- Safeguard records of safe and vault combinations and computer passwords in the office.
- Lock and secure critical and confidential files.
- Shred confidential documents before discarding.
- Safeguard master keys.
- Keep track of copies of keys; be able to account for all keys.
- Maintain a list of commercial tenants who are given keys to restrooms that are kept locked or use electronic locks that require a numeric code or a magnetic swipe card to gain access.
- If a property uses sign-in and sign-out sheets, maintain security by keeping them out of public view.
- Engrave or label all valuable items and equipment with an identification number or name.
- Distribute a list of emergency telephone numbers (building security, managers, police, fire department) to each occupant (residents, commercial tenants).
- Instruct employees NOT to let callers know when persons of authority are out of town or are not on the property.

- Develop programs with public victim services agencies and mental health centers for any victims of crime on the property.

At residential properties, it may be desirable or appropriate to post signs to alert people of possible dangers in less secure, more crime-prone areas of the property.

If appropriate, implement a security system. Review the information in Chapter 3 of this book as a starting point. Seek advice from security professionals regarding appropriate use of safes and vaults, access controls (door locks and other hardware, electronic locks and key pads or swipe cards), intrusion alarms, and closed-circuit television (CCTV) cameras with VCRs as well as the wisdom of employing security patrols using on-site personnel or a contracted security service. Remember, however, that security measures, once implemented, are difficult to alter without raising questions about security being reduced by such a change.

Meet with other property managers to devise a communication network arrangement with the police department that will notify others of specific criminal activity if or when it happens. The network may include sophisticated computer voice-mail systems that automatically contact all users of the system. The arrangement may also include an ongoing program in which property managers meet with police officials to receive periodic updates on crime statistics, trends, and prevention techniques.

It is also a good idea to use an occupant newsletter or occasional flyers to remind residents and commercial tenants' employees to take precautions for their personal safety and to report criminal activity to the proper authorities. Subjects that might be addressed include who to contact if they are the victim of a crime, proper use of dead-bolt locks, safeguarding cash and credit cards, and the need to be aware that pickpockets are more active in areas of heavy retail traffic, especially during lunch hours and holiday shopping seasons.

Investigating Community Crime Reports

Many police departments prepare daily "Criminal Activity Reports," which include reported information on where and when incidents have taken place (not the exact address, but simply the hundred block and street name) and a brief description of the incidents. The listed incidents are unverified, meaning that they have not yet been checked by the police to confirm their occurrence or nature.

The police use these reports to analyze crime trends, assign patrols, gauge the crime rate in given areas, and gain better insight for responding to crime. However, such reports may be of limited use in some communities because they may include only felonies—murder, sexual assault, burglary, auto theft—and not drug arrests or gang activities.

A property manager can use these police reports to obtain information on specific types of crimes—for example, if a car thief is working in the property's vicinity. The reports can also be used to help stop rumors that tend to exaggerate the frequency and seriousness of crime.

Gangs

Gang activity, including violence, occurs when the community at large allows it. However, the effects of gang activity can be minimized. In order to help preserve the safety of people on managed properties—including visitors as well as residents and commercial tenants' employees—and the property itself, property managers should actively combat gang-related activity on their premises.

What can the property manager do? The following list expands on information presented in Chapter 13. While the suggestions are more specific to shopping centers, they may apply as well to residential properties.

- Become aware of gang presence and learn how to detect gang insignia. Youths often identify themselves as members of specific gangs by hand signals, haircuts, jewelry, and styles of dress that include specific colors.

- Establish control. Make it clear that any one who violates property rules will be prosecuted. Gangs repeatedly target properties that have a reputation for being soft on offenders such as vandals. Property managers should work with local police in establishing firm criminal and procedural discipline for gang members who violate property or community conduct policies and show gangs they mean business. Security officers should introduce themselves to individuals known or perceived to be gang members and spell out the rules of the property, which may include a ban on gang-related behaviors and dress.

- Remove graffiti immediately. Graffiti in the form of gang symbols, painted in a process called "tagging," should be painted over or removed immediately to discourage violators from returning and to discourage clashes between gangs who paint over each other's symbols. (Photograph the graffiti before removing it—police may be able to identify which gang was responsible for it.) Graffiti is often used to mark a particular gang's "territory."

- Employ security officers who reflect the demographics of the area surrounding the property to encourage a sense of community. An effective security officer is one who is highly trained and well-equipped, someone who has self-confidence, a professional demeanor, and good communication skills to send a credible message to gang members.

- Create a "gang file." Keep an active record of information concerning gang members. (Police may be able to provide descriptions—and possibly photographs—of locally active gang members.) Such a file will allow property staff to know whom to watch out for.

- Immediately address gang members who are loitering in a particular area. The longer a gang is allowed to remain, the more trouble they may cause.

- Enforce the property's policy, and prosecute criminal offenders consistently. Local police cannot assist a property unless someone is willing to prosecute. A complaint must be signed by a resident or a commercial tenant's representative, the management, or the security staff to effectively combat problems.

Property managers may wish to explore with legal counsel whether effective prosecution is likely to result in gang members being required to make restitution—i.e., to compensate for the cost of cleaning up graffiti or repairing damage from vandalism.

Violence in the Workplace

The information that follows is adapted from an article published in the September/ October 1994 issue of the *Journal of Property Management.*

Workplace attacks—primarily instigated by irate customers, disgruntled employees (both current and former), and estranged lovers or spouses—reflect a stressed-out, downsized business environment and a changing society, says Joseph Kinney, executive director of the National Safe Workplace Institute. "People are increasingly deciding that violence is a way to respond to problems."

According to Alan Bell, manager of Intercon Security Limited's corporate resource group, property managers have no control over commercial tenants' hiring practices or business procedures or whether or not they have security programs in place. Furthermore, commercial tenants tend to keep problems within their own organizations to themselves. Therefore, property managers are encouraged to give heed to early warning signs, particularly when employees are involved. Ignoring potential problems can lead to costly litigation for the companies and properties involved.

What can property managers do to protect their properties against workplace violence? The following are suggested actions that property managers can encourage their tenant-employers to take:

- Design a safe workplace. No one should have access into the inner office of a company unless he or she uses a pass card or the receptionist permits entry by releasing an electromagnetic door lock. Position meeting rooms near the reception lobby to further limit access. To help ensure the safety of the receptionist if he or she is approached by a hostile visitor, install a panic button at the reception desk, which can signal an alarm to building security or the police. Not posting names on office doors makes it difficult for hostile intruders to locate their targets.

- Employ stringent hiring procedures. Pre-employment screening is essential in reducing workplace violence. Criminal, education, and employment background checks reveal patterns that can signal potential problems. For example, substance abuse and incidents of workplace violence go hand in hand.

- Train managers to detect warning signs. Behavioral changes that cause suspicion and merit investigation include sudden drastic changes in employees' personalities, overreaction to changes in the status quo or new corporate policies, persecution complexes, boastful remarks concerning the use of weapons or previous incidents of violence such as spouse abuse, threatening co-workers or supervisors, repeated violations of organizational policies and procedures, increased emotional swings, and symptoms of alcohol or drug abuse.

- Train employees to report threats. Employees should be encouraged to report threats to their personnel departments or supervisors and trust that their concerns are being taken seriously.

- Establish policies and procedures. Threats of violence, intimidation, harassment, or violent acts should not be tolerated. Employees should be made aware of a company's "zero-tolerance" policy and that threats or incidents of violence will result in immediate termination. There should be specific procedures for addressing incidents of violence that occur in a tenant's space, including actions to be taken by employees who encounter threats or experience varying kinds of workplace violence.

- Take precautions when downsizing. Job losses often trigger incidents of workplace violence. Therefore, employers need to handle layoffs and individual dismissals sensitively. "Termination checklists" provided by the property manager are especially important in buildings that employ access control systems. All work-related keys, identification cards, and pass cards that provide access into the building, the commercial tenant's space, and/or the parking garage should be retrieved. Property managers should also be informed by tenants' human resources personnel about the terminations. Unreturned building access cards can be flagged in the system by the property manager, triggering an alarm when the card is used without permission.

Note: Violent reaction to job loss is not necessarily immediate. Sometimes a delayed reaction may occur months later if the individual has difficulty finding new employment. Additional information can be found on the Internet at www.workviolence.com, www.safespaces.com, and www.freemaninstitute.com. See also the listing of Additional Resources at the back of this book.

Crimes Against Elderly People

Nearly every state has enacted legislation addressing abuse, exploitation, or other victimization of elderly people. Elderly people are frequent targets of consumer fraud schemes as well as robbery and physical abuse. They are also more likely to be injured in a criminal incident and to need medical care.

An almost standard feature in adult protection statutes is mandatory reporting of abuse or neglect as defined by law. States vary in stipulating who must report and whether any penalty exists for not revealing known or suspected abuse. That is why it is important for property managers to understand what to look for.

- *Physical abuse* may take the form of sexual assault or rape, making the elderly person fearful. An elderly person may be imprisoned, beaten, or subjected to unnecessary physical restraint. Signs of physical abuse include frequent injuries, especially without plausible explanations, overmedication, and multiple bruises in various stages of healing.

- *Neglect* is akin to physical abuse. It includes deprivation of food and medical care as well as living in a filthy environment. Lack of needed glasses, hearing aids, and/or dentures may signal neglect, as may poor personal hygiene.

- *Emotional or psychological abuse* is not as easily recognized. It may take the form of denying the elderly person any role in decision-making or berating the person as a burden. Signs include sudden dramatic changes in the elderly person's behavior.

- *Exploitation* may involve illegal use of the elderly person's funds, misuse of the guardianship function, or use of the elderly person's funds in a legal manner that is not in the person's best interest—e.g., through guardianship or power of attorney. Signs may include foreclosure on a home or eviction for nonpayment of rent, unusual activity on the person's bank account, and lack of food, clothing, or personal supplies.

Elderly persons whose mental and reasoning abilities may be waning or impaired can also be susceptible to consumer fraud, including fraudulent charitable solicitations.

Managers of residential properties should foster sensitivity among their staff and encourage security personnel to pay particular attention to the welfare of elderly residents, within reason.

Strikes and Demonstrations on the Property

Managers of commercial properties (office buildings, retail properties, industrial facilities) may face the possibility of a strike from a tenant's disgruntled employees. Strikers could be employees who are laid off, fired, or discontent with their work environment, benefits, or wages. The latter may be part of a labor union strategy to obtain management concessions or the result of contract negotiations breaking down. (There are specific rules that both strikers and employers must follow, and property managers should be familiar with them.)

Property managers should be vigilant for threats that may be made by individuals or groups of strikers. Physical attacks may even be made upon the person or property of workers involved in the strike.

Therefore, it is important that before, during, and after the strike, the company involved and the property manager take a firm and clearly expressed position that any type of retaliatory behavior, threats, violence, or intimidation will not be tolerated and that offenders will be dealt with severely. As flare-ups between workers or against the company may likely occur within the first day or two, security forces should be adjusted.

Immediately following the strikers' return to work—or upon arrival of replacement workers—people may be nervous and mishaps more likely to occur.

Demonstrations by people supporting a cause or protesting an action related to a company or organization can lead to similar types of threats and actions. These events are often short-lived. In cities, a permit is usually required, and law enforcement is present to maintain the peace. However, demonstrations have gotten out of hand, resulting in injuries to bystanders, as well as demonstrators, and damage to property. These types of public displays should be subject to the same "rules" as strikes by workers. If the participants in the demonstration have no valid reason to be on the property—if they do not work on the premises—it may be appropriate to consider prosecution for trespassing on private property.

Drugs and Crime

"Crack houses" and other illegal drug operations threaten the sanctity and safety of communities by luring potentially violent customers into the area. While illegal drug manufacturing laboratories may be set up in commercial buildings, drug trafficking is more often seen in residential areas. When drug activity is present or suspected, the property manager should work closely with the police.

Following are lists of warning signs that may indicate possible criminal and/or drug activity taking place on a managed property.

Signs of Drug Activity

The following indicators need not always be present; nor does the presence of any of the indicators mean that criminal or drug activity is taking place. However, taken individually or in an aggregate, they suggest a need to be watchful.

- Regular visits by people in expensive cars to renters who appear to be of modest means.
- Increased traffic to the property by vehicles and pedestrians who stop for only a brief period of time. Traffic may be cyclical—increasing on weekends or late at night, or minimal for a few weeks and then intense for a period of a few days, particularly paydays.
- Visitors who appear to be acquaintances rather than friends.
- Visitors who sit in the car for a while after leaving the residence or who leave one person in the car while the other visits.
- "Lookouts," frequently younger people, who tend to hang around the property during heavy-traffic hours.
- People exchanging small packets for cash; people using drugs while sitting in their cars; syringes on the lawn and other paraphernalia lying about.
- People bringing valuables to the residence, such as televisions, bikes, VCRs, or cameras, and then leaving empty-handed.

- Motorcycle and bicycle riders making frequent late-night trips to and from a property where other indicators of drug activity are being observed.

- A dramatic drop-off of suspected activity within minutes before police arrive; this may indicate that the criminal is using a radio scanner to monitor police broadcasts.

- Unusually strong fortification of a residence or of individual rooms with blacked-out windows, window boards, or extra dead-bolt locks. Large dollar amounts spent on alarm systems. Requests for or willingness to pay high dollar amounts for installation of window bars and other fortifications.

- A willingness to pay rent months in advance, particularly in cash. If an applicant offers six months' rent in advance, resist the urge to accept, and require him or her to go through the application process.

- A tendency to pay in cash combined with a lack of visible means of support.

Methamphetamine (Speed) and Other Drug Laboratories

Managers who have reason to believe that there is a methamphetamine laboratory on their property should leave immediately, wash their face and hands, and call the police. If there is reason to believe exposure has been extensive, they should contact their doctor without delay, as some of the chemicals involved are highly toxic.

The following are some warning signs that indicate the presence of a methamphetamine laboratory. (Some of these indicators may also signal active laboratories that produce other drugs illegally.)

- Strong ammonia smell, similar to a cat litter box.

- Maroon-colored residue on aluminum material in the house. The acid used in the ephedrine process of methamphetamine production leaves this residue but does not have the ammonia smell.

- The presence of flasks and beakers—used for secondary purposes, filled with a mysterious liquid.

- The odor of either chloroform or other solvents.

- Large amounts of baking soda, tin foil, or electrical wiring. These items are used in various drug production or growing operations.

- The presence of unusually sophisticated weight scales, using grams and smaller units of weight.

- Drums and other chemical containers with their labels painted over.

- Individuals leaving the premises just long enough to smoke a cigarette, particularly if other suspicious signs are present

- The presence of ether on the premises. Used in methamphetamine production, ether is highly explosive.

Marijuana Growing Operations

Following are some warning signs that indicate marijuana is being grown:

- General signs of excessive fortifications or overly paranoid behavior.

- A sudden jump in utility bills. Growing operations require strong lighting and excessive electricity.

- Powerful lights on all night in the attic or basement.

- Evidence of tampering with wiring and hooking directly into power lines for growing operations. Sometimes this will overload the power rating for the residence and can burn the wiring, potentially resulting in fires.
- Rewired circuitry. Some operations use 1000-watt bulbs that require 220-volt circuits. The extra circuitry generally exceeds the power rating for the residence and can burn out the wiring, possibly resulting in an electrical fire.
- Basements and attics filled with plants, lights, and highly reflective material which helps speed growing.
- A surprisingly high humidity level in the residence. Growing operations require great quantities of moisture. Peeling paint or mildewed wallboard and carpet may also be observed.

Property managers may find it appropriate to include language in their leases, directly or in an addendum, indicating that drug activities (trafficking, manufacturing, growing) are prohibited in leased premises and that violators will be prosecuted. Legal counsel can best advise on specific language that will stand up to adjudication in a court of law.

During a Crime

The property manager should be able to refer to the property's emergency procedures manual for guidance in responding to criminal activity as it occurs on the premises. The following are some suggested guidelines:

- Report the crime to the police.
    —Stay calm.
    —State the problem.
    —Give the property's address along with the nearest main cross streets.
    —Give the caller's name, address, and telephone number.
    —Let the operator, who is trained to take information about a crime, take control of the conversation. Answer all the operator's questions, and stay on the phone until the operator says that it is all right to hang up.
- The property manager and staff should not subject themselves to physical endangerment at the scene of the crime.
- Never argue or debate with an assailant, an unbalanced person, a thief, or a robber. Many of these people carry weapons and will use them if provoked.
- Never fight back forcibly, unless required in a life-threatening situation.
- If possible, look carefully and get a full description of the perpetrator(s) of the crime:
    —Height, weight, age, sex
    —Facial hair, hair color, hairstyle
    —Distinguishing features, scars, birthmarks
    —Eye color
    —Glasses, jewelry
    —Complexion/skin color
    —Speech patterns
    —Vehicle type, color, license number
    —Method and direction of escape
    —Clothing
    —Weapons
    —Pagers, mobile phones

It may be helpful to have a preprinted form that can be filled out as soon as possible after a criminal incident.

After a Crime

The emergency procedures manual should also provide guidance for responding after a crime has occurred. The following are suggested actions to take:

- Do not disturb anything at the crime scene.
- Keep everyone confined to the building until authorities give the all-clear signal to leave.
- Do not invite a copycat crime by revealing details of the crime to the media.
- Never report large losses and detailed descriptions of stolen items to the media. Readers will know what is being replaced.

21

Bombs and Bomb Threats

Reports of terrorism and major bomb threats have reinforced the need for property managers to educate their staffs about how to properly respond if there is a bomb emergency on the premises.

Areas and Properties at Risk

Though all properties can be vulnerable to bombs and bomb threats, major metropolitan areas are more vulnerable because they offer all the ingredients that terrorists seek—numerous targets, many people whose attention they want to get, and crowds of people among whom they can conceal themselves. Large cities include a wealth of infrastructure and have the media nearby, so a terrorist or terrorist group can get the attention desired.

Security Measures to Thwart Bomb Threats

The property manager may conduct a security review of a property to pinpoint vulnerable areas within the building. A physical assessment of the facility includes checking the access control systems, employee identification (ID) program, alarms, surveillance cameras, and physical barriers. Not all buildings have or need the full array of these security measures.

Building mechanical systems (plumbing, electrical wiring, communications cabling, HVAC equipment) as well as emergency generators should be checked to ensure that they are not easily accessible to the public. A property manager can choose from numerous security measures and options, depending on property type, security needs, and location of the property. Some measures to consider are:

- If the building utilizes security patrols, review the patrol areas and schedule. Are stairwells and corridors patrolled on a regular schedule? Should the frequency of patrols be increased? Should the hours of patrol be extended—earlier in the morning, later in the evening?

- Review the communications systems within the building. Do management staff and security patrols have and use portable communication devices (e.g., two-way radios, cell phones)? Is there a backup system available in the event the primary building-wide system is inoperable?

- Check the lighting systems for elevators and stairwells. Are battery-pack lights available to serve as backup to current emergency lighting systems?
- Check the condition of building exit signs. Are there extra phosphorescent signs posted to facilitate evacuation if lighted exit signs do not work?
- Review methods by which deliveries are made to the property. Do any procedural controls need to be added?

The information derived from the security review can help determine new or additional preventive measures to be implemented. The emergency procedures manual should include procedures for responding to a bomb threat or the discovery of a bomb. The local police department or bomb squad should be consulted for specific guidelines. Recommendations vary regarding evacuation of a building that receives a bomb threat. There is and should be concern that immediate evacuation may expose people to greater danger. Evacuation routes are through public corridors, stairwells, and lobbies—the places most likely to contain an explosive device because they are accessible by "the public." Also, panic during an evacuation could cause injuries to people and damage to property.

Responding to a Bomb Threat

When a property manager receives a bomb threat or word that a bomb has been found on the premises, procedures already in place should be implemented. Response procedures will differ slightly, depending on whether the threat arrives by telephone or by mail. (At a shopping mall, a threat may be presented in person to the individual working at an information desk.)

The following are guidelines for responding to a bomb threat received by telephone.

- Never transfer the call. Try to keep the caller on the telephone as long as possible to obtain information about the bomb and its whereabouts. Depending on the equipment, if sufficient time can be taken, the call may be traceable.
- Never assume the threat is a hoax.
- Never shrug off the threat as a "bomb scare" that can be ignored.
- Never argue with or ridicule the caller.
- Let the caller know that the manager wants to save lives and urge him or her to help.
- Have a prearranged signal with others in the office so that someone can listen in without the caller's knowledge.
- Record the conversation, if possible.
- Have readily accessible a prepared checklist form to help identify the caller.

A bomb threat checklist form is available in quantity at no charge from the Department of the Treasury, Bureau of Alcohol, Tobacco, and Firearms. The contents of that checklist (ATF F 1613.1) are shown on the next page.

The following are guidelines for responding to a bomb or a bomb threat received by mail.

- Save all material received—envelope, packaging material, contents. Do not touch the package if there appears to be an object enclosed.
- Take care in handling the envelope or package so that fingerprints will be preserved.

BOMB THREAT CHECKLIST

1. When is the bomb going to explode?
2. Where is the bomb right now?
3. What does the bomb look like?
4. What kind of bomb is it?
5. What will cause the bomb to explode?
6. Did you place the bomb?
7. Why?
8. What is your address?
9. What is your name?

EXACT WORDING OF BOMB THREAT

_____

_____

_____

_____

_____

_____

Sex of caller: _____   Race: _____

Age: _____   Length of call: _____

Telephone number at which call is received:

_____

Time call received: _____

Date call received: _____/_____/_____

CALLER'S VOICE

_____ Calm   _____ Nasal

_____ Soft   _____ Angry

_____ Stutter   _____ Loud

_____ Excited   _____ Lisp

_____ Laughter   _____ Slow

_____ Rasp   _____ Crying

_____ Rapid   _____ Deep

_____ Normal   _____ Distinct

_____ Slurred   _____ Whispered

_____ Ragged   _____ Clearing throat

_____ Deep breathing   _____ Cracking voice

_____ Disguised   _____ Accent

_____ Familiar _(If voice is familiar, who did it sound like?)_

_____

_____

BACKGROUND SOUNDS

_____ Street noises   _____ Factory machinery

_____ Voices   _____ Crockery

_____ Animal noises   _____ Clear

_____ PA System   _____ Static

_____ Music   _____ House noises

_____ Long distance   _____ Local

_____ Motor   _____ Office machinery

_____ Booth   _____ Other _(please specify)_

_____

BOMB THREAT LANGUAGE

_____ Well spoken   _____ Incoherent
      (education)
                        _____ Message read by
_____ Foul   threat maker

_____ Taped   _____ Irrational

REMARKS: _____

_____

Your Name:

_____

Your Position:

_____

Your telephone number:

_____

Date checklist completed: _____/_____/_____

Characteristics of Mail Bombs

- Excessive postage.
- Fictitious or nonexistent return address.
- Postmark different from the return address city.
- Restricted endorsements—"personal" or "private."
- Distorted handwriting or homemade labels or cut-and-paste lettering for addressee information.
- Unprofessional wrapping with different types of tape, may include special labeling such as "Fragile—Handle With Care" or "Rush—Do Not Delay."
- Irregular shape, soft spots, or bulges.
- Protruding wires, aluminum foil, oil stains, peculiar odor.

Any of these indicators, alone or in combination, should raise suspicions about a parcel. More information can be obtained from the U.S. Postal Inspection Service at www.usps.com/postalinspectors/bombs.htm.

The U.S. Postal Inspection Service recommends observing the following precautions if a suspicious parcel is received (characteristics of mail bombs are shown in the accompanying box):

- Do not open the package.
- Isolate the suspicious parcel and evacuate the immediate area.
- Do not immerse it in water or put it in a confined space (desk drawer, cabinet).
- If possible, open windows in the immediate area to assist in venting potentially explosive gases.
- Contact the Postal Inspection Service and the local police.

The person who receives the threat should immediately report it to supervisory personnel. If the supervisor is not the site manager, the site manager should be notified immediately. At this point, the property management staff should exercise discretion regarding who is informed about the threat in order to avoid panic. Panic over a threat can be as dangerous as an actual bomb. The caller often knows this; seeing the disruption of the property's normal operations may be the objective the caller is trying to achieve.

If the person notified is a site manager, he or she should contact the property manager, who decides what action should be taken based on the property's emergency procedures.

First and foremost, the police department should be called. The police can provide advice about the "threat level," since they are aware of the current activity in the area. Once this call has been made, the property manager could:

- Contact the fire department.
- Inform the property's occupants, and evacuate the property on a voluntary basis.
- Search the property for the bomb.
- Evacuate the entire building or portions of it while searching for the bomb.

The emergency procedures plan should provide options based on the information available. When a bomb threat is made by telephone, the response is based on whether the caller has made threats against the property in the past and the amount and nature of detailed information the caller provides. If the building is evacuated, management staff should perform a visual search as they exit the building. Any suspicious objects or packages should be reported to the property manager or their supervisors or to the police or bomb squad if they are on the scene.

Searching for a Bomb

Every bomb threat should be assumed to be real until it is proved otherwise. It is important to act quickly to prevent an explosion. (Emergency response to an explosion is discussed in Chapter 22.)

The immediate actions may include searching the property for the bomb. *This should preferably be done by local authorities* (police, bomb squad), but it may be necessary to begin a search before they arrive. The emergency procedures manual should list detailed procedures for performing such a search, including (1) how to conduct the search and (2) who makes up the search team. It is recommended that the following steps be followed in the order shown:

- Search the suite and the common areas on the floor where the bomb threat was received.
- Next, search outdoor areas most accessible to intruders.
  —Begin at the lowest level, and search entrances, shrubbery, trash containers and Dumpsters, piles of leaves or refuse, patios and terraces, recreation areas, window ledges, air-conditioning units and equipment, building ornaments, signs, parking lots, parked vehicles, and manholes.
  —Move upward along the exterior of the building, searching fire escapes and roof areas.
  —Extend the search 25 to 50 feet in all directions or to a natural boundary line (e.g., curb, wall, hedge, parking lot, property line).
- Continue with an interior search.
  —Start with the most accessible areas, such as areas open to the public, reception areas, restrooms, areas containing service equipment, and stairwells.
  —Move up through the building systematically, floor by floor.
  —Search each room thoroughly.
  —Listen for unusual sounds. Unplug all electrical equipment to quiet their hums.
  —Divide each room into equal parts, depending on how many items there are in the room and how large an area there is to search. Assign a team member to each part. After the team members have searched their areas, rotate areas and search again.
  —Search in sweeps—from floor to waist height, from waist to chin height, from chin to ceiling, and finally the ceiling area (e.g., light fixtures, false ceiling, smoke alarms).
  —Keep in mind that the use of walkie-talkies while searching for a bomb could activate a device.

Some additional points to look out for as indicators that a bomb may have been hidden inside a building are listed in the box on page 156.

A thorough search can take up to several hours, depending on the size and layout of the building and the number of people on the search team. Who should make up this search team? Suggested team members include:

- Local authorities and trained searchers.
- The on-site management staff.
- People who will be able to identify new, foreign, or unfamiliar objects.

Indications of Tampering

If a bomb threat is received, consider that a bomber will generally only have had access to public areas of the building. While it is logical to search for an object, it is also appropriate to search those public areas of a building looking for signs of an intruder. The following are some indicators to look for:

- Suspicious persons loitering in the area.
- Pictures or other hanging objects that are not hanging straight.
- Disturbed soil in potted plants or potted plants that are moved.
- Broken cabinets
- Furniture or objects recently and obviously moved out of place.
- Torn coverings on upholstered furnishings.
- Ceiling tiles that appear disturbed.
- Doors or door locks that have been tampered with.
- Any object that looks out of place in its surroundings.
- Freshly painted or plastered areas.

- Persons having access to locked doors.
- Trained security guards.
- Trained maintenance crew members.

The emergency procedures manual should list names and current telephone numbers of bomb search team members and designate a clear chain of command. The leader makes the critical decision whether to evacuate, calls the police or fire departments, coordinates the search teams, supervises the command center, and communicates with the media, the public, building occupants, and public agencies (unless another spokesperson has been appointed).

What to Do Once a Bomb Is Found

If a bomb is found (or what is thought to be a bomb), staff should consider the following precautions:

- Do not touch or disturb the bomb or suspicious article unless it is a life-or-death situation.
- Evacuate occupants immediately.
  —Evacuate people to a distance where they will be safe from flying glass and debris, usually at least 300 feet.
  —Do not allow anyone to return to the building until re-entry is officially authorized.
- Call police explosives specialists to take charge of the situation. Property management personnel should never try to defuse a bomb.
- Do not submerge the bomb or suspicious item in water; do not cover it, hoping to diminish its blast. Doing this could hasten explosion and create additional debris.
- Assemble the building's first aid team.
- Initiate damage control procedures at the advice of the police.
  —Open all windows and doors to vent a blast.
  —Shut off all utilities (e.g., gas, fuel oil) that might contribute to fire or explosion.

—Remove any flammable materials.

—Construct a protective barrier around the bomb—but not on top of it—using material that will not fragment (e.g., a double row of sandbags, a mattress, overturned furniture). The material(s) should be placed between the bomb and the nearest vulnerable wall, with the barrier *not touching either.*

Recovering from a Bomb Threat

The property manager's main responsibility after a bomb threat is to ensure the safety of the building occupants. If an evacuation was ordered, the property manager should permit all occupants to return to the building and assure them that the situation is under control. Not all bomb threats result in building evacuation, however.

Finally, no unnecessary mention or public announcement should be made of the bomb or bomb threat. Word of one bomb threat can spawn copycats.

Note: More specific guidance on responding to a bomb threat and searching for a bomb can be obtained from local, state, and federal law enforcement agencies.

22

Explosion

While an explosion may be the result of a bomb being detonated, there are other causes to consider in regard to managed properties. A boiler used to provide steam heat can explode if excess steam pressure builds up. A gas leak ignited by a spark can explode. Chemicals that are themselves not potentially explosive may cause an explosion if exposed to certain other chemicals in an accidental spill. A fire may detonate potentially explosive materials. An explosion outside a building can cause damage to the interior as well as the exterior of the building, and that damage can lead to injuries.

Preventive Measures

If a bomb is discovered because of a bomb threat, it may be possible for an expert to defuse it. Erection of a nonfragmenting barrier can help minimize damage if it does explode (see Chapter 21).

Regular inspection and preventive maintenance can ensure that boilers and other pressure vessels are in good condition and operating at proper settings. Compliance with OSHA workplace safety rules and proper handling of chemicals within tenants' premises can reduce the potential for an explosion to occur accidentally. Information on potential ignitability and reactivity, if known, should be included on the material safety data sheet (MSDS) for an industrial chemical. (Information on preventing gas leaks can be found in Chapter 18; fire prevention measures are discussed in Chapter 14.)

If an Explosion Occurs

If there is an explosion, people should exit the building as quickly as possible, using stairways rather than elevators. (Stairwells and stairs should be checked for stability before using them for evacuation.) There may be smoke or fire, in which case, evacuation procedures for a fire should be followed. The Emergency Management Team should account for building occupants as quickly as possible.

The fire department and rescue squad should be called immediately. If people are trapped in debris, they may also be injured. Rescuers may have to proceed with

---

What to Do If Trapped in Debris

- If possible, use a flashlight to signal your location to rescuers.
- Avoid unnecessary movement so that you don't kick up dust.
- Cover your nose and mouth with anything you have on hand. (Dense-weave cotton material can act as a good filter. Try to breathe through the material.)
- Tap on a pipe or wall so that rescuers can hear where you are.
- If possible, use a whistle to signal rescuers.
- Shout *only* as a last resort. Shouting can cause a person to inhale dangerous amounts of dust.

Source: Federal Emergency Management Agency (FEMA) web site www.ready.gov.

---

caution to avoid destabilizing debris. Even if there is no fire, there is likely to be fine dust in the air. If the explosion is chemical related, there may be toxic gases as well. Rescuers should wear appropriate respiratory protection—at a minimum, dust masks.

If people are trapped and communication is possible, let them know that help is on the way. Devise a signal they can use to help rescuers pinpoint their location. Instructions from the Federal Emergency Management Agency (FEMA) are presented in the accompanying box. This information may be included in resident or tenant handbooks or provided to them as part of fire response/evacuation procedures.

23

Hazardous Materials Incidents

Chemicals are an ever-present and important part of the human environment. They are used every day for laundering clothes, bathing, cleaning equipment, and treating water supplies. They are in the medicines prescribed for humans and animals. However, under certain conditions—very large quantities, higher concentrations, improper use—those same chemicals can be harmful to living beings. There are also chemicals that are hazardous themselves but necessary to the manufacture of equipment, vehicles, and other chemicals.

Materials that pose hazards to life and health are present on most if not all managed properties. If used, stored, and disposed properly, the danger can be minimized. However, a hazardous materials incident can occur anywhere, and incidents occurring in the vicinity of a property, but not on it, can have an impact on the property as well.

Managers of properties located near industrial sites where hazardous materials are used will benefit from an increased understanding of the effects of hazardous materials spills and releases and awareness of preventive measures they can implement to protect people on their properties and the properties themselves.

Areas and Properties at Risk

Chemicals and other hazardous materials are transported by rail and via lakes, rivers, canals, and other inland waterways. They are also moved by truck on roadways, including local streets as well as highways and the Interstate system. Residential and commercial properties located close to these transportation routes are particularly at risk. Properties located near chemical manufacturing plants are also at high risk.

A hazardous materials (hazmat) incident can result from a spill or damage to equipment on site. The property manager should also consider the location of the property and types of incidents that might occur. Based on that information, the property manager should plan for hazardous materials incidents that may accompany a traffic accident, a train derailment, a collision on a waterway. A fire or explosion at a nearby property may release hazardous gases or liquids that pose a danger to occupants of other buildings.

The manager of a property located near an industrial site may want to visit that site to meet with the designated safety officer and discuss the types of hazardous chemicals from the site that might cause problems for their adjacent property, methods of contacting each other in the event of an incident, and safety precautions that could be implemented.

Preventive Measures

Safe handling and storage of chemicals and other hazardous materials is discussed in regard to industrial properties in Chapter 13. Careful handling will generally prevent spills. Immediate cleanup of small spills and proper disposal of the cleaning materials will minimize the consequences of such incidents. The material safety data sheet (MSDS) that accompanies bulk chemicals (or the labels on smaller containers) should provide information on specific hazards and include recommended cleanup procedures. They should also indicate symptoms of exposure and suggested methods of treatment.

The emergency procedures manual should include steps to be taken in the case of small spills as well as larger incidents, possibly off site. The local Poison Control Center can provide guidance on how to respond to chemical poisonings. First aid courses for Emergency Management Team members who choose to receive such training may include treatment for chemical burns. The local chapter of the American Red Cross can provide helpful information. (Bloodborne pathogens are discussed in Chapters 11 and 19 and radiation hazards are discussed in Chapters 33 and 34.)

During a Hazardous Materials Incident

If a hazardous material spill occurs on site—or is witnessed near the property—contact the fire department or other appropriate authority to send a hazmat team. These responders are specially trained and have appropriate protective clothing and equipment. People who are not part of the cleanup team should be kept away from the area of the spill. It may be necessary or appropriate to evacuate the building. Hazmat responders can provide specific guidance regarding evacuation. If the incident is off site but nearby, there are likely to be announcements broadcast on the Emergency Alert System (EAS); see Chapter 15. Alternatively, a siren may sound, building management may be contacted directly by telephone, or emergency personnel may drive by, using a loudspeaker to give instructions.

Authorities will decide whether and when evacuation is necessary and make specific announcements about it. The decision to evacuate is generally based on the type and amount of material released and how long it is expected to affect an area. Other considerations are weather conditions (current and forecast, wind speed in particular), time of day, and how long it is likely to take to evacuate the area. Announcements may include specific evacuation routes to follow. If there is time to do so, shut down the HVAC system—close air intakes and vents and turn off fans in particular—to minimize contamination indoors. Instead of evacuation, authorities may recommend that people shelter in place with all windows and air intake vents closed (see box on page 164).

After a Hazardous Materials Incident

Re-enter the building only when authorities say it is safe to do so. Check exterior and interior surfaces for residue from the spill. Because the residue may be haz-

Exposure to Chemicals

People may be exposed to chemicals in three ways:

1. Inhalation—breathing vapors of a volatile substance or fumes generated when it is exposed to air or water.
2. Ingestion—swallowing the chemical itself or ingesting food, water, or medication contaminated with it.
3. Skin contact—touching the chemical or coming into contact with clothing or other objects that have touched the chemical.

Inhalation and skin contact are most common. Failure to follow label directions and mixing of chemicals such as cleaners are common causes of exposure.

Many chemicals are odorless and tasteless. Exposure may occur even though people may not be able to see or smell anything unusual. Some chemicals may be detected because they present a foul odor or the vapor/fumes they emit cause watering of the eyes. Fumes may also cause an extremely runny nose or other allergic-type reaction.

Symptoms of chemical poisoning include:
- Difficulty breathing
- Irritation of eyes, nose, throat, and/or skin
- Blurring of vision
- Headache
- Dizziness
- Nausea
- Vomiting
- Stomach cramps
- Diarrhea
- Clumsiness or lack of coordination
- Unusual behavior

Chemical poisoning is potentially life-threatening. Emergency medical attention should be sought immediately.

---

ardous, it should be cleaned up and disposed of carefully. Protective clothing and equipment may be necessary or appropriate. Emergency officials may issue instructions for cleanup and disposal.

Care should be taken in restarting HVAC system components. It may be necessary or appropriate to inspect equipment and ductwork for residue and test for contamination of cooling tower water. It may be advisable to clean out ducts, filters, and other system components before restoring full operation. It may also be appropriate to vent the building before occupants are allowed to re-enter it.

Because hazardous materials can contaminate water supplies, including groundwater by leaching through soil, it may be advisable to check with authorities before using water from building faucets for drinking and washing. It may be necessary to boil water for some purposes, especially in a residential property. As an added safeguard, the property manager may have building water tested for chemical contamination.

Sheltering in Place

If instead of ordering an evacuation authorities recommend sheltering in place, the following precautions should be observed:

- Close all windows and doors.
- Turn off HVAC systems and equipment.
- Move to a level above ground, one with a minimum of windows and doors.
- Preferably, stay in a room with a door that can be closed.
- Wet towels and jam them into the crack under the door.
- Tape plastic garbage bags or other suitable plastic sheeting over windows, doors, and vents. It may be appropriate to cover electrical outlets similarly.
- Close window shades, blinds, or curtains if warning includes the possibility of explosion. Stay away from windows to avoid injury.
- Hold a damp cloth over nose and mouth to prevent breathing hazardous vapors.
- Listen to emergency radio for announcements that the area is safe and/or instructions to evacuate.

Sheltering in place may be recommended in the event of a hazardous materials incident. It may also be recommended for some types of severe weather or in the event of a terrorist attack.

Note: Additional information on sheltering in place can be found on the Internet at www.nicsinfo.org/ShelterInPlace.htm and the Centers for Disease Control web site at www.cdc.gov.

Hazardous materials incidents may result in environmental contamination of air, water, and/or soil, especially if the spill involves a large amount of material or covers a large area. Those who manage industrial sites need to be aware of federal and state regulations that must be followed regarding containment of a spill or release and notification of incidents that occur. An incident on managed property may need to be reported specifically to the U.S. EPA and/or to state and local environmental agencies. It may be appropriate to find out what the reporting requirements are—the specific material that is spilled and the nature of the hazard(s) it poses may determine what action is required in this regard.

Note: Additional information on hazardous materials classification, transportation, and spill reporting requirements can be found on the U.S. Department of Transportation web site at http://hazmat.dot.gov/hazhome.htm. Information on hazardous waste disposal can be found on the U.S. Environmental Protection Agency web site at www.epa.gov/epaoswer/osw/. They also publish a *Guide for Industrial Waste Management,* which can be downloaded at www.epa.gov/epaoswer/non-hw/industd/guide.htm. Information on medical wastes, including agencies that regulate them, can be found at www.epa.gov/epaoswer/other/medical/.

24

Tornadoes

Tornadoes are nature's most concentrated and violent weather phenomena. Spawned from powerful thunderstorm conditions, tornadoes are gray or black rotating funnel-shaped clouds that extend from the bases of thunderclouds to the ground. Their whirling winds can reach speeds of up to 300 mph, uprooting trees and buildings and turning harmless objects into deadly missiles transported by their intense velocity A tornado's path of damage on the ground can exceed one mile in width and cover a distance of 50 miles or more. Tornadoes typically travel from southwest to northeast.

Within minutes or even seconds, a tornado can devastate a neighborhood, demolishing properties, tearing roofs from buildings, and leaving a trail of destruction. When it touches down, a tornado sounds like the roaring of a locomotive. An observer witnessing its approach may see blowing debris from a distance. Other indications of a coming tornado are tree branches being blown in circles and the sky becoming very dark with a pea green cast. In coastal areas, a tornado may accompany a tropical storm or hurricane. Weather records indicate that most tornadoes occur in the late afternoon and early evening during the months of April, May, and June although they can occur at any time of year. In an average year, 1,200 tornadoes are reported nationwide, resulting in an average of 70 deaths and more than 1,500 injuries.

Areas and Properties at Risk

Tornadoes are most common east of the Rocky Mountains during the spring and summer months. Although they can occur in any state, Texas has been hit the most. During the spring in the Central Plains, thunderstorms frequently develop along the "dryline" that separates the warm moist air to the east from hot dry air to the west.

The properties that are at greatest risk from tornadoes include wide-span buildings with roofs supported solely by outside walls (e.g., gymnasiums), premanufactured metal buildings, and mobile/manufactured homes. Substantial steel-framed and reinforced-concrete buildings face the least amount of risk.

Categories of Tornadoes

Weak—winds less than 110 mph; duration 1–10 minutes or longer. They represent 88% of all tornadoes and are responsible for <5% of tornado deaths.

Strong—winds 110–205 mph; duration 20 minutes or longer. They represent 11% of all tornadoes and are responsible for 30% of all tornado deaths.

Violent—winds greater than 205 mph; duration 1 hour or longer. They represent <1% of all tornadoes and are responsible for 70% of all tornado deaths.

Source: *Thunderstorms, Tornadoes, Lightning: Nature's Most Violent Storms,* published jointly by NOAA, FEMA, and the American Red Cross, publication numbers NOAA/PA 99050 and ARC 1122; also available for download on the Internet at www.nws.noaa.gov/om/brochures/ttl.pdf.

Weather Advisories and Warnings

Tornadoes are especially deadly because they often strike with little or no warning. However, Doppler radar at weather stations across the United States allows the National Weather Service (NWS) to detect increasing rotation aloft in thunderstorms, which can be indicative of tornadoes. This can allow lifesaving warnings to be broadcast before some tornadoes actually form.

Most tornado-prone communities employ sirens to warn residents of approaching tornadoes. Local weather authorities also utilize public broadcast media such as television, radio, and the NOAA (National Oceanographic and Atmospheric Administration) Weather Radio to announce weather watches and warnings.

Property managers and emergency teams should become familiar with the significance of the following weather alerts in order to understand the severity of approaching tornadoes and initiate the proper emergency response. One of the first indicators that a tornado might develop is thunderstorm conditions.

- A *severe thunderstorm watch* indicates that such storms are possible in the area cited.
- A *severe thunderstorm warning* indicates that severe thunderstorms are present in the specific area. This is issued when winds gust to more than 58 mph accompanied by hail larger than ¾ inch in diameter.
- A *tornado watch* indicates that tornadoes are possible in the cited areas.
- A *tornado warning* indicates that a tornado has been sighted on the ground or indicated on the weather radar.

People should be alert for approaching storms. If there is a warning and the sky becomes threatening—storm clouds dark green or black—everyone should take cover. (The various categories of tornadoes and indications of the damage they can cause are shown in the accompanying boxes.)

Preventive Measures

The following preventive measures can help minimize losses from tornadoes:

- Contact your local emergency management office or American Red Cross chapter. Ask about the threat of tornadoes in the area, and learn about com-

Fujita Scale / Tornado Wind Speed

F0 Gale Tornado—wind speed 40–72 mph; shallow-rooted trees uprooted, tree branches broken off.

F1 Moderate Tornado—wind speed 73–112 mph; moving cars pushed off roads, mobile/manufactured homes overturned, surface peeled off roofs.

F2 Significant Tornado—wind speed 113–157 mph; large trees snapped or uprooted, roofs torn off of frame houses, light objects become missiles.

F3 Severe Tornado—wind speed 158–206 mph; heavy cars lifted off the ground, trains overturned, roofs and some walls torn off of well-constructed homes, most trees in forests uprooted.

F4 Devastating Tornado—wind speed 207–260 mph; cars thrown about; large objects become missiles, well-constructed houses leveled, structures with weak foundations blown some distance off their foundations.

F5 Incredible Tornado—wind speed 261–318 mph; automobile-size missiles move through the air at speeds of more than 100 mph, strong frame houses lifted off foundations and disintegrated, trees debarked.

Note: The Fujita scale bases wind speed on actual damage.

Source: *Tornadoes*, a publication on hurricane preparedness from the National Hurricane Center of the National Oceanic and Atmospheric Administration, available for download from the Internet at www.nhc.noaa.gov/HAW2/english/tornadoes.shtml.

munity warning signals—whether there is a siren, which NOAA Weather Radio frequency is used, etc.
- Check local building codes and ordinances regarding wind-resistant building designs and make needed improvements to comply with structural requirements.
- Know the county or parish in which the property is situated. Warnings use these to identify the tornado's location or projected path.
- Identify designated shelter areas in advance; these may be public buildings, nursing homes, shopping centers.
- Ensure that the building is as structurally sound as possible, and that roofs are firmly secured.
- Seek out and secure outdoor objects that might blow away or damage a structure—e.g., trash containers and Dumpsters, signs, outdoor furniture, tools, and debris. Instruct residents to keep all patio and balcony items (pots, plants) indoors.
- Inspect roofs and catch basins; remove tools and debris. Repair loose gutters, shingles, and coping.
- Prune trees to remove branches that might damage the building.
- Keep a supply of fresh bottled water on hand in case the storm contaminates or disrupts the community's water supply.
- Evacuate low-lying areas and other areas when directed by emergency personnel.
- Be sure the property owner/landlord carries adequate casualty and liability insurance that includes rent loss coverage.
- Check with commercial tenants in office, retail, and industrial properties to ensure that they maintain proper insurance coverages as required by their leases.

During a Tornado

The emergency procedures manual should include directions to both staff and occupants, telling them what to do if a tornado should hit the property. Here are some suggested procedures:

- Listen to local radio or television stations for weather updates.
- Report rotating funnel-shaped clouds to the local police department or weather service.
- Station an emergency team member at a south entrance of the building to watch for the cloud.
- Open windows slightly so pressure will not build and shatter them.
- Stay away from windows, doors, and outside walls. Go to a cellar or basement if possible.
- Advise occupants to seek safe shelter immediately in small interior lower floor rooms without windows; in hallways on the lowest floor; in rooms constructed with reinforced concrete, brick, or block with no windows; or in an interior (windowless) bathroom or other protected areas away from windows.
- If you are in a high-rise building, you may not have time to go to a lower floor or basement. Pick a place in a hallway or the center of the building.
- In a mobile/manufactured home park, advise residents to evacuate immediately to a nearby shelter or to stay with family or friends off site.
- Have members of the Emergency Management Team circulate among management staff, building occupants, and others on the property to ensure that everyone has found a safe place to ride out the tornado.
- If outdoors and there is no shelter nearby, people should lie flat in the nearest ditch, ravine, or culvert with their hands shielding their heads.
- Do not encourage occupants to outdrive a tornado. Tornadoes are erratic and move swiftly.

After a Tornado

Once a tornado has passed, the winds will have noticeably died down. Now is the time for the Emergency Management Team to evaluate the damage.

- Check for injuries among the occupants, and apply first aid as necessary (see Chapter 19).
- Immediately contact local emergency crews if necessary to assist in the location and removal of injured persons. Maintain dialogue between the local authorities and the building contact person to determine when all injured parties have been removed.
- Contact the insurance company, restoration contractor, and building inspector, and request that they visit the site as quickly as possible.
- In the absence of an insurance adjuster, take pictures and/or videos to document damage.
- Assemble building plans and as-built drawings and have on site as soon as possible.
- Inspect the property, and appoint cleanup crews.
- Well-built structures may survive a tornado and appear intact. However, use caution when entering the building. Ensure that the walls, ceiling, and roof are in place and that the structure rests firmly on the foundation.
- Wear a hard hat, sturdy boots, and work gloves, if possible.
- Look out for broken glass and downed power lines.
- Watch for live electrical wires and dangerous debris.

Thunderstorms and Lightning

Only about one percent of thunderstorms spawn tornadoes. Each year, on average, there are 100,000 thunderstorms across the United States, approximately 1,000 of which develop tornadoes.

Severe thunderstorms can produce hail and heavy rains that can lead to flash flooding. Hail can be pea-size or smaller or as large as a softball. It can damage plants and automobiles. Straight-line winds can exceed 100 mph. Thunderstorms are signaled by dark, towering, or threatening clouds, lightning flashes, thunder, and increasing wind. The National Weather Service issues severe thunderstorm watches and warnings.

High winds can be a problem for high-rise buildings. Windows have been blown out of high-rise buildings, causing injuries to pedestrians and damage to vehicles at street level as well as disrupted operations inside the building. If wind damage is a potential problem, the property manager can check with the local building department to see if the issue is addressed specifically in the building code. An architect or structural engineer may be able to advise about preventive strategies. Emergency procedures would need to address interior cleanup and window replacement. Also, movable scaffolding used by window washers and building exterior surface cleaners needs to be secured when not in use and should not be used when there are high winds. If such scaffolding should come loose, it may break windows and cause damage to the building exterior. Workers on the scaffolding may be injured or killed, and there are likely to be injuries to pedestrians and damage to vehicles on the sidewalk and street below.

Lightning, which accompanies all thunderstorms, can cause fires. It can also cause injuries and fatalities. Each year, on average, lightning causes 300 injuries and 80 fatalities. A person struck by lightning has received an electrical shock and may be burned, not only at the site of the lightning strike, but also where the electricity left the body. Being struck by lightning can also cause damage to the nervous system, loss of eyesight or hearing, and broken bones. Injured persons should be given appropriate first aid—they may require CPR—and emergency medical help should be called immediately.

Thunderstorms and lightning can cause power outages. If there is no backup power source, electrical equipment should be unplugged—or electricity may be shut off—to prevent damage from power surges when electricity is restored.

Note: More information can be found on the Internet at www.noaa.gov/lightning .html.

- Open clogged drains and catch basins.
- Prepare for possible flooding from the accompanying storm or from damaged water barriers.
- Be alert for potential fire hazards such as leaking gas lines, pools of water near electrical equipment and appliances, spills of combustible materials, etc. (see Chapter 14).
- If the property is damaged, secure it until local officials and/or a structural engineer has inspected the facility and authorized entry.

- Provide security guards if necessary to prevent looting.
- Apprise the building occupants of the situation and your plans for restoration. Advise them when they can re-enter the premises to collect personal belongings and/or begin the cleanup.

Note: More specific information can be found on the Internet at www.noaa.gov/tornadoes .html. and in *Tornadoes: Nature's Most Violent Storms* published jointly by NOAA, FEMA, and the American Red Cross and available for download at www.nssl.noaa.gov/NWS Tornado/.

25

Hurricanes

Hurricanes are one of nature's most destructive forces. These massive weather phenomena are tropical cyclones with torrential rains and sustained winds of 74 miles per hour or more in which winds blow counter-clockwise (in the northern hemisphere) around a relatively calm center or "eye." Hurricanes may extend up to 400 miles across and can severely damage areas hundreds of miles inland.

Developing hurricanes gather heat and energy through contact with warm ocean waters. The addition of moisture by evaporation from the sea surface powers them like giant heat engines. Around their core, winds grow with great velocity, generating violent seas; and as they move ashore, they can sweep the ocean coastward, spawning tornadoes and causing huge domes of water (storm surges) to crash into the coastline. Widespread torrential rains, often with rainfall amounts in excess of six inches, can produce deadly and destructive floods.

Violent storms can destroy structures. They can result in broken sewer and water mains, loose and dangling electrical wires, power outages, collapsed roads, and widespread destruction. Foundations can be undermined by water and wind. In addition, there is a greater possibility of fire after a hurricane from gas and electrical damage. Timely warnings due to advanced weather technology and communication have greatly decreased hurricane fatalities in the United States, but properties continue to sustain major damage and destruction.

Areas and Properties at Risk

Each year, an average of ten tropical storms (six of which are hurricanes) develop over the Atlantic ocean, Caribbean Sea, or Gulf of Mexico during the peak hurricane months of May through November. Islands in the mid-Pacific are also subject to hurricanes. Although rarely struck by hurricanes, parts of the Southwest United States and the Pacific Coast suffer heavy rains and floods each year from the remnants of hurricanes spawned off of Mexico. Although many hurricanes remain over the ocean, about five hurricanes strike the U.S. coastline every three years. Based on historic tracking, two of these five are usually major hurricanes, with sustained winds of 111–130 mph. The center or eye of a hurricane is relatively calm; the most violent activity takes place immediately around the eye.

Due to limited accessible evacuation routes, barrier islands such as Hawaii and

Saffir-Simpson Hurricane Scale

Category	Winds (mph)	Storm Surge (ft)
One	74–95	4–5
Two	96–110	6–8
Three	111–130	9–12
Four	131–155	13–18
Five	>155	>18

Source: *Hurricanes: Unleashing Nature's Fury* published jointly by NOAA, FEMA, and the American Red Cross, publication numbers NOAA/PA 94050 and ARC 5030; also available for download at www.nws.noaa.gov/om/brochures/hurr/pdf.

Guam are especially vulnerable to hurricanes, while inland areas such as the Midwest experience associated high winds, floods and tornadoes.

Coastal areas, especially near the Gulf of Mexico and along the Eastern Seaboard, are at greatest risk from hurricanes. Inland regions near these areas also are at risk although, generally speaking, the farther away from the coast, the less direct effect a hurricane will have.

The United States is becoming increasingly vulnerable to hurricanes. As shorelines attract large numbers of new homes and condominium towers, cities are being built on coastal sands susceptible to storms. There are more than 45 million permanent residents along the hurricane-prone coastline, with increased populations in the Sunbelt from Texas up through the Carolinas. Florida leads the country in new residents, while holiday populations and tourists further increase the number of potential victims.

Recent technological and communications advances such as geostationary satellites, radar, and military reconnaissance aircraft have enabled authorities to notify residents of advancing hurricanes with sufficient time to evacuate. However, the number of roads and their accessibility have not kept up with growing populations, making evacuation increasingly difficult. Also, residents and properties in hurricane-prone areas may have a false sense of security since 80 to 90 percent of the incoming population has never experienced a "major" hurricane and may be complacent. (Historical data on hurricane tracks can be found on the Internet at http://hurricane.csc.noaa.gov/hurricanes/.)

Structures most at risk from hurricanes are long-span buildings and mobile or manufactured homes. Substantial steel-framed or reinforced concrete buildings are the least risky. On a long-span building, the roof is usually supported solely by outside walls; inside walls are usually false or non-load-bearing. Shopping centers, which traditionally are long-span buildings, are especially vulnerable to roof collapse.

Because of the frailty of mobile homes/manufactured housing, a protective on-site shelter may be included in a mobile home community. In the event of a hurricane, residents should be encouraged to make arrangements to move to such shelters or stay with friends or relatives at the first sign of trouble.

Hurricane Warning Signs

Heavy rains, increasing winds, and thunderstorms in a vicinity are initial signs of approaching hurricanes. The modern technology mentioned above, however, enables

Hurricane Advisories

advisory Official information issued by tropical cyclone warning centers describing all tropical cyclone watches and warnings in effect along with details concerning tropical cyclone locations, intensity, and movement and precautions that should be taken. Advisories are also issued to describe tropical cyclones *prior to* issuance of watches and warnings and subtropical cyclones. (A *cyclone* is an atmospheric closed circulation rotating counter-clockwise in the Northern Hemisphere and clockwise in the Southern Hemisphere. A *subtropical cyclone* is a nonfrontal low-pressure system that has characteristics of both tropical and extratropical cyclones.)

tropical storm watch An announcement for specific coastal areas that tropical storm conditions are possible within 36 hours.

tropical storm warning A warning that sustained winds within the range of 39–73 mph associated with a tropical cyclone are expected in a specified coastal area within 24 hours or less.

hurricane watch An announcement for specific coastal areas that hurricane conditions are possible within 36 hours.

hurricane warning A warning that sustained winds of 74 mph or higher associated with a hurricane are expected in a specified coastal area in 24 hours or less. (A hurricane warning can remain in effect when dangerously high water alone or combined with exceptionally high waves continue, even though winds may be less than hurricane force.)

gale warning A warning of one-minute sustained surface winds in the range of 39–54 mph inclusive, either predicted or occurring and not directly associated with tropical cyclones.

Source: Glossary of National Hurricane Center/Tropical Prediction Center Terms published on the Internet at www.nhc.noaa.gov.

local authorities to convey more advanced warnings on broadcast media such as television, public radio, hurricane sirens, and the NOAA Weather Radio (NWR) operated by the National Oceanographic and Atmospheric Administration.

The National Weather Service (NWS) continuously broadcasts all types of weather advisories and warnings received by NOAA on a special weather radio which can be purchased at radio and sound system retail outlets. These radios alert listeners of approaching weather systems with tone-alert features and provide descriptions of the approaching weather conditions in relevant areas.

Storm surges are abnormally high sea levels accompanying hurricanes that can wash inland one quarter to one half mile, inundating coastal buildings. Residents must evacuate before these surges arrive. Life-threatening torrential rains are captured in gullies and overflow in streams, causing flooding. Residents should evacuate immediately.

Weather Advisories and Warnings

There are five types of hurricane warnings—tropical storm watches, tropical storm warnings, hurricane watches, hurricane warnings, and short-term watches and warnings. All property managers should become acquainted with them in order to understand the current severity of hurricane systems in their areas.

Tropical storm watches are declared when tropical storm conditions are possible in the specified area of the watch, usually within 36 hours. *Tropical storm warnings* are announced when tropical storm conditions are expected within 24 hours in a specified area. *Hurricane watches* are issued when hurricane conditions are possible, usually within 36 hours. During a hurricane watch, prepare to take immediate action in case a hurricane warning is issued. *Hurricane warnings* are issued when hurricane conditions are expected in the area within 24 hours. At this point, all storm preparations should be completed, and evacuation should take place if directed by the local authorities. Short-term watches and warnings provide detailed information on hurricane hazard threats such as floods, tornadoes, and high winds. Tornadoes associated with hurricanes, which can occur for days after landfall, usually are not accompanied by hail or lightning.

Preventive Measures

Today's satellite imagery enables the NWS to track hurricanes for days, so there usually is time for preventive measures to be taken. At the minimum, a property manager should have one day's notice, inasmuch as hurricane watches will be upgraded to hurricane warnings when the hurricane is expected to strike an area within 24 hours. There are a number of measures the property manager can implement during this time to prevent property loss:

- Identify in advance locally designated public shelters in the community.
- Closely monitor the television, radio, or NOAA Weather Radio to keep abreast of storms progressing in the area. They will direct you to areas of public shelter.
- Learn safe routes inland.
- Review the need for and working condition of emergency supplies and equipment such as plywood and nails (for safeguarding windows), flashlights, and battery-powered radios.
- Clear out clogged rain gutters and downspouts; secure loose gutters and downspouts.
- Seek out and secure objects out of doors that might blow away or cause property damage. These include trash cans and Dumpsters, signs, outdoor furniture, and trash.
- Inspect roofs—repair loose gutters, shingles, and coping; remove tools and loose objects; pick up trash.
- Inspect roof-mounted HVAC equipment for loose debris and improperly fastened panels; make needed repairs.
- Inspect storm sewers and catch basins; clear away debris.
- Close and protect windows and glass doors—board up windows, install storm shutters, and apply masking or electrical tape (depending on the fury of the storm) in an X pattern on both sides of the glass.
- If near a coastline, stream or river, shut off gas and electricity.
- Instruct residents to move all patio and balcony items (pots, plants, etc.) indoors. Remove these items from balconies of residents who are not at home.
- Keep a supply of fresh bottled water on hand in case the storm contaminates the community's water supply or damages distribution lines.
- Evacuate low-lying areas and any other areas when so directed.
- Have ice on hand to preserve food in residential complexes, and keep icepacks ready to treat physical injuries.
- Shut down all three-phase electrical service just prior to the hurricane striking.

Hurricane Preparations for Businesses

- Remove papers from lower drawers of desks and file cabinets; place them in containers or plastic bags on top of the desk or cabinet.
- Use plywood to protect glass showcases; alternatively, turn glass side of case toward an inside wall if possible.
- Store merchandise as high as possible off the floor; merchandise that cannot be stored should be moved away from glass areas and covered with heavy plastic or tarpaulin.
- In warehouses, secure goods off the floor; use sandbags to help keep water from entering.

Source: *Surviving the Storm: A Guide to Hurricane Preparedness* published by the U.S. Department of Homeland Security/Federal Emergency Management Agency and available for download on the Internet at www.fema.gov/hazards/hurricanes/survivingthestorm.shtm.

- Move elevators to the second floor level and lock them off in the event of flooding. Secure elevator doors at lower levels to prevent entry into the shaft.

The National Institute of Building Sciences (NIBS) at the direction of FEMA has developed a standardized methodology, called HAZUS, for assessing losses from hurricane wind damage. Information about HAZUS is available on the Internet at http://nibs.org/hazusweb/methodology/wind.php. HAZUS software is available at no charge from FEMA.

Hurricane-Proofing a Property

Plans to protect a property should be developed well in advance of hurricanes. Permanent storm shutters offer the best protection for windows, although an alternative is to board up windows with 5/8-inch marine plywood that is pre-cut to fit and ready to install.

Each property should be inspected for compliance with local building codes to ensure maximum safety and qualification for insurance coverage. Many roofs destroyed by hurricanes have been found to be in violation of local building codes.

Flood insurance is a necessity in hurricane-prone areas. Flood insurance should be purchased well in advance, as there is normally a five-day waiting period before it takes effect. (See Chapter 27 for more information on flood insurance.)

The Emergency Management Team should know how to shut off utilities, where gas pilot lights are located, and how the heating and air-conditioning systems are controlled. The need for backup systems should be considered, such as battery-operated portable pumps to remove flood water, battery-powered emergency lighting, and alternate power sources such as gasoline-powered generators. Preparations should include measures for securing hazardous materials or plans for removing them from the property.

During a Hurricane

The emergency procedures manual should tell both the Emergency Management Team and the building's occupants what to do during a hurricane. Here are some suggestions:

- Frequently listen to broadcast updates of the storm's status.
- Inspect and secure mobile home tie-downs.
- Turn off gas and electricity.
- Follow evacuation instructions of local officials. Hurricane winds are especially strong at higher elevations, so occupants of high-rise buildings should waste no time in evacuating.
- Stay away from windows and doors, even if they are covered. Take refuge in a small interior room or hallway, where structural support is strongest.
- Remain indoors—go to designated shelters or basement areas.
- Do not be fooled by the eye of the hurricane if it passes over you. If it is directly overhead, there will be a lull in the wind lasting several minutes to half an hour or more, and then strong winds and weather will recur.
- Be alert for tornadoes, which can happen during a hurricane or after it passes.
- Avoid using the phone except for serious emergencies; local authorities need first priority in using telephone lines.
- Advise occupants of multiple-story buildings that are located away from the water to go to the first or second floors and take refuge in halls or interior rooms, away from windows.
- Wear a hard hat, if possible.

After a Hurricane

After a hurricane, the Emergency Management Team should continue to use the utmost care in ensuring the safety of building occupants and the property. Suggested actions include:

- Continue listening to public broadcast announcements. Wait until an area is declared safe before entering.
- Care for injured persons (See Chapter 19).
- Be extremely careful in moving around the property. Watch for live electrical wires, shattered glass, splintered wood, and debris as well as structural damage.
- Inspect the property, and appoint cleanup crews.
- Call the property's insurance company, restoration contractor, and building inspector, and get them to the site as soon as possible.
- Set up a manageable schedule to repair the property. Be aware of symptoms of stress and fatigue.
- Have available materials for making temporary repairs, such as tools, hardware, plywood, sawhorses, and barricades.
- Do not turn on the electricity unless it has been officially declared safe to do so by the utility company.
- Report broken gas, sewer, or water mains to the respective utilities.
- Open clogged pipes and catch basins.
- Prepare for possible flooding from the storm or damaged water barriers.
- Be alert for potential fire hazards such as leaking gas lines, pools of water near electrical equipment and appliances, spills of combustible materials, etc. (see Chapter 14).
- If occupants are permitted by local authorities to evacuate, advise them of safe and unflooded evacuation routes and roads. Drive only when necessary, as flooding may continue and roads my weaken and collapse.
- Replenish emergency supplies.

Note: More specific information can be found on the Internet at www.noaa.gov/hurricanes
.html.

26

Winter Storms

Property managers who live and work in snowbelt communities know that severe winter storms and the heavy snowfall and extreme cold that accompany them can paralyze a city and immobilize an entire region.

Severe snowstorms or blizzards bring heavy snow, ice, strong winds, and battering freezing rain. They can disrupt communities by impeding road travel for people seeking medical attention, retrieving supplies, and obtaining assistance from emergency services such as fire departments. The powerful winds can knock down trees, utility poles, and power lines. Structures can be severely damaged from wind gusts of 100 mph or more, and heavy snow and ice can cause structural damage, including roof collapse, and power outages. Delivery of vital services can be delayed for days.

Four physical factors characterize severe winter storms—strong winds, extreme cold, ice storms, and heavy snowstorms.

- Storms with strong winds create blizzard conditions with blinding, wind-driven and drifting snow and dangerous windchills. Powerful winds accompanying intense cold fronts and storms can knock down trees, damage roofs, and weaken other building structural elements.

- The extreme cold (near freezing temperatures or below, depending on the average area climate) that accompanies a storm or follows in its aftermath can become life-threatening to humans and animals. Pipes may freeze and burst in buildings that are poorly insulated or unheated, and ice jams may form on rivers and streams and result in flooding.

- Ice storms characterized by freezing rain or hail can cause overwhelming accumulations of ice, which can bring down trees and utility poles and lines, disrupting power and communications for days. Even small accumulations of ice can cause slippery conditions that are hazardous for pedestrians as well as motorists.

- Heavy snowstorms can bring such large accumulations of snow that traffic cannot move and building structures collapse under the weight. The cost of snow removal and restoration, as well as loss of business, can cause significant economic losses for property owners.

The physical effects of severe winter storms on human beings and animals can be fatal. People exposed to cold weather for prolonged periods of time face the risks of frostbite, hypothermia, and other medical problems. Infants and elderly people are especially susceptible to the cold. These weather phenomena can create a challenge for an unprepared property manager.

Areas and Properties at Risk

Properties located in areas that routinely experience heavy snowstorms are at risk of experiencing similar weather patterns in the future. Because weather systems are so variable and unpredictable, even areas that normally experience mild winters can fall prey to severe winter storms. In fact, these areas may be even more vulnerable, as neither the properties nor the municipalities may be prepared to meet the needs of residents and commercial tenants or the community. For example, water pipes may not be as well-insulated as in traditional cold-weather climates, and municipal services may not be able to respond to severe snow emergencies.

From the Mid-Atlantic Coast to New England, the classic storm is called the Nor'easter. These storms originate off the Carolina coast and move north, encouraging wind-driven waves to batter the coastline and creating snow and ice storms in susceptible regions.

The Gulf Coast and Southeast are generally unaccustomed to snowstorms due to the warm, moist Gulf waters and tropical air heading northward from the equator. Many of the local municipalities may not be prepared with proper snow removal equipment if a snowstorm should hit.

Winter storms in the Midwest and Plains areas tend to develop in the lee (eastern) side of the Rockies and move east or northeast to produce heavy snow and blizzard conditions. They are intensified by the colder air coming from the north and the moisture from the Gulf of Mexico. Other storms in these areas draw Arctic air from the north and move across the Plains to the Great Lakes.

The Pacific Coast can experience strong storms that draw on the vast moisture of the Pacific Ocean. Snowfall is particularly intensified on the windward (western) side of the Sierra Mountains and in canyons, where wind speeds can reach 100 mph, damaging roofs, structures, and power lines and closing freeways. Homes and businesses literally become inaccessible.

In Alaska, intense storms and wind-driven waves can cause coastal flooding and drive large chunks of sea ice inland, destroying buildings near the shore. In the mountains, the snow builds glaciers, but heavy accumulations of snow can also cause avalanches or collapse building roofs. High winds across the Arctic coast can combine with loose snow to produce blinding blizzards and windchill temperatures of $-90°F$. Temperatures of $-40°F$ to $-60°F$ and ice fog may last for days.

Weather Advisories and Warnings

The National Weather Service and public broadcast facilities provide warnings and advisories on the progress of severe winter storms and other weather conditions. In order to be prepared for snowstorms, the property manager should be familiar with the following weather terms:
- Snow may be characterized as one of the following.
  —Flurries are short periods of light snow fall with little or no accumulation.
  —Showers are brief periods of snow falling at varying intensities with some accumulation possible.

Winter Weather Advisories

advisory Winter weather conditions are expected to cause significant inconvenience and may be hazardous, especially to motorists.

winter storm watch Conditions are right for severe winter weather such as heavy snow or ice to develop within 36–48 hours.

winter storm warning Life-threatening severe winter weather conditions have begun or will begin within 24 hours.

blizzard warning Severe weather conditions are likely to produce deep drifts, life-threatening wind chills, and blinding snowfall with near-zero visibility. Blizzards consist of large amounts of falling or blowing snow with sustained winds of at least 35 mph.

frost or freeze warning Below-freezing temperatures are expected.

Specific advisories may also address freezing rain, sleet, blowing and/or drifting snow, and expected amounts of snowfall (depth in inches).

- —Squalls, best known in the Great Lakes region, are brief, intense snow showers accompanied by strong, gusty winds and significant accumulation of snow.
- —Blowing snow is wind-driven snow that reduces visibility and causes significant drifting. The snow may be falling and/or loose snow on the ground that is picked up by the wind.
- —Blizzard is a situation of winds in excess of 35 mph with snow and blowing snow reducing visibility to near zero.
- Freezing rain is rain that freezes when it hits the ground or other surfaces and creates a coating of ice on roads, cars, and walkways.
- Sleet is rain that turns to ice pellets before reaching the ground, causing roads to freeze and become slippery.

Winter weather advisories prepare area residents for coming storms (see accompanying box).

Preventive Measures

The emergency procedures manual may include guidelines that can be followed to minimize loss in the event of a severe winter storm. Suggestions include:

- Establish procedures for facility shut down and early release of employees. Also address late opening in the event a storm occurs overnight or over a weekend.
- Every fall, winterize ground-based sprinkler systems (shut off water, blow system dry with compressed air) and HVAC systems (winterize equipment, drain cooling water).
- Drain or install heat tape on all equipment that needs freeze protection.
- Supply emergency heating sources, such as space heaters. Use with caution.
- Protect water pipes that may be vulnerable to freezing (insulation; heat tape).
- Establish procedures to be followed if water pipes freeze (see Chapter 17).

- Store nonperishable foods for occupants.
- Replenish snow and ice control supplies and equipment—salt, chemical pellets, sand, snow shovels, etc.
- Prepare contracts for winter snow removal. Be sure contracts include the time of day, frequency, and weather conditions under which plowing or snow control can occur.
- Keep maintenance personnel on call if a storm threatens.
- Instruct maintenance staff that clearing walks of snow and ice should not be started more than one hour prior to the majority of tenants' arrival at or departure from the building.
- Winterize residential property to conserve energy by doing the following:
  —Insulate walls (and attics if appropriate).
  —Install storm windows, or cover windows with plastic, when necessary.
  —Caulk and weatherstrip doors and windows.
- Make plans to accommodate staff who may have to stay on site at commercial properties (e.g., food, cots, blankets).

During a Severe Winter Storm

Certain steps should be taken during a snowstorm to help minimize the harsh effects of these weather conditions. Suggestions include:

- Advise building occupants, if possible, to wear layered clothing for extra warmth.
- Keep entrances and walkways clear of snow.
- Be careful when shoveling snow. Overexertion can cause heart attacks—a major cause of death in the winter.
- Inspect the amount of snow on rooftops, and remove if necessary. Heavy, wet snow can cause a roof to collapse. Flat roofs are especially vulnerable to freezing, thawing, and refreezing, which can plug roof drains and add weight.
- When using alternative heating, employ safeguards. If no heat is available, close off unused rooms.
- At night, cover windows and stuff towels or other materials under doors to help eliminate drafts.
- If evacuation is not possible, encourage occupants to consume food and drink fluids; food provides the body with energy to produce its own heat, and fluids prevent dehydration.
- Watch for signs of frostbite—a loss of feeling and a white or pale appearance of areas of the extremities, including fingers and toes. If symptoms are noticed, seek medical help immediately.
- Watch for signs of hypothermia—memory loss, uncontrollable shivering, disorientation, incoherence, drowsiness, and exhaustion. Seek medical help if symptoms are observed.
- Be alert for potential fire hazards, especially if alternative heating devices are used.

After a Severe Winter Storm

After a snowstorm, review mechanical and heating systems and any other equipment that may have been exposed to cold or moisture (snow, ice) to determine if there is any weakening or minor damage to repair. The performance of snow removal contractors should be reviewed, and notes should be made of needed adjustments to the contract. Likewise, the performance of maintenance personnel should be reviewed and adjustments made in the procedures followed. Notify your insurance company if any damage has occurred.

When the snow begins to melt, flooding may occur. Make sure all street and building drains are cleared of debris and snow.

Note: More specific information can be found on the FEMA web site at www.fema.gov/hazards/winterstorms/winterweatherf.shtm and in *Winter Storms: The Deceptive Killers,* published jointly by NOAA, FEMA, and the American Red Cross and available for download on the Internet at www.nws.noaa.gov/om/brochures/winterstorm.pdf.

27

Floods

Floods are the most common natural disaster (except for fire). Any property manager who has endured catastrophic flooding on a property can attest that flooding is one of the worst natural disasters that can occur. Flooding causes more property damage in the United States than any other natural disaster, averaging losses of several billion dollars each year. Most natural floods are due to melting snow, the effects of tsunamis and hurricanes, and prolonged and heavy rainfall although floods can also result from overflow of inland tidal waters, failure of a dam or levee, a mudflow, or an unusual and rapid accumulation or runoff of surface waters from any source. (Tsunamis are discussed in Chapter 30, and hurricanes are addressed in Chapter 25.)

Flooding inside buildings can be caused by broken water lines and frozen or bursting pipes. It can also be caused by an unexpected accident. In April 1992, basements of downtown Chicago buildings were flooded when a piling driven into the Chicago River bottom pierced the city's long-abandoned underground freight tunnels.

In the case of natural flooding, management should listen to flood forecasts and warnings to determine the possibility of a flood, its expected severity, and when and where it may begin. Severe conditions may require evacuating buildings. Floods can be slow or fast-rising, but they generally develop over a period of days. Flash floods, however, are like walls of water that develop in minutes. These can be caused by intense storms or failure of a dam.

While a flood can cause extensive property damage, it can also cause other potential disasters, including electrical outages, which could impede rescue operations and result in electrocution of occupants. Drowning is a strong possibility in large regional floods, and—depending on the type of property—food, fuel, and water shortages can also occur. In thunderstorm updrafts, which may accompany floods, dangerous hail the size of baseballs can fall at speeds of 100 mph.

Areas and Properties at Risk

Properties with the highest risk of flooding are those located on a flood plain and in areas with histories of flooding. It is wise for property owners and managers to check with their local FEMA field office to review the potential flood risks of their properties. FEMA periodically updates flood zone maps which are available to the public. Flood hazard maps can be found on the Internet at www.fema.gov/mit/tsd. Also, the

Advanced Hydrologic Prediction Service (AHPS) of the National Weather Service provides improved flood forecasting and offers tools to assist in flood emergency planning at www.nws.noaa.gov/om/water/Ahps.shtml.

There are several types of floods, each having its own risk factors. River floods—flooding along rivers—occur seasonally when winter or spring rains, coupled with melting snows, fill river basins with too much water too quickly. They also occur when floating ice accumulates at a natural or man-made obstruction (an ice jam) and stops the flow of river water, eventually causing an overflow. Torrential rains from decaying hurricanes or tropical storms can also produce river flooding.

Coastal floods occur when winds generated from tropical storms and hurricanes or intense offshore low-pressure systems drive ocean water inland. Escape routes can be cut off and blocked by high water. Coastal flooding can also be produced by tsunamis, which are ocean waves produced by earthquakes or volcanic activity.

Flash floods are the number one thunderstorm killer, resulting in more than 140 fatalities each year. Most fatalities occur at night and when people are trapped in automobiles. Urban flash floods occur where land has been converted from fields or woodlands to paved roads and parking lots and the ground surface loses its ability to absorb rainfall. Urbanization increases runoff by two to six times compared with runoff on natural terrain. During periods of urban flooding, streets can become swift-moving rivers, and basements can become deathtraps as they accumulate water.

Warning Signs and Weather Advisories

Except for flash floods, the average natural flood is preceded by a few potential warning signs. A roaring sound upstream may herald an impending flood. Rapidly rising water in a river or stream and/or water turning muddy is another sign. Continuous heavy rains for several days can lead to flooding in low-lying areas. (Areas that have been flooded in the past often exhibit telltale signs of old waterlines on the sides of buildings.) When skies darken and thunderstorms are forecast, look and listen for increasing winds, flashes of lightning, sounds of thunder, and static on your radio. Severe thunderstorms often lead to flooding and flash flooding.

Local radio and TV stations and NOAA Weather Radio broadcast watches and warnings regarding flooding in specific areas. A flood *watch* means a flood is possible in the areas cited. A flood *warning* means flooding is already occurring or will occur soon in the area and necessary precautions should be taken at once. Authorities may advise evacuation. The same applies for flash flood watches and warnings. Urban and small stream advisories are issued when flooding of small streams, streets, and low-lying areas, such as railroad underpasses and urban storm drains, is occurring. Property managers should refer to their emergency procedures guidelines to determine what actions should be taken in each circumstance.

Preventive Measures

Certain measures can be implemented to prevent losses that can occur from flooding. Here are some suggestions:

- Ask your local emergency management office whether your facility is located in a flood plain. Learn the elevation of your facility in relation to streams, rivers, and dams. Check on the history of flooding in the area.
- Review the community's emergency plan. Learn the community's evacuation routes and where there is high ground in your vicinity.
- Purchase an NOAA Weather Radio with a warning alarm tone and battery backup. Listen for flood watches and warnings.

Flood Insurance

U.S. government-backed flood insurance is available to any business owner, homeowner, or renter whose property is located in a community that participates in the National Flood Insurance Program (NFIP). Participating communities must adopt and enforce local flood plain management ordinances that are designed to reduce the risk of flood losses in the future. In such communities, flood insurance can be purchased from a licensed insurance agent or company—the same one who writes the owner's property policies, for example. Flood insurance is the best means of recovering losses from flood damage. It should be purchased well beforehand because policies do not take effect immediately. The effective date is normally 30 days after purchase.

Following are some items a standard flood insurance policy will cover:

- Structural damage
- HVAC damage
- Cleanup of flood debris
- Damage to floor surfaces (e.g., tile, carpeting)

It is also possible to obtain flood insurance coverage for building contents—furnishings, collectibles, and other personal property.

Note: Information on the National Flood Insurance Program can be found on the Internet at www.fema.gov/nfip or www.floodsmart.gov.

- Contact the National Flood Insurance Program (NFIP) to find out if the community in which the property is located participates in the program.
- Ask your insurance carrier about flood insurance for your property. This is a separate policy; regular property insurance does not cover flooding (see accompanying box).
- Inspect areas in your facility subject to flooding. Identify equipment and records that can be moved to a higher location and make plans to move them if a flood is expected.
- Consider the feasibility of floodproofing your property (see box on page 186).
- Consider the need for backup systems.
  —Alternate power sources (generators, gasoline-powered pumps)
  —Portable pumps to remove flood water
  —Battery-powered emergency lighting
- Consider the feasibility of relocating vital equipment (e.g., fire pump motors) if these items would not be easily moved out of the path of flood water entering the building.
- Consult with a local building contractor or building official as to the best structural materials advised in flood-prone areas. For example, wood has a high water-absorption capacity, and average wallboard acts like a sponge, drawing water up above the flood level.
- Know where asbestos-containing materials (ACM) have been used in the building. Flood-damaged materials that contain asbestos require special handling; services of an asbestos contractor may be needed.
- Use site planning techniques—sloping lawns, raised patios, improved drainage, flood walls, and levees—to protect a property against floods.

Floodproofing Methods

According to FEMA, there are three basic methods for floodproofing a property.

Permanent Floodproofing

- Elevate the facility on walls, columns, or compacted fill. (This is most applicable to new construction.)
- Reinforce walls to resist water pressure and seal them to prevent or reduce seepage.
- Install check valves to keep flood water from entering the building by backing up through sewer lines.
- Build watertight walls around equipment or work areas within the facility that are particularly susceptible to flood damage.
- Construct floodwalls or levees outside the building to help keep water away.

Contingent Floodproofing

- Install water-tight barriers called flood shields to prevent flood water from entering through windows, doors, ventilation shafts, or other openings.
- Install permanent watertight doors.
- Construct movable flood walls.
- Install permanent pumps to remove flood waters.

Emergency Floodproofing

- Build walls with sandbags.
- Construct a double row of walls with boards and posts to create a "crib" and fill the crib with soil.
- Construct a single wall by stacking small beams or planks.

Permanent floodproofing measures are undertaken before a flood occurs and require no human intervention when flood waters rise. Contingent floodproofing measures are also taken prior to a flood, but some additional action is required when flooding occurs. Emergency floodproofing measures, while generally less expensive than the other types, require substantial advance warning of a flood and do not satisfy minimum requirements for floodproofing as set forth by the National Flood Insurance Program (NFIP).

Source: *Emergency Management Guide for Business and Industry* published by the Federal Emergency Management Agency (FEMA 141/ October 1993) and available for download from the Internet at www.fema.gov/pdf/library/bizindst.pdf.

- Keep a supply of sandbags, plastic sheeting, lumber, and plywood for waterproofing at strategic locations and entrances.
- Keep auxiliary pumps on hand.
- Move valuable items to higher ground and advise building occupants to do likewise.
- Disconnect electrical appliances before flooding begins. Do *not* do this while standing in water.
- Identify a safe and elevated location for evacuees to assemble.

- Address dangerous and acceptable conditions for driving from the building. If a car stalls during evacuation, it should be abandoned immediately, and occupants should move to higher ground.
- Participate in community flood-control projects.

The National Institute of Building Sciences (NIBS) at the direction of FEMA has developed a standardized methodology, called HAZUS, for assessing losses from flood damage. Information about HAZUS is available on the Internet at http://nibs.org/hazusweb/methodology/flood.php. HAZUS software is available at no charge from FEMA.

During a Flood

The emergency procedures manual should outline what management should do during a flood or immediately after a flood warning is issued. Possible actions include:

- Give priority to the protection of power plant and fire pumps, keeping them in service if at all possible. In the event flood waters overwhelm defenses and enter the building, vital fire pump motors or engines should be protected. If they can be moved, they should be relocated. The same should be done for important motors, controls, and emergency power generation equipment.
- If possible, shut down the electricity in the building and distribute emergency flashlights.
- Open basement or low-level windows to equalize water pressure on the building's foundation and walls.
- Use no open flames (there may be gas escaping from ruptured mains).
- Watch for and avoid live electrical wires.
- If water enters the building and evacuation becomes impossible, move to an upper floor and wait for rescuers.
- While evacuating, avoid attempting to drive through floods or rising water; nearly half of all flash flood fatalities are auto-related!

It is especially important to develop a specific flood evacuation plan for low-rise residential and commercial buildings because these types of structures are particularly vulnerable to collapse.

After a Flood

It is important to check the safety of a building before anyone re-enters it after a flood. If there is standing water next to the outside walls of a property, do not go in. The building may not be safe or structurally sound. Walk around the building before entering it and check for loose power lines and gas leaks; a distinctive putrid odor will signal the latter. The property manager should either call or appoint someone to call the appropriate utility company if either of these conditions is observed.

The emergency procedures manual should specify what actions to take after flood water recedes. Suggestions include:

- Begin to assess the property damage and potential loss. Contact the property's insurance company or agent to file a claim under the flood insurance policy.
- Appoint and supervise cleanup crews.
- If the electricity is still on, it should be turned off immediately. If someone has to step into water to turn it off, call an electrician to do the job.

- Breaker boxes should be turned off using a dry stick while standing on a dry surface.
- Watch for and avoid live electrical wires; do not turn on any electrical appliances until an electrician says it is okay to do so.
- Pump out water gradually to minimize further structural damage (e.g., one-third of the water each day for three days).
- Drain basements carefully. Draining too quickly could allow the pressure outside the basement to collapse the walls.
- Get fresh air moving throughout the building to reduce moisture and dissipate leaking gas.
- Properly dehumidify the building and other areas to avoid unhealthy conditions. Use dehumidifiers in conjunction with turbo fans to create laminar air movement and speed up evaporation.
- Affected areas will need to be treated with an antimicrobial solution to kill bacteria and prevent the growth of mold and mildew. Growth of bacteria, mold, and mildew in ductwork is especially dangerous. Water damage or mold/mildew growth may necessitate complete removal of some items. (If a building is flooded for 24 hours or more, it may be appropriate to engage a qualified professional to identify and eliminate potential mold and mildew growth.)
- Cover holes in the roof, walls, or windows with boards, tarpaulins, or plastic sheets.
- Temporarily repair sagging floors or roof sections by suing 4×4s as braces in weak areas.
- Check for broken or leaking water pipes. If any are found, turn off the water supply.
- Be prepared for looting; secure the property to guard against trespassers.

The building should be inspected at the earliest opportunity to assess its condition. The exterior should be inspected before anyone is allowed to enter the building. The interior should be inspected before cleanup is started or power is restored.

- Check the foundation for cracks and examine overhangs for missing structural supports. If obvious damage is observed, the property manager could ask the city building inspector or fire chief if the building is safe to enter.

- Inside, check ceilings for signs of sagging. If a ceiling is holding water, the wet plaster or wallboard will be very heavy and could be dangerous if it falls. Carefully poke or drill a hole in the ceiling at the edge of the sagging area and away from electrical fixtures so any water trapped there can begin to drain. (Walls made of plasterboard or other water-absorbent materials should also be checked for signs of sagging and treated appropriately.)

- Inspect building mechanical systems prior to restoring power to components.

- Determine whether flood damage requires full removal or if cleaning and/or other treatment will suffice. For example, once drywall has been saturated, it generally needs to be replaced.

Note: Additional information can be found on the Internet at www.noaa.gov/floods.html and in *Floods: The Awesome Power* published jointly by NOAA, FEMA, and the American Red Cross and available for download at www.nws.noaa.gov/om/brochures/Floodsbrochure_9_04_low.pdf.

28

Drought

Drought results when there is a lack of sufficient precipitation to sustain normal function of a geographical area. It can be devastating to farmlands around the world and life-threatening to residents of third-world countries that rely solely on their crops and water supply for sustenance. Although droughts do not directly threaten the lives of most Americans, they can make properties more susceptible to fires and endanger the lives of building occupants.

Droughts not only sap the water out of vegetation to make it dry and brittle, but also deplete valuable life-saving water reservoirs that aid communities in fighting fires. This leaves properties more susceptible to fires, which can arise from intense solar heat and prime dry conditions, arson, or disasters of natural or human origin (see the discussion of wild fires in Chapter 29).

Where most other types of disasters occur suddenly, often without warning, droughts develop slowly and insidiously over time. Communities susceptible to drought conditions can plan ahead by creating water reservoirs and monitoring water usage.

Areas and Properties at Risk

Though many natural disasters occur only in limited parts of the United States, droughts can occur nationwide. Areas most susceptible to droughts may be geographically situated away from abundant natural mountain runoffs and where precipitation is rare. However, freak weather conditions can also lead to droughts in areas where precipitation occurs frequently.

In an area where there is drought, every property type will feel the impact. Residential and commercial buildings alike can be vulnerable to its effects. (For information on the drought status of specific areas, the National Weather Service Climate Prediction Center publishes a U.S. Drought Assessment on the Internet at www.cpc .ncep.noaa.gov/products/expert_assessment/drought_assessment.html.)

Preventive Measures

Droughts increase the risk of fire due to the dry, flammable condition of brush, crops, and grass. Moreover, if there is a fire, fighting it may be especially difficult due to low water pressure. For these reasons, all of the steps that are taken to prevent human and property loss from fires should be adhered to when there is a drought in the area. (See the discussions of preventive measures for fires and wild fires in Chapters 14 and 29, respectively.)

During a Drought

The emergency procedures manual may include a section outlining what should be done during a drought. Recommended precautions include:

- Review ongoing water conservation measures.
  —Periodically check for and repair water leaks (faucets, toilets).
  —Consider the advisability of installing water flow control devices (e.g., flow-restricting aerators in faucets, low-flow shower heads at residential properties).
  —Consider the advisability of inserting water displacement devices or flow regulators in toilets or possibly replacing them with newer toilets that use less water to flush.
  —Encourage residents to wash only full loads of laundry or dishes using the shortest cycle possible.
- Educate residents on water conservation measures.
- Encourage occupants (residents, commercial tenants' employees) to report plumbing leaks.
- Check with the local water department for recommendations on water-saving measures and any incentives they may offer.
- Obey all municipal requests regarding the use and rationing of water.
- Be aware of increased fire hazards:
  —Keep flammable chemicals in cool, dark places.
  —Remove flammable items and dead plants that, if ignited, could endanger property.
  —Keep fire extinguishers and a property's limited water supply easily accessible to prevent fire from spreading once it is detected.
  —Familiarize staff and building occupants with precautionary fire safety measures and instruct them to report any fire hazard conditions on the property.

In some areas, it may still be permissible to burn leaves and/or trash on one's property. Especially during a drought, people should avoid using fire out of doors close to areas of natural vegetation.

Note: More information on water conservation can be found on the National Weather Service Hydrologic Information Center web page on drought at www.nws.noaa.gov/oh/hic/current/drought/, which includes links to national, regional, and state/local resources. The American Red Cross has also published a fact sheet on water conservation on the Internet at www.redcross.org/services/disaster/keepsafe/drought.html.

After a Drought

As with the gradual onset of a drought, the aftermath of a drought is not marked by a sudden change. The emergency procedures manual should outline a gradual return to normal operations.

- Continue to use water conservation measures. Stay in compliance with rationing orders until they are lifted by local authorities.

- Consider implementing permanent measures for reducing the property's water consumption such as installing low-pressure showerheads and low-flow toilets and recycling water.

- Consider changing the property's landscaping to reduce water requirements. Properties in the Southwest, for example, might consider desert plants rather than grass. In any geographic area, vegetation that is native to the area is likely to be less sensitive to changes in water availability.

Note: Additional resources are available on the Internet. The National Oceanic and Atmospheric Administration maintains a drought information center at www.drought.noaa.gov/. The National Drought Mitigation Center web site at www.drought.unl.edu/error_files/ndmc_redirect.htm contains information on planning for and mitigating drought and understanding its impact.

29

Wild Fires

In certain parts of the United States, forest and brush fires—i.e., wild fires—pose a particular threat to properties. Susceptible regions have been known to yield thousands of acres to raging fires that have started in open prairies, fields, or forests, or on properties on which the flames spread by contact with dry grass or vegetation. This devastation has occurred within days. According to the National Interagency Fire Center (NIFC), one of the worst years for wild fires in the United States was 2000 when there were 122,827 fires involving 8,422,237 acres. In 2003, the most recent year for which statistics were available, there were 85,943 wild fires involving 4,918,088 acres.

While they often begin unnoticed, wild fires spread quickly, igniting brush, trees, and buildings in their path. Drought conditions contribute to wild fires, but most are started by people who are careless with fire.

Areas and Properties at Risk

Wild fires occur in chaparral regions, areas characterized by hot dry summers and cool moist winters and dominated by dense growth of mostly small-leaved evergreen shrubs, predominantly in California and the West. Although brush, canyon, and forest fires can occur at any time, the principal fire season is from May through October. Obviously, any properties that are in or near wooded areas could be subject to damage by forest fires.

Preventive Measures

A number of measures can be implemented to minimize human and property loss attributable to wild fires:

- Obtain local building codes and weed abatement ordinances that apply to structures built near wooded areas and take steps to comply with them as appropriate.
- Use landscaping as a fire prevention measure.
  —For at least 30 feet—or to the property line, whichever is nearer—trim any brush that could catch fire to a maximum height of 2 inches.

—For another 70 feet—or to the property line, whichever is nearer—trim all brush to a maximum height of 18 inches.
—Prune trees away from roofs. Clip trees and shrubbery that overhang adjoining properties.
—Prune branches to a height of 8–10 feet and keep trees adjacent to buildings free of dead wood.
—Plant fire-resistant ground cover (e.g., perennial grasses, ivies, ice plants).
—Do not remove low-growing ground cover.
- Properly dispose of all waste material, including dead vegetation, daily trash, accumulated waste, trimmed and clipped brush, and roof debris.
- Practice other fire-prevention tactics:
—Screen chimney openings, using ½-inch-thick mesh, to prevent sparks from escaping.
—Keep piles of fire wood away from combustible items.
—Keep long garden hoses hooked up and ready to use around the property to squelch fires if necessary.
—Keep lawn chairs, wicker and canvas furniture, and patio umbrellas away from buildings on the property.
—Coordinate with adjoining properties to take preventive measures.
- Use caution when clearing open spaces, especially if electrical or gasoline-powered equipment is being used. Sparks generated when equipment runs into rocks or other foreign items can cause a fire. Keep hoses connected and ready to extinguish any fire that starts. Having a cell phone available will expedite calling the fire department.

Note: Federal grants may be available to property owners through National Park Service programs to help pay the costs of major investments in fire prevention. The Wildland Urban Interface Initiative (WUII) to protect areas where homes meet wildlands is an example. Information on the National Wildland/Urban Interface Initiative can be found on the Internet at www.firewise.org/pubs/operationWater/nwu_initiative.html. There is a Western States Wildland-Urban Interface Grant Program through the National Park Service (www.nps.gov).

During and After a Wild Fire

If a building catches fire as a result of a wild fire, the procedures that should be followed during and afterward are the same as for other types of fires. The plan and procedures presented in Chapter 14 are equally applicable here.

Also, people should proceed with caution when returning to an area burned by a wild fire. Lingering hot spots can burst into flame without warning. It is important to check for sparks and extinguish them.

Property managers should also be aware of potentially devastating consequences of wild fires, including landslides and debris flow (mudslides). In areas where vegetation is destroyed, surface soil has nothing to hold it in place. Heavy rains can wash the surface soil away, taking structures with it (see Chapter 32).

Note: More information on wild fires can be found on the National Interagency Fire Center (NIFC) web site at www.nifc.gov.

30

Earthquakes

Earthquakes occur when the tectonic plates that form the earth's crust grind and scrape against each other along a fault line. Earthquakes strike suddenly, violently, and without warning. The tumultuous effects of major earthquakes can be catastrophic—causing buildings and bridges to collapse, downing of telephone and power lines, fires, explosions, and landslides. Earthquakes can also cause tsunamis, which are huge ocean waves that travel long distances over the water until they crash into coastlines.

An earthquake can be identified by the rolling, rumbling sound that often heralds it as well as the severe shaking motion. A building's structure and items in and around it may shake, shatter, rattle, fall, or break. Shaking may begin in different ways—gently, growing violent in one or two seconds, or with a violent jolt like a sonic boom.

Injury can result from flying glass, which is of special concern in high-rise structures; overturned bookcases, wall units, and other heavy furniture; and fallen power lines, bricks, and concrete. Severe damage also can be caused by fires, which can break out due to broken gas lines and electrical short circuits.

Electricity and telephone service may be disrupted. Gas, water, and sewer pipelines may be broken. Fire protection systems are often triggered, and sprinklers go on. Strong drafts created by the breakage of exterior windows may make the situation even worse. Normal police, fire, medical, and other services may not be accessible, possibly for extended periods of time. Looting may be a possibility to contend with as well.

Aftershocks may occur over a period of several days, creating more damage. Tsunamis may occur in coastal areas as a result of the earth's movement (see box on page 196). Still another concern after earthquakes is the threat of landslides resulting from a new imbalance in ground structure, which can cause both structural and nonstructural damage.

Areas and Properties at Risk

Earthquakes occur most frequently west of the Rocky Mountains, although other parts of the United States are also susceptible. Thirty-nine states are potential targets of earthquakes. The area of greatest earthquake risk east of the Rockies is the New Madrid seismic zone, which extends more than 120 miles southward from Cairo, Illi-

Tsunamis

Tsunamis are ocean waves that are produced by earthquakes or underwater landslides. They can travel upstream in coastal estuaries and rivers, causing damage inland as well as on the coast. Often referred to incorrectly as a tidal wave, a tsunami is a series of waves traveling at speeds averaging 450–600 mph in open ocean. While wave heights have exceeded 100 feet, waves 10–20 feet high can be very destructive. Tsunamis are a Pacific Ocean phenomenon affecting California, Oregon, Washington, British Columbia in Canada, and Alaska as well as the Hawaiian Islands and U.S. territories in the Pacific Basin. They also affect countries along the west coast of Central and South America and across the ocean, including Japan, the Philippine Islands, and Indonesia. While U.S. coastlines are vulnerable, tsunamis are infrequent events and damaging tsunamis are very rare.

People living along the seacoast should consider an earthquake or sizable ground rumbling as a warning signal. A noticeable rapid rise or fall in coastal waters is another sign of an approaching tsunami. The following bulletins may be issued regarding tsunamis:

- An *advisory* indicates that an earthquake has occurred in the Pacific basin that might generate a tsunami. Subsequent hourly bulletins are issued regarding the situation.
- A *watch* is issued when a tsunami was or may have been generated, but it will take at least two hours for it to arrive onshore; preparation to evacuate may be advised.
- A *warning* indicates a tsunami that could cause damage was or may have been generated; people in the affected area will be advised to evacuate.

A tidal wave is a sea wave that sometimes follows an earthquake, but it may also be a great rise of water along an ocean shore due to exceptionally strong winds. A similar phenomenon called a seiche may occur inland on landlocked lakes (e.g., the Great Lakes). A seiche is an oscillation of the lake surface that may be caused by local variations in air pressure, sometimes aided by winds and tidal currents. The oscillation can vary in frequency from a few minutes to several hours and may continue for some time after the atmospheric pressure differences no longer exist.

Note: More information can be found on the National Oceanic and Atmospheric Administration web page for tsunamis at www.noaa.gov/tsunamis.html and in *Tsunamis: The Great Waves* published jointly by NOAA, the International Tsunami Information Center, Laboratoire de Geophysique in France, and the UNESCO/ Intergovernmental Oceanographic Commission and available for download at www.prh.noaa.gov/itic/library/pubs/great_waves/great_waves_en_2002.pdf).

nois, where the Mississippi and Ohio Rivers converge, into Arkansas and parts of Kentucky and Tennessee.

The property manager should determine if his or her state has a history of earthquakes, the likelihood of another quake occurring in the area, and the amount of damage typically caused by quakes in the vicinity. If the property manager determines that earthquakes are a potential threat to the property, then an earthquake emergency plan is needed.

It is not surprising that the closer a property is to the center of an earthquake, the greater the likelihood of severe damage. Structures built on solid ground run a smaller risk of serious damage than those built on alluvial or fill soils. Structures most likely to suffer extensive structural damage include the following:

- Properties with asymmetrical towers
- L-shaped structures
- Masonry, brick, concrete block, adobe, and stone buildings with no reinforcing steel
- Reinforced concrete frame buildings with nonductile or brittle joints (i.e., structures supported by column beam frames and no load-bearing walls)
- One- and two-story commercial and industrial buildings that have concrete or masonry walls and wood roofs
- Long-span buildings in which only outside walls support the roof (e.g., shopping centers, warehouses, gymnasiums)
- Mobile/manufactured homes
- House-over-garage structures
- Buildings that have not been constructed according to earthquake building codes
- Buildings anchored to their foundations improperly or not at all

Buildings located adjacent to hills or situated on cliffsides should be constructed with extra structural reinforcement to withstand forceful landslides that can uproot structural foundations and thrust dislocated soil and debris into building interiors.

Preventive Measures

There are two categories of damage a property may sustain during an earthquake, structural and nonstructural. In the structural category is damage to foundations; outside and inside load-bearing walls; floor and roof sheathing, slabs, and decking; beams, girders, and joists; and posts, pillars, and columns.

Nonstructural damage is much more broadly defined. It can consist of damage to ceilings and light fixtures, windows, office equipment and computers, air conditioners, files, electrical and utility equipment, merchandise and inventory, furnishings, and personal property. Damage caused by moving or falling objects, whether during the earthquake or resulting from it, is also considered nonstructural.

Although structural damage is difficult to prevent, it may be possible to reduce future damage by incorporating earthquake-specific upgrades during major renovation projects. Building codes evolve, and newer codes are more likely to address earthquake damage mitigation. It is a good idea to know when the building you manage was built and what new building codes might apply.

Following are some simple steps that can be taken to avoid *nonstructural* damage.

- Secure the following items by whatever means possible:
  —Exterior ornamentation
  —HVAC equipment
  —Piping
  —Suspended ceilings
  —Light fixtures, especially suspension type
  —Wall hangings and hanging plants
  —Computers and other office equipment
  —Heavy furniture

        —Shelves
        —File cabinets (install locks) and other cabinets and cupboards (install
           sturdy latches on doors)
        —Water heaters
        —Gas and electrical appliances
        —Top-heavy items

- Inspect for and repair:
  —Defective electrical wiring
  —Leaky or inflexible gas connections
  —Deep cracks in ceilings and foundations
- Store heavy items on lower shelves.
- Locate heavy wall hangings, shelving units, and the like where they will do the least damage to persons and property if they fall.
- Bolt foundations to buildings and mobile/manufactured homes, when necessary.
- Ensure that sewer lines and other underground utility connections are structurally secure.

It may be desirable to measure and record earth movement on a property to help in planning preventive measures. This is usually done in consultation with a geotechnical engineer or other appropriate professional.

Note: More specific information on earthquake preparedness can be found on the FEMA web site at www.fema.gov/hazards/earthquakes/. The California Governor's Office of Emergency Services also has a number of publications on earthquake preparedness available for download at www.oes.ca.gov. Select Publications Inc. (www.select-publications.com) offers two publications that may be helpful: *Homeowners' Guide to Earthquake Safety and Environmental Hazards* and *The Commercial Property Owner's Guide to Earthquake Safety.* Property managers may wish to list these resources in an occupant handbook.

During an Earthquake

A practiced response to an earthquake is essential. For this reason, the emergency plan should specify what each person should do during the earthquake to avoid personal injury. This applies to occupants as well as members of the management staff. The appropriate response depends on where the person is when the earthquake occurs.

If you are indoors:
- Turn off the gas and utilities within immediate reach.
- Locate a sturdy table or desk to protect you. If it is near a window or exterior wall, move it against an interior wall. Crouch under the table or desk, tucking your head to your knees and protecting your head with your arms.
- If the furniture moves, move with it.
- Watch for and avoid falling objects—plaster, light fixtures, heavy items on shelves or in cupboards or closets, mirrors, wall hangings, glass from windows, swinging doors.

If you are in a hallway:
- Kneel against the nearest interior wall.
- Tuck your head to your knees.
- Cover your head with your arms.

If you are in an elevator
- Remain clam.
- Be prepared for the elevator's power to shut down and the lights to go off

and for the possibility that the elevator may become jammed in the shaft; even if the latter does occur, the shaft should be safe from falling objects.
- Wait for an emergency rescue team when the quake is over. Be patient; it may take some time for help to arrive.

If you are outdoors:
- Quickly get as far away as possible from buildings.
- If you cannot move to an open area, position yourself in a building doorway.
- Watch for and avoid falling power lines, chimneys, building and roof ornaments, walls, glass, television antennas, and other airborne objects.

After an Earthquake

The earthquake itself probably will last only a few seconds, although the time span may seem like minutes or even hours. Likewise, recovery time usually is brief, but it can be chaotic and difficult. The property manager may have to cope with limited fire, police, and medical help. Power may be out, and water and sewer facilities may be unavailable for up to 72 hours or even longer.

To get through this post-earthquake period as smoothly as possible, the emergency plan should outline actions that the Emergency Management Team, as well as building occupants, can take. Here are some suggestions:
- Do not rush to the exits when the shaking stops. Crowds pushing down stairs or surging through doorways can be as dangerous as the earthquake itself. Moreover, aftershocks may follow immediately.
- Tend to the injured. Do not move seriously injured persons unless it is a matter of life and death.
- Listen to the radio for emergency information. Do not use the phones to obtain this information.
- Put on protective clothing.
- Use flashlights only (no matches or candles because of possible gas leaks).
- Avoid fallen and falling glass and equipment.
- Do not flick light switches either on or off. This may ignite leaking gas.
- Turn off utilities at main switches, if appropriate.
- Turn off appliances, such as computers, copiers, and washing machines and dryers, that were operating when the earthquake occurred.
- Check immediately for evidence of structural damage that could worsen during aftershocks. Such evidence could be in the form of:
  —Cracks in chimneys, which have a propensity to fall during aftershocks.
  —Parking structure instability.
  —Damage to building skin.
- Check immediately for nonstructural damage that could cause secondary problems. The following warrant special attention:
  —Broken or leaking gas lines.
  —Shorts in electrical equipment or wiring.
  —Leaks in diesel fuel lines.
  —Damaged and nonfunctioning elevators (see box on page 200).
- Make arrangements for the cleanup of dangerous or flammable substances spilled during the quake (e.g., medicines, cleaning solutions, fuels, chemicals).
- Extinguish secondary fires caused by broken natural gas lines and electrical short circuits; use only fire extinguishers designed for these types of fires.
- Secure the building against looting.

Earthquake Damage to Elevators

- Elevator cars may stop between floors.
- Hoistway doors may bind so they cannot be opened.
- Hoistway door locks may break, allowing doors to sag and leaving the hoistway open.
- Counterweight rails and guide shoes may be loosened.
- The suspension system may fail due to loosened beams and/or deflector sheaves or broken ropes.
- Machine room equipment may be damaged.

- Do not turn on utilities until given the go-ahead by the appropriate utility companies. Then, restore electrical power one floor at a time, one piece of equipment at a time, to avoid a power surge.
- Check sewer main lines before attempting to use toilet facilities. If sewers are inoperable, use plastic bags to line wastepaper baskets for temporary toilet facilities; close bags after each use and dispose after several uses.
- Open cabinet, cupboard, and storage area doors slowly and cautiously to avoid being injured by items that tumble out.
- Make people at the property as comfortable as possible for as long as necessary.
  - —Provide playing cards, books, and magazines from the property's emergency provisions.
  - —Provide food and drink, which goes a long way toward calming nerves and avoiding panic.
  - —Pay particular attention to anyone who may be injured and to elderly persons, those with disabilities, and children.
- Prepare for landslides and tsunamis, if applicable (see Chapter 32 for more information on landslide hazards).

It may be necessary or appropriate to have a structural engineer inspect the building. If the property owner is responsible for water, sewer, and other underground utilities between the building and the connections to the main lines—often the case even though the utility may have performed the installation—it may be necessary to have appropriate professionals check out the integrity of such utility lines and connections. A plumber can detect breaks in sewer lines using a video camera.

The National Institute of Building Sciences (NIBS) at the direction of FEMA has developed a standardized methodology, called HAZUS, for assessing losses from earthquakes and other natural hazards. HAZUS uses geographic information system (GIS) software to calculate, map, and display earthquake hazards and damage. Information about HAZUS is available on the Internet at http://nibs.org/hazusweb/ methodology/earthquake.php. HAZUS software is available at no charge from FEMA.

Note: Additional information can be found at the U.S. Geological Survey National Earthquake Information Center web page at http://neic.usgs.gov and in *Earthquakes* by Kaye M. Shedlock and Louis C. Pakiser published by the USGS on the Internet at http://pubs.usgs.gov/ gip/earthq1/.

31

Volcanic Eruptions

Volcanic eruptions can create rivers of molten rock or spew tons of fine ash into the air. Mauna Loa in Hawaii is an example of the former, Mount St. Helens in Washington state the latter. Volcanoes can hurl hot rocks for distances of 20 miles or more, and airborne ash can travel hundreds of miles. Dangerous floods and mudflows can occur in valleys leading away from volcanoes. Molten rock and mudflows can block roadways, uproot trees, and destroy buildings and bridges.

Areas and Properties at Risk

Volcanic eruptions are most likely to occur in the Pacific Rim, including the states of Alaska, Washington, Oregon, California, and Hawaii. The greatest likelihood of damage to populated areas is around the active volcanoes in Alaska and Hawaii although active volcanoes in the Cascade Mountain Range in California, Oregon, and Washington have also created problems. While the danger area around a volcano covers approximately a 20-mile radius, there may be some danger 100 miles or more from a volcano, which means Montana and Wyoming are also at risk.

Emergency Planning

People who live near a known volcano, whether it is active or dormant, should be ready to evacuate at a moment's notice. Emergency preparations for volcanic eruptions should anticipate other hazards that can accompany them, including earthquakes, tsunamis, flash floods, landslides and mudflows, airborne ash, and acid rain.

Managers of properties in areas near volcanoes should find out how the local community warns residents about volcanic eruptions. Emergency plans should include procedures to be implemented before, during, and after an eruption. It may be appropriate to inquire about the likelihood of ashfall—e.g., past incidents in the general area—to determine what emergency procedures may be needed. The various hazards that can accompany volcanic eruptions should also be addressed, especially if they are not among the commonly expected emergencies for the locale. Specific preparations might include:

- Compile information to facilitate evacuation of the building and departure from the area. Include area evacuation routes in occupant emergency procedures.
- Ensure that everyone on the property knows and understands how warnings of a volcanic eruption will be announced and what to do to evacuate the building and the area.
- Stockpile disposable dust masks and goggles for property personnel (also for occupants if possible and practical to do so). Encourage occupants to have these available for themselves.
- Purchase or prepare appropriate covers to protect sensitive equipment. For some items, covers of plastic sheeting may be adequate. Equipment with slots or vents may need closely fitted covers to keep out volcanic ash.

During a Volcanic Eruption

During a volcanic eruption, people should avoid areas downwind of the volcano. If there is time to take precautions, close building windows and doors; turn off machinery and equipment and protect it from dust. This is especially important for rooftop installations (e.g., HVAC equipment). People who are out of doors should seek shelter. If caught in a rockfall, they should roll into a ball to protect their heads. Avoid low-lying areas where poisonous gases can collect. If caught near a stream, be aware of mudflows. Mudflows occur when rain falls through clouds containing volcanic ash or when rivers are dammed during an eruption. If you hear a mudflow approaching, move upslope. Mudflows are most dangerous in areas close to stream channels.

After a Volcanic Eruption

After a volcanic eruption, listen to a battery-powered radio or television for updates on the emergency, including how widespread ashfall has become. Stay away from areas of volcanic ashfall. Wear protective goggles and a dust mask, and keep skin covered to avoid burns or irritation. People with respiratory ailments are especially vulnerable to injury from breathing volcanic ash. Because volcanic ash is very heavy and can cause buildings to collapse, it should be cleared off of roofs as soon as possible.

Note: More specific information can be found on the Internet at www.noaa.gov/volcanoes and http://volcanoes.usgs.gov/. The USGS site includes information on specific volcanoes in the United States. The FEMA web site includes background information and a link to a fact sheet on volcanoes at www.fema.gov/hazards/volcanoes/volcano.shtm. States with active volcanoes include emergency information on their web sites (e.g., the State of Washington web site at http://access.wa.gov/emergency/volcano.aspx).

32

Landslides

Landslides are a global phenomenon. In the United States alone, they are estimated to cause $2 billion in damage and 25–50 deaths each year. Typically associated with periods of heavy rainfall or rapid snow melt, they tend to worsen the effects of flooding that accompanies such events. While landslides often move very rapidly, causing deaths and destroying property suddenly and unexpectedly, they can also move very slowly and cause damage gradually. The force behind landslide movement is gravity. A number of factors allow gravity to overcome resistance to landslide movement, including steepening of slopes by erosion, alternate freezing or thawing, and saturation by water as well as earthquake shaking and volcanic eruptions.

Areas and Properties at Risk

Landslides are common to almost every state in the United States. They are more likely to occur in areas where vegetation has been destroyed by wild fires or development, on steep slopes or slopes that have been modified for construction of roads and buildings, in channels along a river or stream and where surface runoff is directed, and areas where landslides have occurred previously. Heavy rains after an extended period of drought can also precipitate landslides. Even if a property is not in the path of a landslide, it can be impacted by landslide damage to electrical, gas, water, and sewer lines and disruption of road and rail transportation.

Preventive Measures

Because they are so widespread, it is important to learn about the risk of landslides in your area and your property's vulnerabilities.

- Contact local, state, and/or federal authorities to find out if landslides have occurred in your area previously.
- Find out about local emergency and evacuation plans.
- Develop an evacuation plan for the property. This might include alternate driving routes to be recommended to staff and occupants in the event nearby roads are affected by a landslide. Plan for the possibility that people may not be able to leave the building.

Mudslides

Landslides result from disturbances in the natural stability of a slope. They occur when masses of rock, earth, or debris move down a slope. Mudslides or debris flows are a common type of fast-moving landslide. They are rivers of rock, earth, and other debris that develop when the ground becomes saturated. Mudslides often occur without warning in areas where they have never been seen before. They can travel at avalanche speeds, growing in size as they pick up boulders, trees, cars, and other materials in their path. Mudslides are covered under the National Flood Insurance Program (see Chapter 27); however, landslides are not.

Mudslides usually begin on steep slopes and can be activated by natural disasters. Those that accompany volcanic eruptions are among the most destructive. The debris flow that resulted from the eruption of Mount St. Helens in Washington state in 1980 is a spectacular example. Wildfires followed by heavy rains can also lead to mudslides.

Note: More information can be found on the California Geological Survey web site at www.consrv.ca.gov/CGS/information/publications/cgs_notes/note_33/index.htm.

- If your property is in an area prone to landslides, consider having a consultant—civil engineer, structural engineer, geotechnical engineer—evaluate the property and recommend corrective measures. (Local authorities may be able to advise you of the best type of professional to contact.)

- Consult your insurance agent about specific coverages—debris flow may be covered under the National Flood Insurance Program (see box).

- Avoid gas and water leaks by replacing rigid pipe fittings with flexible ones.

- Observe storm-water drainage patterns on slopes in your area, especially areas where runoff water converges. Look for signs of soil movement, progressive tilting of trees, and other small changes that may signal potential for a landslide.

- Consider using Visqueen or other heavy plastic sheeting to prevent a slide from occurring on a slope.

During Intense Storms

Emergency information regarding intense rainfall will be broadcast on radio, television, and NOAA Weather Radio. The following are some indicators that a landslide may be imminent.

- A sudden *increase* in water level in a stream or creek may indicate a debris flow upstream. A trickle of flowing mud may precede a larger flow.

- A sudden *reduction* in water level may indicate a debris jam upstream that could eventually cause a more forceful flow when the dam breaks.

- Tilting trees, telephone poles, walls, or fences may indicate shifting of topsoil.

- Unusual sounds, trees cracking, boulders knocking together, general rumbling noises may indicate a landslide or mudflow is approaching.

- If a landslide is imminent, getting out of its path is the best protection. People in buildings may be advised to move above the first floor.

During a Landslide

The best place to be during a landslide or if a landslide is imminent is the inside of a building. Steps that can be taken if a landslide occurs include the following.

If inside a building:
- Stay inside.
- Take cover under a desk, table, or other piece of sturdy furniture.

If outdoors:
- Try to get out of the path of the landslide or mudflow. Run to the nearest high ground in a direction away from the flow path.
- If rocks and other debris are approaching, run for the nearest shelter such as a group of trees or a building.
- If escape is not possible, curl into a tight ball and protect your head.

After a Landslide

Even though a landslide has stopped, there may be danger of additional slides or flooding. The site of the landslide should be avoided until the area is declared safe. Actions that may be taken at a managed property include the following:

- If possible to do so without entering the slide area, check for people who are injured or trapped in debris near the area of the landslide. Direct rescuers to assist them.
- Watch for signs of flooding.
- Report broken utility lines to appropriate authorities.
- Check the building foundation and surrounding land for damage.
- Consult a geotechnical expert for advice on further reducing landslide risks.
- Replant damaged ground to prevent further erosion.
- Remember that flooding may occur after a landslide or mudflow, especially if heavy rain precipitated it.

Cleanup of building interiors—removal of water, mud, and debris—may require specialized equipment. A restoration consultant may be able to suggest appropriate vendors who provide this service.

Note: More specific information on landslides can be found on the USGS web site at http://landslides.usgs.gov/html_files/nlicsun.html and http://walrus.wr.usgs.gov/elnino/landslide-guidelines.html. Information on landslide emergency preparedness can be found on the American Red Cross and FEMA web sites at www.redcross.org/services/disaster/keepsafe/landslide.html and www.fema.gov/hazards/landslides/landsli.shtm, respectively.

33

Nuclear Accident

Designed to provide an efficient means of generating electricity, nuclear power plants have been operating in the United States for decades. As of 2003, there are 104 commercial nuclear power reactors licensed to operate at 65 locations in 31 states.

There are two basic types of reactors used in nuclear power production:

1. Boiling water reactors, which generate steam to turn a turbine that produces electricity, and
2. Pressurized water reactors, which circulate water through the reactor under pressure to heat it. The heated water moves to a steam generator where it heats another, secondary water supply to make steam that spins the turbine.

While nuclear accidents are very rare, the 1979 incident at Three Mile Island in Pennsylvania and the 1986 incident in Chernobyl, Ukraine, in the former USSR have proven that the threat of nuclear accidents exists. Managers of properties located near nuclear power plants will benefit from an increased understanding of the effects of nuclear accidents and awareness of preventive measures they can implement to protect people on their properties and the properties themselves.

Each power plant is equipped with extensive safety systems to prevent or cope with an accident. Unlike the familiar images of a nuclear attack, with an atomic bomb exploding and creating a fireball and a mushroom cloud, nuclear accidents do not cause explosions. Instead, they release radioactive gases into the atmosphere. The effects of such accidents represent only a small fraction of the concentrated capacity of a nuclear explosion. However, all nuclear accidents should be taken seriously because exposure to radiation could be fatal. The specific hazard depends on the type of accident, the amount of radiation released, and the weather conditions at the time of and after the accident.

In addition to accidents at nuclear power plants, a radiological incident could occur anywhere that radioactive materials are used, stored, or transported, including hospitals, research laboratories, industrial plants, and major highways, railways, and shipyards.

Government Regulation of the Nuclear Industry

The Nuclear Regulatory Commission (NRC), successor to the Atomic Energy Commission, was created in 1975 to regulate the various commercial and institutional uses of nuclear energy, including power plants. Under its responsibility to protect the public health and safety, the NRC has three principal functions:

1. Establish standards and regulations,
2. Issue licenses for nuclear facilities and users of nuclear materials, and
3. Inspect facilities and users of nuclear materials to assure compliance with regulatory requirements.

The NRC is also responsible for assuring that the risks of accidental nuclear emissions are maintained at acceptably low levels. The NRC regulatory program also establishes limits for exposure of the general public to radiation.

In 1979, the President of the United States appointed the Federal Emergency Management Agency (FEMA) to take the lead in off-site planning and response to radiological emergencies, and the NRC is to assist FEMA in carrying out this role while also carrying out its statutory responsibilities for public health and safety. Currently, federal oversight of emergency planning for licensed nuclear power plants is shared by the NRC and FEMA.

After the Three Mile Island incident, the NRC issued regulations stating that before a plant could be licensed to operate, the Commission must have "reasonable assurance that adequate protective measures can and will be taken in the event of a radiological emergency." In addition, emergency plans must be prepared for evacuation or other actions to protect the residents in the vicinity of nuclear plants. These plans usually cover an area about 10 miles in all directions around each nuclear plant. The utility has its own emergency plan to notify government officials and provide them with information and recommendations in the event of a potential or actual radiological emergency. State and local governments also have detailed plans for sheltering and evacuation of residents, if necessary. In the event of a nuclear accident, the NRC is responsible to closely follow how the utility company responds to the accident and to investigate its causes. These emergency plans are tested through emergency exercises that simulate a serious reactor accident. The exercises may sometimes include small-scale evacuation drills for schools, nursing homes, and other institutions.

In addition, Congress has established a system of "no-fault" insurance for nuclear power plants to provide liability coverage in the event of a major reactor accident. Initiated under the Price-Anderson Act, the program combines commercial insurance and self-insurance by the nuclear industry. Large nuclear plants are required to have the maximum amount of liability insurance commercially available. The Act also provides liability insurance coverage for actual damages incurred by anyone affected by a major reactor accident.

It is important for the property manager to become familiar with the regulatory provisions for nuclear power plants, especially if the property is located near a nuclear facility. This knowledge will aid the manager in determining where to turn for guidance in developing emergency procedures and provide assurance of the many regulatory safeguards currently in place to protect the public.

Note: Additional information can be found in *NRC: Regulator of Nuclear Safety* published by the U.S. Nuclear Regulatory Commission and available for download on the Internet at www.nrc.gov.

Areas and Properties at Risk

There are two zones for emergency preparation, and a property's location within either of these zones will affect how it should prepare for and respond to a nuclear accident. The first zone is the area within a 10-mile radius of a nuclear power plant.

Potassium Iodide

Radioactive iodine (I^{131} in particular) released in a nuclear accident can cause thyroid cancer if inhaled or ingested. Children are especially vulnerable. Potassium iodide (KI) has been found to be a safe and effective means of protecting against thyroid cancer when exposure cannot be prevented by evacuation, sheltering, or control of food and milk supplies.

As a general rule of thumb, the Food and Drug Administration (FDA) recommends that adults age 18 and over receive 130 mg of KI and children ages 3–18 receive 65 mg. The dose of KI should be taken daily until there is no longer risk of significant exposure to radioiodines. (More specific information can be found in the FDA publication *Guidance: Potassium Iodide as a Thyroid Blocking Agent in Radiation Emergencies,* which can be downloaded on the Internet at www.fda.gov/cder/guidance/index.htm.)

Federal policy regarding KI was revised in 2002 such that the decision to use KI to protect the general public has been left to the discretion of individual states and, in some cases, local governments. As of October 2003, the following 18 states have received KI tablets through FEMA: Massachusetts, Connecticut, Maryland, Vermont, Delaware, Florida, Alabama, Arizona, New York, New Jersey, North Carolina, South Carolina, Pennsylvania, California, Ohio, Virginia, Mississippi, and New Hampshire.

In this area, direct exposure to radiation from an accident is possible and potentially harmful. The second zone is the area within a 10- to 50-mile radius. In this zone, indirect exposure to radiation is possible if radioactive particles enter the food chain through contamination of water, crops, or grazing lands. Although the areas and properties closest to a nuclear power plant are at greatest risk, the entire United States could suffer the effects of indirect exposure.

Preventive Measures

An emergency plan for nuclear accidents is built around three methods to minimize radiation exposure:

1. Shielding—Placing heavy, dense materials between oneself and the radiation source. The more of such materials, the better.
2. Distance—Placing as much distance between oneself and the source of radiation. In a serious nuclear accident, local officials will likely call for evacuation.
3. Time—Limiting the amount of time spent near a radiation source. Radioactivity weakens fairly quickly (the concept of half-life).

The property manager may develop guidelines and procedures for evacuating occupants to shelters, depending on the amount of radioactive material released, based on public announcements and his or her own visual judgment.

Inclusion of potassium iodide (KI) tablets in the property's emergency supplies or first aid kit may be advisable. Authorities may recommend taking KI in the event of a nuclear accident (see accompanying box). A medical professional may be able to advise the property manager regarding the need for and use of potassium iodide

(KI). It may be desirable to encourage occupants (residents, commercial tenants' employees) to acquire their own supplies of KI.

Every community near a nuclear power plant is legally required to have an emergency plan in place. Managers of properties within such communities should find out what plans the local government has in place and what is recommended for the private sector. Radioactive gases released into the atmosphere may require the same precautions as fallout from a nuclear attack. The next chapter, which addresses nuclear attack, contains additional information that may apply to nuclear accidents.

In addition to power generation, radioactive materials are used in medical diagnosis and treatment and in some manufacturing processes. Consequently, it is possible that such materials may be present at managed properties such as medical office buildings and industrial sites. If that is the case, it may be appropriate to consider addressing this issue in the lease. In particular, the tenant may be required to comply with NRC regulatory requirements regarding use, storage, disposal, and transportation of radioactive materials and to have appropriate liability insurance coverage.

The property manager may wish to consult with the owner's insurance agent or other risk management advisor regarding emergency plans for the property and potential liabilities that may arise out of a nuclear accident.

Note: All uses of radioactive materials are highly regulated. Radioactive materials used in medical and industrial applications are likely to be sought after for use in creating a so-called dirty bomb (see Chapter 35).

During a Nuclear Accident

Actions to be taken are somewhat similar to those for a nuclear attack:

- Listen to radio or television for official information regarding the incident. This may include instructions to evacuate the area or to shelter in place (see Chapter 23).
- All persons should shield themselves from potential radioactive gas or runoff water by creating a barrier between themselves and the contaminants, such as staying indoors in a basement.
- If officials order an evacuation, all persons should immediately evacuate to a designated shelter. Radioactive gases can travel rapidly, especially if there is wind. Seeking shelter should take priority over anything else.
- If there is no designated shelter, seek cover in building mechanical areas or stairwells.

After a Nuclear Accident

Radioactive contamination could affect areas as far as 50 miles away from the accident site. Government authorities will indicate when it is safe to return to the affected area.

- Continue to listen to radio and television for updated emergency information.
- Do not drink from community water supplies, which could be contaminated. Local authorities will advise when water is safe for drinking and hygienic uses (bathing, dishwashing, laundry).
- Be prepared for looting during any evacuation or chaos that might ensue.
- Buildings and soil at properties may be contaminated with radioactivity from a nuclear accident. Have the condition of the building evaluated professionally. It may be necessary to demolish the building. Radioactive soil and construction materials should be removed from the site and disposed of properly.

Depending on the type of radioactive material released and the extent of the area involved in a nuclear incident, it may be a very long time before anyone can get close to a contaminated property.

Note: Additional information on nuclear accidents can be found on the FEMA web site at www .fema.gov/hazards/nuclear/. The Centers for Disease Control and Prevention web site includes information on preparing for a radiation emergency at www.bt.cdc.gov/radiation/ index.asp.

34

Nuclear Attack

Explosion of a nuclear bomb produces an intense pulse or wave of light, air pressure, heat, and radiation. While it is unlikely that a country, group, or individual would attack an area in the United States with nuclear weapons, the availability of nuclear weaponry at military compounds around the world demands attention. It would benefit the property manager to become aware of ways to safeguard the property he or she manages in the event such a tragedy should occur.

The damage and other consequences of a nuclear attack differ from those resulting from an accident at a commercial nuclear power plant (see Chapter 33). Nuclear weapons are created specifically to cause the maximum damage possible. They are capable of killing or injuring very large numbers of people and destroying or damaging properties over very wide target areas.

The fireball from a nuclear explosion vaporizes everything in its path, including soil and water, and forms an upward rising mushroom cloud. As the vaporized radioactive material cools, it condenses into dust-like particles and falls back to earth. This "fallout" can travel long distances on wind currents, spreading to areas miles away from the explosion and contaminating anything it touches, including food and water supplies.

The immediate effects of a nuclear attack are unmistakable. They include a flash of intense light followed by a blast of heat and radiation. The secondary effects are from radioactive fallout. The extent of immediate and secondary effects will depend on several factors:

- The size and type of nuclear device exploded.
- The use of the area affected by the blast.
- The height of the explosion above the surface of the earth.
- The distance of people and objects from the explosion.
- Weather conditions during and after the explosion (stronger winds will intensify the damage and disseminate fallout over a larger area; rain may concentrate the radiation in an area).
- The thickness of protective material between the person and the fallout (e.g., bagged sand or gravel, concrete, bricks, wood, or earth).
- The amount of time spent in a shelter after the initial explosion.

People near the explosion most likely would be killed or seriously injured by the initial blast, heat, or radiation. People several miles away from the explosion would be

Health Effects of an Atomic Blast

Injury or death may result from the blast itself or from debris thrown by the blast. Human skin may receive moderate to severe burns. Those who look directly at the fireball could experience temporary blindness or even retinal burns. While severe burns may appear in minutes, other effects may take days or weeks to appear. These effects range from mild (e.g., reddening of the skin) to severe (e.g., cancer, death), depending on the type of radiation, the radiation dose (amount absorbed by the body), the route of exposure (e.g., external by absorption through the skin or internal by inhalation or ingestion), and the duration of exposure.

endangered by the initial blast, heat, and subsequent fires. Others may survive but would be exposed to dangerous radioactive fallout.

Areas and Properties at Risk

Areas of the United States that are at greatest risk of a nuclear attack are those with significant military, political, and economic importance. Properties located around military bases may be particularly vulnerable, especially during wartime. The risk of exposure to radiation from fallout extends well beyond the boundaries of cities and military bases.

Preventive Measures

Local government agencies may have constructed shelters or designated certain structures (buildings, subway tunnels) as fallout shelters. However, these may not accommodate everyone in the area who needs shelter.

The only precaution a property manager can take to prevent loss due to a nuclear attack is to provide an emergency shelter for those on the property at the time of an attack. The shelter could be a special building or underground bunker, where possibility for destruction from the impact of the nuclear blast is minimized. The property manager should determine ahead of time—as part of the emergency planning process—where the safest areas(s) of the building might be. Water and non-perishable food may be stored in the shelter to sustain its inhabitants over a period of days or weeks. This is called sheltering in place, which is discussed briefly in Chapter 23.

Because building occupants (property staff, commercial tenants' employees) cannot be forced to shelter in place at their workplace, it is important to involve them in the planning process to maximize their cooperation in the event of a disaster. Planning to shelter in place at the workplace might include:

- Determining whether all personnel will shelter in place or if some will leave the building before shelter procedures are implemented. The process involves sealing doors and windows, which would not be unsealed until an "all clear" has been signaled by authorities.
- Developing an accountability system. This may include sign-in sheets to document who is entering and leaving the designated shelter area. Plan for visitors to the building as well as regular occupants.

- Assigning specific duties to individuals and making backup assignments.
- Planning and conducting drills, assessing the drills for needed improvements.

In a large building, the manager may wish to encourage individual tenants to make plans and preparations for their employees to shelter in place. The National Institute for Chemical Studies has published *Shelter in Place at Your Office: A General Guide for Preparing a Shelter in Place Plan in the Workplace* on its web site at www .nicsinfo.org.

If an underground shelter is not available, the property manager could advise people on the property to seek safety at an alternative location in a building that has walls and a roof thick enough to absorb radioactivity emitted by fallout.

Inclusion of potassium iodide (KI) tablets in the property's emergency supplies or first aid kit may be advisable. Authorities may recommend taking KI in the event of a nuclear attack (KI is discussed in Chapter 33).

The same preventive measures may apply in the event of a terrorist attack that releases biological or chemical agents or explodes a dirty bomb (see Chapter 35).

During a Nuclear Attack

In the event of a nuclear attack, federal, state, and local governmental agencies would activate a national emergency response plan. Suggested steps for people to take at a managed property may include:

- Immediately evacuate to a designated shelter. Radioactive fallout travels rapidly, so seeking shelter should take priority over anything else.
- If there is no designated shelter, seek cover in mechanical areas or stairwells in the building.
- Shield your body from the explosion using solid material such as sandbags.
- Protect your eyes; do not look at the light from the blast.

The World Health Organization (WHO) has published suggested actions for individuals to take under different circumstances, depending on where they are when a nuclear attack occurs. These are outlined in the accompanying box. (Additional information can be found on the Centers for Disease Control and Prevention web site at www.bt.cdc.gov/radiation/nuclearfaq.asp).

After a Nuclear Attack

After the intense heat, rumbling noise, and obvious fallout have noticeably ceased, a person in a shelter may think that it is safe to leave the shelter area. However, this is not the case. Radioactive dust and other particles can remain airborne for extended periods of time, and the earth may still be subject to fallout. Once these particles hit the ground, they decay fairly rapidly; but it is recommended that people remain inside the shelter for as long as physically possible to avoid radiation exposure. Here are some actions to consider.

- Stay indoors for at least the first 24 hours after the initial explosion. This is the most dangerous period, when radioactive particles fall to the earth's surface.
- While in the shelter, continue to listen to radio and television for announcements about affected areas and when it is safe to leave shelter. It may not be necessary to remain in the shelter more than one or two weeks. People may be able to leave the shelter for short periods of time after a few days.

Suggested Actions to Take During a Nuclear Attack

Emergency procedures for building occupants may include the following actions suggested by the World Health Organization (WHO). These are primarily actions for people to take individually.

People near the blast should:
- Prevent damage to your eyesight by turning away from the blast and closing and covering your eyes.
- Lay face down with your hands under your body.
- Remain flat until the heat and two shock waves have passed.

People who are outside when a blast occurs should:
- Use a handkerchief or other cloth to cover your nose and mouth.
- Go to a ventilated area and brush, shake, or wipe dust from your clothing; keep your mouth and nose covered while doing this.
- Remove clothing (it may be contaminated); if possible, take a shower, wash your hair, and put on fresh clothing before entering the shelter.
- Move to shelter (preferably a basement or other underground area located away from the direction of the wind).

People in a shelter or basement should:
- Listen to local radio or television stations for information about the areas affected by the blast and instructions to follow. Authorities may direct people to shelter in place or evacuate to a safer location.
- Keep your mouth and nose covered with a face mask or cloth until the fallout cloud has passed.
- Clean and cover any open wounds on your body.
- Turn off the ventilation system and seal doors and windows until the fallout cloud passes. After it has passed, unseal doors and windows to allow for air circulation.
- Stay inside until authorities say it is safe to come out.
- Use stored drinking water and food; do not drink water from open water supplies or eat local fresh food until told it is safe to do so.
- If you go out, cover your nose and mouth with a damp towel.

- Do not drink from community water supplies, which could be contaminated. Local authorities will advise when water is safe for drinking and hygienic uses (bathing, dishwashing, laundry).
- Be prepared for looting during any evacuation or chaos that might ensue.
- Buildings and soil at properties may be contaminated with radioactivity from the nuclear blast. Have the condition of the building evaluated professionally. It may be necessary to demolish the building. Radioactive soil and construction materials should be removed from the site and disposed of properly.

Note: More specific information on radiological emergencies, including nuclear blast, can be found on the Centers for Disease Control and Prevention web site at www.bt.cdc.gov/radiation/index.asp.

35

Terrorist Acts

Terrorism is the unlawful use of force or violence against persons or property for purposes of intimidation or coercion. The goal of terrorism is to create fear of the unknown and the unknowable. A terrorist can strike at any time, anywhere. The Federal Bureau of Investigation (FBI) differentiates two types of terrorism—domestic and international—referring not to where an incident takes place but to the origins of those responsible for it.

- Domestic terrorism involves groups or individuals who direct terrorist activities at elements of the U.S. government or population without foreign direction. Most such incidents in the United States have involved small extremist groups who use terrorism to achieve a specific objective. The bombing of the Murrah Federal Building in Oklahoma City in 1995 is one example.

- International terrorism involves groups or individuals whose terrorist activities are foreign-based and/or directed by countries or groups outside the United States or whose activities transcend national boundaries. The September 11, 2001, attacks are examples.

All manner of man-made disasters could be acts of terrorism. Explosions are usually more spectacular than arson fires, but the latter can also be a component of a terror campaign. Sabotage of infrastructure components is a possibility. An explosive device detonated at a nuclear power plant could result in the release of radioactive material while also causing a power outage. An obstacle on railroad tracks could derail a train and possibly disrupt freight shipments and passenger train travel for a period of time. Even a bomb threat, whether real or a hoax, is a terrorist act.

A terrorist act may rely on chemical or biological warfare materials to cause harm. Terrorist devices can employ high-powered explosives combined with radioactive material—a "dirty bomb." Most published information about terror threats focuses on these three types of potential attack. While there is likely to be property damage, possibly extensive, from the conventional explosives used in a dirty bomb, biological and chemical weapons are used strictly to kill and injure people. The three types of terror threats are discussed later in this chapter.

In the event of a terrorist attack, the aftermath is likely to be chaotic.

- There are likely to be large numbers of casualties and extensive damage to buildings and city infrastructure. Employers should have up-to-date information on employees' emergency contacts (e.g., spouse, parent, or other family member).

- Increased law enforcement at all levels of government (terrorism is a crime) may include more visible police and other law enforcement personnel and restrictions on people's movements.
- Large numbers of people may be evacuated from the affected area.
- Hospitals and mental health facilities in affected communities are likely to be strained, even overwhelmed.
- Buildings (i.e., workplaces, schools) may be closed—or they may be commandeered for use by government emergency personnel. There may be restrictions on travel inside and outside the United States.
- Media coverage will be extensive. Strong public fear is likely.
- International implications and consequences of the event can continue for a long time.
- Clean-up may take a long time—months or even years.

Regarding media coverage, unedited video footage and repeated images of a terrorist attack and people's reactions to it can be very upsetting. This is especially true for children who may think the event is happening over and over again. People may want to gather in groups and take turns listening to the news so they can be informed without being psychologically and emotionally overwhelmed. Property managers whose buildings include live media displays in lobbies or common areas need to be sensitive to the need for information while also being aware that the media have a need to fill air time.

Areas and Properties at Risk

The nature of terrorism is such that all areas of the United States and all types of managed properties can be considered at risk. Because possible targets include infrastructure components, it is likely that those properties near nuclear power plants, chemical manufacturing plants, transportation centers (railway stations, airports), and utilities are at greater risk than those located away from such facilities. Major high-rise buildings, especially named buildings that may be considered emblems of America, could be specific targets, and any adjacent properties would likely experience some devastation because of their proximity. High-profile landmarks, monuments, and major international sporting events might also be targets.

Preventive Measures

Because the specifics of terrorist acts are unpredictable, property managers should be prepared to respond to a wide variety of possibilities. General precautions recommended for other types of disasters would apply for a terror attack as well. Written emergency procedures that address bombs and bomb threats, power outages, elevator emergencies, fire, hazardous materials incidents, nuclear accidents, and medical emergencies will cover many types of terrorist acts and their consequences. Additional precautions to consider include:

- Check the effectiveness of security measures implemented at the property. Consider having a security professional conduct a risk assessment to identify potential vulnerabilities, especially in regard to a terrorist attack. Implement additional measures if appropriate.
- Consider making arrangements to increase security (e.g., contract for security guards to patrol the property—as a supplement to current patrol levels or as an added measure if there are no patrols currently) when the homeland security advisory level is raised above "high" (yellow)—i.e., to "elevated" (orange) or "severe" (red). The Homeland Security Advisory System is outlined in the accompanying box.

U.S. Homeland Security Advisory System

The U.S. Department of Homeland Security (DHS) established a color-coded threat alert system to advise citizens and businesses when they need to take action to protect themselves from possible terrorist acts. There are five levels to the system. Each successive level of recommended actions builds on and incorporates the previous one. The information presented here has been summarized.

Low risk (green)—Businesses (and individuals) should develop written emergency plans that address likely hazards, including terrorist acts and their consequences. This should include an emergency communication plan to notify employees about specific emergencies and a designated off-site location for employees to gather. A plan for continuing operations, possibly at an alternate location, is also advisable (see Chapter 1).

Guarded (general) risk (blue)—Staff should be alert for suspicious activity and report it to the proper authorities. Consult with local authorities, emergency management agencies, and utilities about emergency preparedness. Ensure that the emergency communication plan is updated to include purchase of needed equipment if this has not been done.

Elevated (significant) risk (yellow)—Have a private security consultant conduct a security risk assessment to determine vulnerabilities and need to implement additional security measures (see Chapter 3).

High risk (orange)—Review emergency plans regarding continuity of operations and be prepared to respond to the media. Determine whether and how much to restrict access to the building and whether private security support is needed. Check with suppliers and vendors to confirm their emergency response procedures.

Severe risk (red)—Determine whether to close the building based on circumstances and the written emergency plan. Be prepared to work with a smaller staff. Listen to radio and television for current information and instructions—authorities may recommend evacuation or sheltering in place. In general, this level of protective measures is not intended to be sustained for substantial periods of time.

During periods of elevated and higher levels of risk, people's ability to travel to and from work or from city to city may be limited. There may be traffic delays and restrictions. Security at railway stations and airports may be increased. Access to public buildings may be restricted, and there may be baggage searches.

Note: Homeland Security Advisory System recommendations for businesses are outlined on the American Red Cross web site at www.redcross.org/services/disaster/beprepared/hsas/business.pdf. It may be advisable to seek out more comprehensive information such as the recommended actions for fire chiefs and first responders published by the International Association of Fire Chiefs on the Internet at www.iafc.org/downloads/hscoloralert.pdf. State and city web sites include information about homeland security, the advisory system, and emergency preparedness specific to their areas.

Qualifying Residential Rental Applicants as a Preventive Measure

Because it is possible that terrorists may be planning to attack apartment buildings, many in the multifamily industry are taking greater care in qualifying rental applicants to avoid problems on their properties. Some options to consider include:

- Verify the identity of all rental applicants. Require all adult applicants (over age 18) to complete a written rental application form and provide original documents to verify identity (social security card, driving license, or other government photo-ID), show evidence of employment (pay stub, W-2 form) or school enrollment (student ID, current class schedule), and proof of U.S. citizenship or the applicant's right to live in the United States (birth certificate; visa or green card for non-citizens).

- Obtain consumer reports to verify identity and authenticity of social security numbers and other information provided by the applicant regarding his or her financial/credit status. If there is no credit record, a search can be made based on the applicant's social security number (this is done by a service separate from the credit reports). Such a search can verify social security numbers, identify addresses and employers associated with the applicant over time, provide additional names the applicant may have used, and help identify application fraud. It is also possible—and desirable—to obtain a rental history and information on any landlord-tenant disputes.

- Review the information to be sure that the information on identification documents and credit reports is consistent across all the documents and in agreement with that provided on the application form (i.e., social security numbers, names, addresses, birth dates, etc., are the same in all instances).

It is also a good idea to ask for and verify personal references. To comply with fair housing laws, applicant screening procedures should be the same for all applicants. Also, confidential information provided in the application process should be protected to prevent inadvertent or improper disclosure, which could lead to identity theft.

- Ask commercial tenants to provide a list of names and telephone extensions for all of their employees. This should include phones in unoccupied offices or workstations and other locations in their leased premises. In the event of a terrorist attack or if there is an intruder in the building, this information can help emergency response personnel locate the site of a reported incident (i.e., by linking the caller who reports an incident to a specific phone in a particular location).

- Review and strengthen rental applicant screening procedures at residential properties (see accompanying box).

- Designate one employee (or one from each work shift if applicable) to be the safety coordinator and make decisions relating to employee and customer safety, perhaps including the safety of the property itself. This person should know how to contact the building owner or manager at all times.

- If you have a voice mail system, designate one extension for emergency use to record messages for employees and building occupants. Make sure the phone number is provided to all who may need it.

- If you have programmable call forwarding, use that feature to reprogram phones to ring elsewhere.

- Use UL-listed battery backup systems and surge protectors for sensitive equipment such as computers (see Chapter 15).

- Ensure that cabinet doors and drawers have secure locks or latches to prevent them from opening and dumping their contents in the event of an explosion.

- Install automatic fire sprinklers if the building has none.

- Consult your insurance agent about types and levels of insurance coverage in place and what might be advisable adjustments. Business continuity insurance should be considered. Valuable equipment and personal property may be covered under special riders. It may be possible to obtain specific insurance coverage for terrorist acts (see *Insurance, Finance, and Regulation Primer for Terrorism Risk Management in Buildings* published by FEMA and available for download at www.fema.gov/fima/rmsp.shtm).

Property managers can prepare the people who live and work in the buildings they manage—and the buildings themselves—by finding out what types of incidents local police and fire departments and area hospitals are preparing for. However, government preparations are likely to be broader in scope than those needed for an individual property or location, and information the authorities share may be for "public consumption"—information they are required to provide—rather than specifics. On the other hand, there may be an opportunity to work with local authorities to the benefit of your property by volunteering to participate in their planning processes.

Note: For property managers who may wish to seek more specific information regarding preventive measures, the Lawrence Berkeley National Laboratory has published "Advice for Safeguarding Buildings Against Chemical or Biological Attack" on their web site at http://secure buildings.lbl.gov/. There is also a publication from the National Institute for Occupational Safety and Health titled *Guidance for Protecting Building Environments from Airborne Chemical, Biological, or Radiological Attacks*. This can be found on the Internet at www.cdc.gov/niosh/bldvent/2002-139.html.

FEMA offers a series of risk management publications that can be downloaded at www.fema.gov/fima/rmsp.shtm; several are related specifically to terrorism. Additional information on terrorism preparedness and mitigation can also be found on the FEMA web site at www.fema.gov/hazards/terrorism/. The American Red Cross includes terrorism-related information sources on their web site at www.redcross.org/pubs/dspubs/terrormat.html. Many of the documents can be downloaded directly.

Specific Terror Threats

The following sections discuss the different types of terrorist attacks, including descriptions of some likely chemical and biological agents. Both categories include many more agents than are mentioned here. In the event of a biological or chemical attack, authorities are likely to instruct people to either seek shelter where they are and seal the premises (i.e., shelter in place; see Chapters 23 and 34) or evacuate immediately.

The Centers for Disease Control and Prevention provides information on large numbers of potential biological and chemical agents on its web site at www.cdc.gov

Real Estate Information Sharing and Analysis Center (ISAC)

The real estate industry has taken a proactive approach to preventing terrorism and responding to terrorist acts when they occur. Specifically, the Real Estate Roundtable organized the Real Estate Information Sharing and Analysis Center (ISAC). The ISAC serves three roles:

1. Disseminate information from the federal government, including terror alerts and advisories, to real estate industry participants.
2. Facilitate real estate industry reporting to government authorities regarding credible terrorist threats to real estate assets.
3. Bring together private- and public-sector experts to share useful information on specific issues, including risk assessment, building security, and emergency response planning.

Founding members of the real estate ISAC include the National Association of REALTORS® (NAR), the Institute of Real Estate Management (IREM®) which is an affiliate of NAR, the Building Owners and Managers Association (BOMA) International, the International Council of Shopping Centers (ICSC), the National Association of Industrial and Office Properties (NAIOP), and the National Association of Real Estate Investment Trusts (NAREIT). Information on the organization, current alerts, and incident reporting as well as links to member web sites and resources can be found on the Internet at www.reisac.org.

Other industries—including the chemical, electric power, financial services, food, information technology, oil and gas, telecommunications, and water industries—also operate ISACs in partnership with the federal government as part of efforts to protect America's critical infrastructure from terrorist attacks.

under Emergency Preparedness and Response. The section also includes information on dirty bombs. Fact sheets on radiation and radioactive materials, including dirty bombs, can be found on the Nuclear Regulatory Commission web site at www.nrc.gov/reading-rm/doc-collections/fact-sheets/. A concise summary of information about dirty bombs and some specific biological and chemical agents has been developed at the Center for Technology and National Security Policy at the National Defense University. Titled *Coping with an Attack: A Quick Guide to Dealing with Biological, Chemical, and "Dirty Bomb" Attacks,* the information has been published on the Internet at www.ndu.edu/ctnsp/wmd-tipsheet.htm. (It is also included on the CD-ROM that accompanies this book.) Property managers can find real estate industry specific information and resources on homeland security and emergency preparedness on the Real Estate Information Sharing and Analysis Center web site at www.reisac.org (see accompanying box).

Biological Attack

A biological attack is the deliberate release of bacteria, viruses, or other biological agents that can cause illness and, in some cases, death. Some agents (e.g., the smallpox virus) are potentially contagious—i.e., they can be spread by contact with people who are infected. Others (e.g., anthrax) are not contagious. Unlike an explosion, a biological attack may not be immediately obvious. As with the anthrax mailings subsequent to September 11, 2001, local health care workers may report increased numbers of sick people seeking emergency medical attention or a pattern of unusual illness. The general population will most likely learn of the danger from media reports. The illnesses caused by smallpox and anthrax are described below.

Smallpox is a serious, contagious, sometimes fatal disease caused by the variola virus. Except for laboratory stockpiles, the variola virus has been eliminated. Smallpox is spread by prolonged face-to-face contact with an infected person, direct contact with contaminated body fluids, bedding, or clothing. The most common form of smallpox—variola major—is also the most severe. Symptoms include extensive rash and high fever, and there is a fatality rate of about 30 percent. The less common form—variola minor—is much less severe, with a fatality rate of one percent or less. Symptoms develop after an incubation period of one to two and one-half weeks. Initial symptoms include fever, malaise, headache, and body aches; sometimes there is vomiting. After two to four days, a rash emerges; about four days later, the rash becomes open sores. Smallpox is most contagious during the first 7–10 days after the onset of rash, but contagion continues until the last smallpox scab falls off. Treatment is symptomatic. The disease does not respond to antibiotics.

Anthrax is caused by *Bacillus anthracis,* a spore-forming bacterium. Anthrax can be contracted from eating undercooked meat from infected animals, handling infected animal products, or inhaling spores from infected animal products such as wool. Anthrax can also be used as a weapon. Because anthrax is likely to be sent through the mail, the postal service and on-site mailrooms in commercial buildings are likely to be points of contact. Symptoms of anthrax infection depend on the method of exposure. Skin contact may produce a small sore that develops into a blister and then into a skin ulcer with a black center. None of these are painful. Ingestion can cause loss of appetite, nausea, bloody diarrhea, and fever followed by stomach pain. Inhalation produces cold or flu-like symptoms, including sore throat, mild fever, and muscle aches. Symptoms can appear within seven days of contact; however, symptoms following inhalation may take up to six weeks to develop. Anthrax can be treated with antibiotics, usually for 60 days. Success depends on the method of exposure and how soon treatment is started. Antibiotics can also be used to prevent infection in persons exposed to anthrax but who have not yet become ill. Anthrax can be prevented by a vaccine, but that has not been available to the general public.

Managers of buildings that include an on-site mail center can find information on emergency planning for such facilities in U.S. Postal Service publication 166, *Mail Center Security Guidelines,* which can be downloaded from the Internet at www.usps.com/publications/pubs/welcome.htm.

In addition to smallpox and anthrax, there are numerous other biological agents that could be used in a terrorist attack. These include plague and tularemia, which are bacterial infections, hemorrhagic fevers caused by viruses, and botulism caused by a bacterial toxin.

During a Biological Attack

Public health officials may not be able to provide information immediately in the event of a biological attack. It will take time to determine the nature and cause of the illness, how to treat it, and who is in danger. Official news on radio, television, and the Internet will release particulars, which are likely to include:

- What geographic area or population group authorities consider in danger.
- The signs and symptoms of the disease caused by the agent.
- Whether medications or vaccines are being distributed and where to obtain them.
- Who should receive medications and/or vaccines. Segments of the population—infants, children, the elderly—may be especially vulnerable and need to seek treatment or may be cautioned against using specific medications or vaccines.
- Where those who become sick should go to obtain emergency medical care.

People who are potentially exposed to a biological agent should follow instructions of doctors and public health officials. They should expect to receive medical evaluation and treatment. (Note, however, that some medical facilities may not accept victims out of fear that they will contaminate the hospital population.) If the disease is contagious, those exposed may be advised to stay away from other people or deliberately quarantined.

Chemical Attack

A chemical attack is a deliberate release of a toxic substance (solid, liquid, gas) that can poison people and contaminate the environment. There are many chemicals that could be used for this purpose, among them nerve agents such as sarin (a liquid), hydrogen cyanide (a flammable colorless gas or liquid) and chlorine (a gas that is heavier than air), and sulfur mustards (heavy, yellow to brown, strong-smelling liquids). Ricin toxin from castor beans is considered both a chemical and a biological agent. Chemical agents can be inhaled, ingested, or absorbed through the skin and eyes, and their effects can appear fairly quickly. Many people may suddenly exhibit common symptoms such as redness and watering of the eyes, difficulty breathing, choking, twitching, loss of coordination or other indications of a nervous disorder such as drooling, excessive sweating, and confusion. Large numbers of sick or dead animals, birds, fish, or insects may also be an indicator. The effects of sarin and ricin are described below.

Sarin is a man-made chemical warfare agent that acts on the nervous system. In its pure form, sarin is a clear, colorless, odorless, tasteless liquid that can evaporate into a gas. People can be exposed to sarin in the air by skin or eye contact or inhalation. Because sarin readily mixes with water, it can be used to poison water and food. Symptoms of exposure to low or moderate doses of sarin by inhalation, ingestion, or skin contact may develop within seconds or over a period of hours. These include runny nose, blurred vision, cough, tightness of the chest, rapid breathing, diarrhea, drowsiness, confusion, headache. Large doses of sarin can cause convulsions, paralysis, loss of consciousness, and respiratory failure leading to death. There are antidotes to sarin but they must be used quickly to be effective. Treatment consists of removing sarin from the body as soon as possible and providing supportive medical care at a hospital.

Ricin is a deadly poison. It is present in the waste "mash" when castor oil is extracted from castor beans. It can be injected into the body, dispersed in a mist or powder, or used to contaminate food or water. Accidental exposure is highly unlikely; it would take an intentional act to make ricin and use it as a poison. Symptoms of ricin poisoning depend on the route of exposure and the amount received. Inhaling ricin would likely cause difficulty breathing, cough, nausea, and fever with heavy sweating within eight hours after exposure. Ingestion in food or water would likely lead to vomiting and diarrhea accompanied by severe dehydration in less than six hours. Exposure of skin or eyes to ricin mist or powder can cause redness and pain. In severe cases, death could take place in 36–72 hours. There is no antidote for ricin. Victims should receive supportive medical care by treating the symptoms they exhibit.

During a Chemical Attack

People who see signs of a chemical attack should try to find clean air as quickly as possible.

- If possible, try to define the affected area or identify where the chemical is coming from.
- Leave the area immediately.
- People inside a building where the chemical agent is present should get out of the building (without passing through the contaminated area, if possible).
- Those who are unable to exit the building should move as far away from the contamination as possible and shelter in place.
- People who are outside during an attack should quickly decide on the fastest way to find clean air (leave the area or enter the closest building and shelter in place).

Those who think they have been exposed to the chemical—i.e., they are exhibiting symptoms—should immediately remove their clothing and wash themselves with any source of water at hand, preferably with soap, but being careful not to scrub the chemical into the skin. Then they should seek medical attention. (Exposure to chemical agents can be fatal. There is no assistance an untrained person can offer that would likely be of any value to the victims of chemical agents.)

Dirty Bomb Attack

Basically, a dirty bomb combines a conventional explosive (e.g., dynamite) with a radiation source. The conventional explosive would be more lethal than the radioactive material. This is because the difficulty and danger in obtaining high-level radioactive materials (from a nuclear power plant, for example) make it more likely that low-level sources (e.g., materials used in medical diagnosis and treatment or at industrial sites) would be used in a dirty bomb. Such sources are unlikely to yield enough radiation to kill people or cause serious illness. However, it is also possible that a powerful source of radioactivity could be hidden in a public place (e.g., a waste receptacle in a subway or train station) so that people passing close to the source might receive a significant dose of radiation.

Radioactive materials are carefully regulated in the United States. Users are licensed, and licensees are required to secure the materials from unauthorized access and theft. Lost or stolen material must be reported immediately, and local authorities make a determined effort to recover it. Government continues to tighten controls on high-risk radioactive sources.

The extent of local contamination from a dirty bomb would depend on the amount and type of radioactive material, the size of the explosive, and weather conditions. Because radiation cannot be seen, felt, tasted, or smelled, those at the scene of an explosion will not know whether radiation was released.

After a Dirty Bomb Explosion

The following actions are recommended for people at or near the scene who have not been severely injured by the blast:

At the blast site:

- Follow instructions from emergency personnel; stay in the area until you are released.
- Stay calm; decontamination does not have to start immediately.
- Cover your nose and mouth with a handkerchief.

Near the blast site:

- Stay calm.
- Cover your nose and mouth with a handkerchief.
- Leave the area—preferably on foot. To avoid contaminating vehicles, do not take public transportation. If driving a car or truck do not use the heater or air conditioner.
- As soon as possible, remove clothing. Shower twice and wash your hair thoroughly. (Preferably remove clothing outdoors and seal it in a plastic bag.)
- Listen to local radio or television stations for information about the emergency and the response to it. If radioactive material was released, people will be advised where to report for monitoring, blood testing, etc., to determine whether they were exposed. News broadcasts will also advise how to discard contaminated clothing and clean your vehicle.

As with a nuclear accident, it is important for people to limit the amount of radiation they are exposed to by using shielding, distance, and time (see Chapter 33). Those who become ill from radiation exposure in the range of 75–200 rem may have nausea, vomiting, fatigue, and loss of appetite. Recovery make take a few weeks. Higher doses of radiation (>300 rem) can cause bleeding and changes in blood cells, and exposure in excess of 600 rem causes hair loss and suppresses the ability to fight infections—this is usually fatal. For perspective, the natural environment includes a certain amount of low-level radioactivity that does not harm humans. Radiation exposure from a chest x-ray is equivalent to 1/100 rem.

Note: Because potassium iodide (KI) only protects the thyroid gland from exposure to radioactive iodine and it is unlikely that a dirty bomb would contain radioactive iodine, KI would probably not be beneficial.

Appendices

Glossary

automatic external defibrillator (AED)   A medical device used to provide electrical stimulation to the human heart in the event of cardiac arrest. Such devices are often installed in shopping centers and other commercial buildings to which the public is invited.

avalanche   A fall or slide of a large mass of snow or rock down a mountainside.

biological half-life   The time required for a biological system, such as that of a human, to eliminate, by natural processes, half of the amount of a substance (such as a radioactive material) that has entered it.

blizzard   In general, a very heavy snowstorm with high winds. More specifically, a violent snowstorm with winds of 35 mph or more with snow and blowing snow reducing visibility to less than one-quarter mile for a period of at least three hours.

bloodborne pathogens   Pathogenic microorganisms that are present in human blood and can cause disease in humans. These pathogens include, but are not limited to, human immunodeficiency virus (HIV/AIDS), hepatitis B virus (HBV), and hepatitis C virus (HCV). Considered an occupational hazard—exposures to blood and other body fluids occur across a wide variety of occupations, including cleaning personnel and emergency response and public safety personnel as well as health care professionals.

cardiopulmonary resuscitation (CPR)   A basic emergency procedure for life support consisting of artificial respiration and manual external heart massage.

combustible   Capable of burning. A characteristic of some chemicals (e.g., volatile solvents such as benzene); a type of hazard. Also, something that ignites and burns readily.

corrosive   Capable of causing corrosion or eating away. A characteristic of certain chemicals (e.g., acids) that when skin is exposed to them, the tissue is "eaten away," causing chemical "burns"; a type of hazard.

emergency   An unforeseen combination of events or circumstances, or the result of such events or circumstances, that requires immediate action. A usually distressing event (e.g., fire, flood, earthquake; explosion, civil disorder) that can be planned or prepared for but not necessarily foreseen.

emergency preparedness   Having in place established procedures for addressing various types of distressing incidents or events and ensuring that building occupants are trained to follow them.

emergency procedures   Procedures developed in order to minimize injury to people and damage to property in the event of natural or man-made disasters, usually including specific procedures for evacuating buildings.

emergency response team   A group of individuals, usually at a commercial property and comprising members of the management staff and representatives of the tenants, who are trained to respond to various types of emergencies and to expedite *evacuation* of the building.

exposure incident   Defined by OSHA to mean a specific eye, mouth, other mucous membrane, non-intact skin, or parenteral contact with blood or other potentially infectious materials that results from the performance of an employee's duties.

external exposure   Used in referring to contact with radioactivity from outside the body (e.g., on the skin).

fallout   The descent of particles through the atmosphere; used in referring to radioactive particles resulting from or dispersed by a nuclear blast as well as to the particles collectively. The term is sometimes applied in other contexts, as fallout from a biological or chemical weapon.

flammable   Easily ignited. A characteristic of some chemicals; a type of hazard.

frostbite   Freezing of the skin or any other part of the body. The fingers, toes, and nose are usually the first parts affected.

Good Samaritan laws Laws aimed at protecting those who choose during an emergency to aid others who are ill or injured. They typically protect people from being sued for negligence but not for gross or willful negligence or reckless misconduct.

half-life The time in which one half of the atoms of a particular radioactive substance disintegrates into another form. The measured half-life of a substance can vary from millionths of a second to billions of years; also called physical or radiological half-life.

hazmat Abbreviation for *hazardous material*. When used in reference to firefighters and other trained professionals who respond to hazardous material (usually chemical) incidents and spills, a *hazmat team*.

HAZUS Multihazard Loss Estimation Methodology A standardized, national methodology for assessing losses from natural hazards—earthquakes, flood, wind—implemented through PC-based geographic information system (GIS) software.

heat exhaustion A condition resulting from exposure to heat in which depletion of body fluids causes weakness, dizziness, nausea, and often collapse; also called *heat prostration*. The condition can be alleviated by rest and administration of fluids and electrolytes to replace those lost through excessive sweating.

heat stroke A severe condition resulting from impairment of the body's temperature-regulating mechanisms because of prolonged exposure to excessive heat. Heat stroke is characterized by high fever, hot dry skin, cessation of sweating, severe headache, and, in serious cases, collapse and coma.

hypothermia An abnormally low body temperature.

Incident Command System A structured system for managing emergency incidents developed by a federal interagency task force. Originally designed for management of wildland fires, the concept is applicable across a wide range of emergencies and may be applied in the private sector. Activities and personnel assignments are divided among five categories—command, operations, planning, logistics, and finance/administration.

indoor air quality (IAQ) An environmental concern related more specifically to the work environment (e.g., office buildings). In particular, certain symptoms in employees have been related to poor IAQ *(sick-building syndrome)*. The four major contributors to IAQ, as defined by the U.S. Environmental Protection Agency, are outside air sources, HVAC systems, activities of building occupants, and construction materials. The American Society of Heating, Refrigerating, and Air-Conditioning Engineers (ASHRAE) has established an IAQ standard specific to ventilation rates in relation to occupancy levels. Other IAQ issues continue to be considered for establishment of specific standards.

internal exposure Used in referring to contact with radioactivity by ingestion (eating contaminated food or drinking contaminated water) or inhalation (breathing contaminated air).

Legionnaires' disease A lobar pneumonia caused by the bacterium *Legionella pneumophila,* so-named because its first recognized occurrence was during the 1976 American Legion convention. It is transmitted to individuals who inhale water mists (e.g., from fouled cooling towers, showerheads, drinking fountains, etc.) that contain levels of bacteria sufficient to cause infection.

material safety data sheet (MSDS) A compilation of information regarding the hazardous properties of chemicals. Usual information includes composition, physical and chemical properties, and known hazards (e.g., toxicity, flammability, explosion potential); recommended cautions for handling (e.g., protective clothing and devices), storage, and disposal; clean-up procedures, and first aid treatment in the event of exposure. An MSDS is provided when chemicals (e.g., solvents, cleaning compounds) are shipped in bulk in pails or drums and when the information cannot be fitted on the labels of small containers. These documents must be retained for reference by maintenance and other on-site personnel.

mitigation Any sustained action taken to reduce or eliminate long-term risk to human life and real property from a hazard event; also known as *prevention* when undertaken before a disaster. The goal of mitigation is to decrease the need for response to a disaster as opposed to simply increasing the response capability.

nuclear power plant An electrical generating facility using a nuclear reactor as its heat source to provide steam to a turbine generator.

occupational exposure   Defined by OSHA as reasonably anticipated skin, eye, mucous membrane, or parenteral (i.e., by injection, including needlesticks) contact with blood or other potentially infectious materials (body fluids and/or tissues other than blood) that may result from the performance of an employee's duties.

rad   Abbreviation for *radiation absorbed dose;* the amount of energy from any type of ionizing radiation (e.g., alpha, beta, gamma, neutrons, etc.) deposited in any medium (e.g., air, water, living tissue).

radioactivity   The spontaneous emission of radiation from the nucleus of an unstable isotope, generally alpha or beta particles, often accompanied by gamma rays. Also, the rate at which radioactive material emits radiation (measured in units of becquerels or disintegrations per second).

rem   Abbreviation for *roentgen equivalent man;* a standard unit of measure of the effects of ionizing radiation on humans.

rolling blackout   Intentional power outage scheduled by a utility to reduce electrical output for a set period of time during peak usage hours in order to prevent large-scale grid failures. Specific areas are blacked out at different times in an alternating sequence, hence the name rolling blackout.

seiche   An oscillation of the surface of a lake or other landlocked body of water that varies in frequency from a few minutes to several hours. A seiche is thought to be initiated by local variations in air pressure, sometimes aided by winds and tidal currents. The oscillation may continue for some time after the atmospheric pressure differences no longer exist.

shelter in place   A precaution intended to keep people safe while remaining indoors. Sheltering in place means selecting a small interior room with few windows or none and taking refuge there. A recommended response when/if chemical, biological, or nuclear contaminants are released into the environment. It does not mean sealing off an entire residence or office building.

storm surge   An abnormal rise in sea level accompanying a hurricane or other intense storm, and whose height is the difference between the observed level of the sea surface and the level that would have occurred in the absence of the cyclone. Storm surge is usually estimated by subtracting the normal or astronomic high tide from the observed storm tide.

storm tide   The actual level of sea water resulting from the astronomic tide combined with a storm surge.

terrorism   As defined in the U.S. Code of Federal Regulations, the unlawful use of force and violence against persons or property to intimidate or coerce a government, the civilian population, or any segment thereof, in furtherance of political or social objectives.

tidal wave   An unusual rise of water along the seashore, often capable of causing destruction; a swell or crest of ocean water as from a storm or a combination of strong wind and high tide.

toxicity   The quality of being toxic or poisonous; also, the degree to which a substance is toxic. A characteristic of some chemicals; a type of hazard.

tsunami   An earthquake under the ocean; also a very large wave produced by movement of the sea floor or an under water volcanic eruption.

Additional Resources

This list provides information on a wide variety of resources that property managers might consult to assist them in developing emergency plans and procedures. It includes government agencies, private organizations, publications, and web sites but is not intended to be all-inclusive. State and local government web sites include emergency planning information relevant to their jurisdictions; these have not been included here. Citation in this list is for information purposes only and does not constitute endorsement by the Institute of Real Estate Management. In particular, readers should be aware that information and web addresses on the Internet are subject to change.

Federal Government Agencies

The Access Board, 1331 F Street, N.W., Washington, DC 20004 (phone: 202-272-0080; fax: 202-272-0081; web site: www.access-board.gov).

   A federal agency committed to accessible design, the web site includes information on evacuation planning for employees with disabilities.

Centers for Disease Control and Prevention (CDC), 1600 Clifton Road, Atlanta, GA 30333 (phone: 404-639-3534; web site: www.cdc.gov).

   Web site includes information on emergency preparedness and response for a wide range of weather and other emergencies, including power outages, nuclear blasts, and bioterrorism.

Department of Homeland Security (DHS), Washington, DC 20528 (web site: www.dhs.gov).

   Web site includes listings of State Homeland Security and Emergency Services with links to the states' home pages. DHS is closely linked to FEMA and offers resources and tips on preparing for terror attacks at a separate web site, www.ready.gov.

Environmental Protection Agency (EPA), 1200 Pennsylvania Avenue, N.W., Washington, DC 20460 (phone: 202- 272-0167; web site: www.epa.gov).

   Federal entity responsible for protecting human health and safeguarding the natural environment; web site includes information about various environmental hazards and planning for and responding to environmental emergencies.

Federal Emergency Management Agency (FEMA), 500 C Street, S.W., Washington, DC 20472 (phone: 202-566-1600; web site: www.fema.gov).

   Web site includes fact sheets on specific hazards as well as the current threat level and information on current weather-related and other emergencies. *Citizen's Protection Guide* details opportunities for citizens to become involved in FEMA's Citizen Corps initiative and Community Emergency Response Team training program. The Emergency Management Institute offers interactive web-based training in the Incident Command System that includes an examination. It is also possible to print hard copies of instructional materials for self study and take an examination online. The interactive course and printed materials can be accessed on the Internet at www.training.fema.gov/emiweb/is/is195.asp.

General Services Administration,1800 F Street, N.W., Washington, DC 20405 (web site: www.gsa.gov).

   Agency charged with procuring buildings and supplies and providing security to personnel employed by the federal government.

National Institute for Occupational Safety and Health, part of the Centers for Disease Control and Prevention, 1600 Clifton Rd, Atlanta, GA 30333 (phone:800-311-3435; web site: www.cdc.gov/niosh/homepage.html).

   Provides information and guidelines for preventing work-related injuries and illnesses, including *Criteria for a Recommended Standard: Working in Confined Spaces* (Publication 80-106), *NIOSH Guide to Industrial Respiratory Protection* (Publication 87-116), and *Personal Hearing Protection Devices* (Publication 96-110).

National Interagency Fire Center (NIFC), 3833 South Development Avenue, Boise, ID 83705 (phone: 208-387-5512; web site: www.nifc.gov).

> Provides information and statistics on wild fires.

National Oceanic and Atmospheric Administration (NOAA), National Weather Service (NWS), 1325 East West Highway, Silver Spring, MD 20910 (web site: www.nws.noaa.gov).

> Web site includes a glossary of weather-related terms in addition to national and local weather forecasts, weather safety information, and historical information on weather-related disasters.

Nuclear Regulatory Commission (NRC), Washington, DC 20555 (phone: 301-415-7000; web site: www.nrc.gov).

> Web site includes information on radiation (sources, exposure effects, ways to minimize exposure) and radiological emergency preparedness, fact sheets on nuclear radiation topics, and a glossary of related terms.

Occupational Safety and Health Administration (OSHA), 200 Constitution Avenue, N.W., Washington, DC 20210 (web site: www.osha.gov).

> Web site includes telephone and fax contact numbers for regional offices, downloadable publications, and information about various types of workplace emergencies. OSHA also offers free safety consultations. The site includes an Evacuation Plans and Procedures e-tool designed to help small, low-hazard service or retail businesses implement an emergency action plan and comply with OSHA emergency standards. (The e-tool can be downloaded at www.osha.gov/SLTC/etools/evacuation/index.html.)

U.S. Fire Administration (USFA), 16825 South Seton Avenue, Emmitsburg, MD 21727 (phone: 301-447-1000; fax: 301-447-1052; web site: www.usfa.fema.gov).

> An entity of the Department of Homeland Security and the Federal Emergency Management Agency. Co-sponsor of www.firesafety.gov, which includes a Fire Safety Directory with links to residential fire safety resources.

Private Organizations

Alliance of Information and Referral Systems (AIRS), 11240 Waples Mill Road, Fairfax, VA 22030 (phone: 703-218-2477; fax: 703-359-7562; web site: www.airs.org).

> Organization working with the American Red Cross, the Salvation Army, United Way of America, and other organizations to provide coordinated disaster assistance to individuals and families.

American Association of Retired Persons (AARP), 601 E Street N.W., Washington, DC 20049 (phone: 888-687-2277; web site: www.aarp.org).

> An organization of retirement-age persons (age 50 or over) devoted to informing its members of all rights and benefits to which they are entitled.

American Red Cross (ARC), 2025 E Street, N.W., Washington, DC 20006 (phone: 202-303-4498; web site: www.redcross.org).

> Web site includes definitions and descriptions of emergency situations, causes of weather-related emergencies, information on what to do before, during, and after different types of emergencies, and addresses for local chapters. Disaster relief services include shelter, food, and health and mental health services. They also feed emergency responders, help victims communicate with their families, and provide assistance in accessing other available resources.

American Society for Industrial Security (ASIS International), 1625 Prince Street, Alexandria, VA 22314 (phone: 703-519-6200; fax: 703-519-6299; web site: www.asisonline.org).

> Organization of security professionals; provides training toward and awards the Certified Protection Professional (CPP) designation. Web site includes information on security topics and disaster preparedness. Monthly periodical, *Security Management,* is resource on security strategies and devices; also accessible online at www.securitymanagement.com.

The Business Forum, 9297 Burton Way, Beverly Hills, CA 90210 (phone: 310-550-1984; fax: 310-550-6121; web site: www.bizforum.org).

> Independent West Coast organization which is a source of information for senior decision makers in business, government, and academia.

Disaster Resource Guide, P.O. Box 15243, Santa Ana, CA 92735 (phone: 714-558-8940; fax: 714-558-8901; web site: www.disaster-resource.com).

> Published by Emergency Lifeline Corporation, the site includes information about emergency-related professional certifications and training as well as articles and links to organizations.

Emergency Food and Shelter National Board Program, 701 North Fairfax Street, Alexandria, VA 22314 (phone: 703-706-9660; fax:703-706-9677; web site: www.efsp.unitedway.org).

> A public/private partnership created to distribute federal funds to local communities to help people in need of emergency assistance.

The Humane Society of the United States, 2100 L Street, N.W., Washington, DC 20037 (phone: 202-452-1100; web site: www.hsus.org).

> Web site includes information on disaster preparedness for pets.

International Foundation for Protection Officers, P.O. Box 771329, Naples, FL 34107 (phone: 239-430-0534; fax: 239-430-0533; web site: www.ifpo.org).

> Organization of security professionals; provides training toward and awards Certified Protection Officer (CPO) and Certified Security Supervisor (CSS) designations. Web site includes information on security issues and emergency planning.

National Fire Protection Association (NFPA), 1 Batterymarch Park, Quincy, MA 02169 (phone: 617-770-3000; fax: 617-770-0700; web site: www.nfpa.org).

> Nonprofit association that develops scientifically based fire protection codes for buildings and educates the public on fire safety.

National Institute for Chemical Studies (NICS), 2300 MacCorkle Avenue, S.E., Charleston, WV 25304 (phone: 304-346-6264; fax: 304-346-6349; web site: www.nicsinfo.org.

> Works with government at all levels to address issues related to chemical emergencies.

National Institute of Building Sciences (NIBS), 1090 Vermont Avenue, N.W., Washington, DC 20005 (phone: 202-289-7800; fax: 202-289-2092; web site: www.nibs.org).

> A consortium of building construction-related organizations; developer of HAZUS Multi-hazard Loss Estimation Methodology under a cooperative agreement with FEMA. Currently, there are HAZUS models for earthquakes, flood, and wind storms; software can be obtained from FEMA.

National Organization on Disability (NOD), 910 Sixteenth Street, N.W., Washington, DC 20006 (phone:202-293-5960; fax: 202-293-7999; web site: www.nod.org).

> Organization created by disabled individuals to expand the participation and contribution of Americans with disabilities in all aspects of life by raising disability awareness through programs and information. Through its Emergency Preparedness Initiative, NOD has developed an emergency responders *Guide on the Special Needs of People with Disabilities*.

National Voluntary Organizations Active in Disaster (NVOAD), 5960 Kingstowne Center, Alexandria, VA 22315 (phone: 703-339-5596; fax: 703-339-3316; web site: www.nvoad.org).

> Coordinates national and local voluntary organizations to prepare communities before disaster strikes (each state has its own VOAD) and ensure more effective disaster relief service; member of the Coordinated Assistance Network.

The Salvation Army, National Headquarters, 615 Slaters Lane, P.O. Box 269, Alexandria, VA 22313 (web site: www.salvationarmyusa.org).

> International social service and charitable organization whose mission is to fight hunger, homelessness, poverty, and abuse in the struggle for basic human dignity and hope. They also provide disaster relief in the form of shelter, food and water for both victims and emergency responders, and recovery assistance.

United Way of America, 701 North Fairfax Street, Alexandria, VA 23314 (phone: 703-836-7112; web site: www.unitedway.org).

> Provides fund-raising and other program support to national, regional, and local United Way organizations.

Real Estate Organizations

Building Owners and Managers Association (BOMA) International, 1201 New York Avenue, N.W., Washington, DC 20005 (phone: 202-408-2662; fax: 202-371-0181; web site: www.boma.org).

Institute of Real Estate Management (IREM), 430 North Michigan Avenue, Chicago, IL 60611 (phone: 312-329-6000; fax: 312-661-0217; web site: www.irem.org).

International Council of Shopping Centers (ICSC), 1221 Avenue of the Americas, New York, NY 10020 (phone: 646-728-3800; fax: 212-589-5555; web site: www.icsc.org).

Statistical Research

Teenage Research Unlimited, 707 Skokie Boulevard, Northbrook, IL 60062 (phone: 847-564-3440; web site: www.teenresearch.com).

Company conducts marketing research on teenagers, including how they respond to advertising, what they buy and how much they spend.

Workplace Violence Research Institute, 1281 North Gene Autry Trail, Palm Springs, CA 92262 (phone: 800-230-7302; fax: 888-486-8996; web site: workviolence.com).

Disaster-Related Services

AmeriVault, 60 Hickory Drive, Waltham, MA 02451 (phone: 800-774-0235; web site: www .amerivault.com).

Provider of online data storage services.

Barton Protective Services, 11 Piedmont Center, Atlanta, Georgia 30305 (phone: 800-866-1122; web site: www.bartonsolutions.com).

In addition to contract security personnel services, the company provides paramedic services, life safety education, intellectual asset protection, security surveys and risk assessments, and terrorism consulting.

Beyondcom.Inc., 7701 N.W. 29th Street, Margate, FL 33063 (phone: 954-346-0350; fax: 954-346-7883; web site: www.beyondcom.com).

Provider of data recovery and business resumption planning services.

BMS Catastrophe, 303 Arthur Street, Fort Worth, TX 76107 (phone: 800-433-2940; fax: 817-332-6728; web site: www.bmscat.com.

Company specializes in large-scale commercial and industrial property restoration following disasters.

Corig•elan, LLC, 1945 South Halsted Street, Chicago, IL 60608 (phone: 312-563-1430; fax: 312-873-3762; web site: www.corigelan.com).

Offers business continuity and disaster recovery planning and implementation services.

Database Systems Corp. (phone: 602-265-5968; web site: www.databasesystemscorp.com).

Web site offers call center technology that includes collection and organization of call lists to be used for broadcast telephone messages about specific emergencies. Directed specifically to communities, the technology may apply as well to managed properties with large numbers of occupants. May be purchased as a system or contracted as a service.

Emergency Planning Services, 2181 Stevens Creek Boulevard, Cupertino, CA 95014 (phone: 408-342-9035; fax: 408-873-9179; web site: www.epserve.com).

Source for templates for developing an emergency action plan and related training materials.

Insurance Restoration Services, 1300 Brighton Road, Pittsburgh, PA 15233 (phone: 412-322-1135; fax: 412-322-7304; web site: www.disastercontractor.com).

A full-service disaster recovery firm providing emergency response, reconstruction, building drying, records recovery, disaster planning, and consulting services.

MLC & Associates, Inc., P.O. Box 635, Port Orchard, WA 98366 (phone: 253-857-3124; web site: www.mlc2resq.com.

Company provides consulting services on business continuity and disaster recovery planning.

Otis Elevator Company, 1 Farm Springs Road, Farmington, CT 06032 (phone: 860-676-6000; web site: www.otis.com).

Web site provides information about elevators and escalators, including equipment maintenance and upgrades.

Precision Service, Online Backup Services Division, 517 Oothcalooga Street, Calhoun, GA 30701 (phone: 706-625-2657; fax: 706-625-2699; web site: www.precisionbackup.com).
Provider of online data backup services.

Premiere Network Services, Inc., 1510 North Hampton Road, DeSoto, TX 75115 (phone: 972-228-8881; fax: 972-228-8889; web site: www.rewireit.com).
Offers disaster recovery planning services

Strohl Systems Group, Inc., 631 Park Avenue, King of Prussia, PA 19406 (phone: 610-768-4120; fax: 610-768-4135; web site: www.strohlsystems.com.
Company offers business continuity planning and disaster recovery services and software. Web site includes articles on disaster recovery and business continuity planning.

Publications

AEDs Secure Their Place in Office Buildings by Jeannette Keton, *BOMA.org* January 2002, pages 3 and 5.

Are You Ready: A Guide to Citizen Preparedness published by the Federal Emergency Management Agency; available for download at www.fema.gov/are you ready.

Arming Against Workplace Violence, by Marcy Mason, in the September/October 1994 issue of the *Journal of Property Management.*

Business Resumption Planning, by Edward S. Devlin, et al., copyright 1997 by Auerbach Publications, a division of CRC press (www.crcpress.com).

Business Resumption Planning: A Progressive Approach, by Wayne Freeman; article published online at www.itsecurity.com/papers/wayne1.htm.

Business Resumption Planning: Justification, Implementation and Testing, by Paul Rosenthal, in *The Business Forum;* published online at www.bizforum.org/whitepapers/calstatela.htm.

The Commercial Property Owner's Guide to Earthquake Safety, published by Select Publications Inc. Purchase information can be found at www.select-publications.com.

Consultation Services for the Employer, published by the Occupational Safety and Health Administration, revised 1997; available online at www.osha.gov/Publications/osha3047.pdf. Explains the free OSHA safety consultation program.

Coping with an Attack: A Quick Guide to Dealing with Biological, Chemical, and "Dirty Bomb" Attacks published by the Center for Technology and National Security Policy at the National Defense University; available for download at www.ndu.edu/ctnsp/wmd-tipsheet.htm.

Critical Elements of a Disaster Recovery & Business/Service Continuity Plan, by Pat Moore; article published online at www.disaster-resource.com; copyright 2003 by Disaster Resource Guide.

Critical Incident Protocol—A Public and Private Partnership, copyright 2000 by Michigan State University; available for download at www.cj.msu.edu/~outreach/CIP/CIP.pdf.

The Definitive Guide to Business Resumption Planning, by Leo A. Wrobel, copyright 1997 by Rothstein Associates Inc. Can be purchased online from Disaster Recovery Journal at www.drj.com.

Disaster Preparation Guide published online by American Society for Industrial Security at www.asisonline.org/newsroom/crisisResponse/disaster.pdf; copyright 2003 by ASIS International. Includes a checklist of major planning considerations related to emergencies, including communications, facility shutdown, evacuation, shelter, health/medical, and security.

Disaster Preparedness for People with Disabilities published by the American Red Cross; available for download at www.redcross.org/pubs/dspubs/terrormat.html,

Disaster Preparedness for Seniors by Seniors, published online by the American Red Cross at www.redcross.org/services/disaster/beprepared/seniors.html.

Disaster Recovery and Business Resumption Planning, by Dana Turner, published online at www.bankersonline.com/security/sec_disasterrecovery.html.

Disaster Recovery Journal, P.O. Box 510110, St. Louis, MO 63151 (phone: 314-894-0276; fax: 314-894-7474; web site: www.drj.com).

Earthquakes, by Kaye M. Shedlock and Louis C. Pakiser, published by the U.S. Geological Survey on the Internet at http://pubs.usgs.gov/gip/earthq1/.

Emergency Management Guide for Business and Industry copyright October 1993 by the Federal Emergency Management Agency; available for download at www.fema.gov/pdf/library/bizindst.pdf. Offers a step-by-step approach to emergency planning, response, and recovery for companies of all sizes.

Emergency Preparedness Initiative Guide on the Special Needs of People with Disabilities for Emergency Managers, Planners & Responders published online by the National Organization on Disability at www.nod.org/pdffiles/epiguide2004.pdf.

Emergency Procedures for Employees with Disabilities in Office Occupancies published online by the U.S. Fire Administration (publication FA154, June 1995); available for download at www.fire.nist.gov/bfrlpubs/fire95/PDF/f95043.pdf.

GSA Security Resource Guide: A Guide to Federal Security, published in 2003 by U.S. General Services Administration; available on the Internet at www.usda.gov/da/physicalsecurity/gsa.htm.

Guidance for Filtration and Air-Cleaning Systems to Protect Building Environments from Airborne Chemical, Biological, and Radiological Attacks published in 2003 by the National Institute for Occupational Safety and Health (Publication NIOSH 2003-136); available for download at www.cdc.gov/niosh/docs/2003-136/pdfs/2003-136.pdf.

Guidance for Protecting Building Environments from Airborne Chemical, Biological, or Radiological Attacks copyright 2002 by the National Institute for Occupational Safety and Health; available for download at www.cdc.gov/niosh/bldvent/2002-139.html. Provides specific recommendations, including physical security.

Guidance: Potassium Iodide as a Thyroid Blocking Agent in Radiation Emergencies copyright 2001 by the U.S. Food and Drug Administration; available for download at www.fda.gov/cder/guidance/index.htm. Provides detailed information on the use of potassium iodide in preventing thyroid cancer.

Guide to Writing a Shopping Center Security Manual (New York: International Council of Shopping Centers).

Guide to Writing a Shopping Center Tenant Manual (New York: International Council of Shopping Centers).

Helping Young Children Cope with Trauma published by the American Red Cross; available for download at www.redcross.org/pubs/dspubs/terrormat.html.

Homeowners' Guide to Earthquake Safety and Environmental Hazards, published by Select Publications Inc. Purchase information can be found at www.select-publications.com.

How to Develop a Disaster Action Plan for Older, Distant Relatives, by Jane Irene Kelly, published May 2003 by the American Association of Retired Persons in the AARP Bulletin Online at www.aarp.org/bulletin/yourlife/Articles/0505_sidebar_11.html.

How to Plan for Workplace Emergencies and Evacuations published by the U.S. Department of Labor, Occupational Safety and Health Administration, OSHA 3088, 2001 (revised); available for download at www.osha.gov/Publications/osha3088.pdf. Provides an overview of OSHA standard 29 CFR 1910.38.

Introduction to Employee Fire and Life Safety, edited by Guy Colonna; copyright 2001 by the National Fire Protection Association. (See especially Chapter 3, Developing a Preparedness Plan by Jerry L. Ball and Chapter 6, Emergency Evacuation Drills by David P. Demers and Jon C. Jones.)

Mail Center Security Guidelines copyright 2002 by the United States Postal Service (Publication 166), available for download at www.usps.com/publications/pubs/welcome.htm.

NFPA 1600 Standard on Disaster/Emergency Management and Business Continuity Programs copyright 2004 by the National Fire Protection Association. Recommended by the American National Standards Institute (ANSI) to become the national standard on disaster preparedness. The standard can be downloaded on the Internet at www.nfpa.org.

NIOSH Pocket Guide to Chemical Hazards (NPG), third edition, published 2003 by the National Institute for Occupational Safety and Health (Publication 97-140); available for download at www.cdc.gov/niosh/npg/npg.html.

NRC: Regulator of Nuclear Safety published by the U.S. Nuclear Regulatory Commission and available for download at www.nrc.gov.

Occupant Emergency Program Guide published in 2002 by U.S. General Services Administration; can be downloaded in Word format at www.gsa.gov/federalprotectiveservices.

On the Homefront: A Proactive Approach to Homeland Security Emergency Preparedness by Regina Raiford Babcock, *Buildings* 97(5):28, May 2003.

Pets and Disasters: Get Prepared, developed by the Humane Society of the United States in cooperation with the American Red Cross and published online at www.disasterrelief.org/Library/Prepare/pets.html.

Planning and Preparedness Remain Keystones of Emergency Preparedness Plans, *BOMA.org* June 2002, pages 1, 21–22.

Practices for Securing Critical Information Assets copyright 2000 by the Critical Infrastructure Assurance Office; available for download at www.infragard.net/library/pdfs/securing_critical_assets.pdf. (While directed to agencies of the U.S. government, some information—especially Chapter IV, Security Incident Planning, which relates to computers and technology—can be applied in the private sector. Infragard is affiliated with the FBI.)

Protecting the Home Front: Experts Recommend Practical Steps to Help You Plan for the Unthinkable, by Barbara Basler, published May 2003 by the American Association of Retired Persons in the AARP Bulletin Online at www.aarp.org/bulletin/yourlife/Articles/a2003-06-26-protecting.html.

Risk Management: An Essential Guide to Protecting Critical Assets copyright 2002 by the National Infrastructure Protection Center; published on the Internet at www.nipc.gov/publications/nipcpub/P-Risk%20Management.pdf. Includes models for assessing risk related to key personnel, computers, and communications and applicable to both private and public sectors.

Safety First: The Critical Issues—and Planning—of Fire and Life Safety by Robin Suttell, *Buildings* 97(5):32–37, May 2003.

Shelter in Place at Your Office: A General Guide for Preparing a Shelter in Place Plan in the Workplace published by the National Institute for Chemical Studies and available for download on the Internet at www.nicsinfo.org.

Spotlight on Security for Real Estate Managers by Lawrence J. Fennelly and John H. Lombardi, copyright 1997 by the Institute of Real Estate Management.

Surviving the Storm: A Guide to Hurricane Preparedness published by the U.S. Department of Homeland Security/Federal Emergency Management Agency; available for download at www.fema.gov/hazards/hurricanes/survivingthestorm.shtm.

Tsunamis: The Great Waves published jointly by NOAA, the International Tsunami Information Center, Laboratoire de Geophysique in France, and the UNESCO/Intergovernmental Oceanographic Commission available for download on the Internet at www.prh.noaa.gov/itic/library/pubs/great_waves/great_waves_en_2002.pdf.

2000 Emergency Response Guidebook, developed jointly by the U.S. Department of Transportation (DOT), Transport Canada, and the Secretariat of Communications and Transportation of Mexico (SCT) for those who respond to hazardous materials transport spills; available for download at http://hazmat.dot.gov/erg2000/erg2000.pdf.

Vendrell, Ernest G.: The Incident Command System: A Proven Tool for the Management of Emergency Operations, June 2001; published online by the International Foundation for Protection Officers (IFPO); available for download at www.ifpo.org/articlebank/incident_command_system.htm.

Warehouse Superstores: Hazards of Shopping in a Working Warehouse, by John M. Mroszczyk, in *Professional Safety;* copyright March 2002 by the American Society of Safety Engineers.

Workplace Violence: Awareness and Prevention, published on the Internet at www.freemaninstitute.com/violence4.htm.

Specific Web Sites

www.anss.org is the web page of the Advanced National Seismic System of the U.S. Geological Survey. It includes maps and information specific to earthquakes.

www.apa.org/practice/drnindex.html is the web page for the American Psychological Association Disaster Response Network, a pro-bono service of the APA and its membership that provides information on traumatic stress, its warning signs, and its management.

www.avalanche.org is a web page operated by the American Avalanche Association, which is dedicated to the study, forecasting, control, and mitigation of snow avalanches.

www.CANinfo.net is the information site for Coordinated Assistance Network, a collaboration of several disaster relief agencies to help disaster victims receive assistance more quickly through a single registration in a central data base. The American Red Cross is a member organization.

www.cern.us is the web site for the Community Emergency Response Network of Howard County, Maryland. In addition to information on disaster planning for families, the site includes a template for creating a wallet-sized emergency communication (contact information) card.

www.citizencorps.gov, web site of the Citizen Corps, which was created to coordinate volunteer activities related to disaster preparedness in local communities. Coordinated nationally by the Department of Homeland Security, which works closely with state and local governments as well as other federal entities, first responders, and emergency managers. The site includes citizen disaster preparedness publications from FEMA and other sources, which can be downloaded at www/citizencorps.gov/ready/cc-pubs.shtm.

www.contentisking.com offers information on household emergencies related to gas leaks, plumbing, and electricity.

www.contingencyplanning.com is a source for information on off-site data storage and remote electronic data vaulting.

ww.cpc.ncep.noaa.gov, the web site for the National Weather Service Climate Prediction Center, provides local weather assessments and forecasts.

www.disabilityinfo.gov provides a directory of government web links relevant to people with disabilities.

www.disasterrelief.org provides access to disaster preparedness materials published on the Internet by the American Red Cross in conjunction with FEMA and other governmental agencies and private organizations.

www.fema.gov/mit/saferoom, part of the FEMA web site, provides information and guidelines for preparing safe rooms and community shelters.

www.firesafety.gov is operated by the U.S. Fire Administration.

www.FirstGov.gov is the U.S. government's official web portal for contacting federal agencies.

www.geo.mtu.edu/volcanoes, web page of the Michigan Technological University Keweenaw Volcano Observatory, provides information to assist in volcano hazard mitigation.

www.ir-net.com, the Information and Referral Resource Network, provides directory information and Internet links to providers of medical and social services nationwide.

www.missfireprevention.com, a web site sponsored by the Baltimore County Volunteer Fire Association, includes fire prevention information and tips.

www.nwac.noaa.gov is the Internet home of the Northwest Weather and Avalanche Center provides weather and snowpack information related to potential avalanche hazards.

www.pdc.org is the web site for the Pacific Disaster Center, which provides information related to disaster management and humanitarian assistance for communities of the Asia Pacific region and beyond.

www.ready.gov is a combined DHS/FEMA/USFA resource for information on preparing for terrorism.

www.reisac.org, the acronym stands for Real Estate Information Sharing and Analysis Center, whose role is to disseminate information from the federal government, facilitate real estate industry reporting to the government, and bring private- and public-sector experts together to share useful information. The Institute of Real Estate Management (IREM), Building Owners and Managers Association (BOMA) International, and the International Council of Shopping Centers (ICSC) are all members of REISAC.

www.safespaces.com is the online successor to the National Safe Workplace Institute. Web site includes articles on workplace safety and security, including violence in the workplace.

www.safetyinfocur.com, operated by System Interface Consultants, Inc., is an online source for fact sheets and other publications from OSHA.

www.securebuildings.lbl.gov, web site of the Lawrence Berkeley National Laboratory, contains advice for building operators and emergency personnel on safeguarding buildings against chemical or biological attack.

www.seismo.berkeley.edu, operated by Berkeley Seismological Laboratories of the University of California, provides information on earthquakes in California.

www.211.org provides information on communities participating in the 211 disaster relief telephone registration program.

www.us-cert.gov, web site of the U.S. Computer Emergency Readiness Team, contains information to help computer users and corporate computer professionals prepare for and respond to computer and network emergencies.

Federal Emergency Management Agency Publications
Community Shelter (FEMA 361)
Design Guidelines for Flood Damage Reduction (FEMA 15)
Disaster Mitigation Guide for Business and Industry (FEMA 190)
Preparedness in High-Rise Buildings (FEMA 76)

National Oceanic and Atmospheric Administration Publications (published jointly with FEMA and the American Red Cross; downloadable versions can be accessed at www.nws.noaa.gov/om/brochures.shtml)
Floods: The Awesome Power (NOAA/PA200253 © 2002)
Hurricanes: Unleashing Nature's Fury (NOAA/PA 94050 © 2001)
Thunderstorms...Tornadoes...Lightning: Nature's Most Violent Storms (NOAA/PA 99050)
Winter Storms: The Deceptive Killers (NOAA/PA 200160 © 2001)

National Fire Protection Association Publications
Facility Security (© 2002)
Fire Protection Handbook: Business and Industry Edition (© 2003)
Introduction to Employee Fire and Life Safety (© 2001)
NFPA Ready Reference: Fire Safety in High-Rise Buildings (© 2003)
NFPA Ready Reference: Human Behavior in Fire Emergencies (© 2003)

American Red Cross Training Programs and Materials
Community First Aid and Safety
First Aid/CPR/AED Program

Risk Assessment Questionnaire

Fire Protection
- Is there an automatic fire detection system? If yes, what type?
  —Direct to fire and police
  —Local, within the building
  —Monitored central station
- Is there a fire detection system or smoke alarm system in the building?
- Is this system inspected and serviced at least annually?
- Are there sufficient numbers of fire extinguishers—
  —On each floor?
  —In each office suite or store space?
- Are the fire extinguishers readily identifiable?
- Are the fire extinguishers inspected and recharged at least annually?
- Are there automatic sprinklers and/or standpipes and hoses in the building?
- Are they inspected at least annually?
- Are fire protection system components tested on a regular schedule or as required?

Electrical
- Are all panel boards, switches, and fuses enclosed in metal cabinets that close securely?
- Are all circuits easily identifiable?
- Are all fuses or breakers properly sized for the equipment and lighting they control?
- Are there recurring problems with fuses or circuit breakers being continually tripped?
- Do metal-enclosed switch gears receive periodic preventive maintenance?
- Are ground fault interrupters (GFIs) utilized in potentially wet or damp areas?
- Are surge protectors used on phone systems, computers, and office equipment? Is this required of commercial tenants (i.e., under their leases)?
- Are extension cords used as permanent power sources in lieu of hard wiring or adding an outlet?
- Are space heaters being used to augment the HVAC system?
- Are tenants reminded periodically
  —Not to use extension cords as permanent power sources?
  —Not to use space heaters?
- Is adequate clear space or appropriate protective material provided between recessed light fixtures and insulating materials?
- Is the emergency generator inspected and tested on a regular schedule?
- Are electrical rooms and cabinets that are accessible from common areas kept locked?

Plumbing
- Are water and drain pipes, seals, etc., inspected periodically for leaks?
- Are pipes properly insulated?
- Is heating tape used to prevent pipes from freezing?

HVAC
- Has the HVAC system been inspected and serviced within the past year?
- Is HVAC service provided by an outside contractor?
- Is the boiler's low water cutoff/water supply flushed out every month during the heating season?
- Does the boiler room meet fire code requirements concerning noncombustible materials and proper fire-rated doors and closers?
- Is the boiler room properly ventilated?
- Is the room inspected periodically to ensure that no combustible materials are stored there?

- Are vents and chimney flues inspected annually for clear passage?
- Is there a program in place for cleaning ductwork and diffusers?
- Does HVAC equipment receive regular preventive maintenance—changing/cleaning of air filters, changing/cleaning of water filters, seasonal cleaning of condensers and coils?
- Is cooling water tested regularly? Are water treatment chemicals maintained at proper levels?

Exits and Stairwells

- Are all fire exits clearly marked?
- Are all exit doors in working order, free of any hindrance, debris, or obstruction?
- Do all fire doors open outward?
- Are the stairwell sides of all exit doors marked with LARGE bright-colored floor numbers? Are floor numbers clearly marked on the stairwell wall next to the exit doors?
- Are stairwell fire exit doors kept locked (from the stairwell side) at all times for security reasons?
- Are there any designated egress points (i.e., selected floors) other than the ground floor?
- Are these electronic locks that use a card reader or keypad to open them?
- Are the electronic locks wired into the fire alarm system so they can be automatically released (opened) in the event of a fire or other need for evacuation?
- Do fire doors to the outside have panic hardware?
- Are all fire escapes inspected and serviced at least quarterly?
- Are there sufficient emergency lighting units?
- Is the emergency lighting system tested periodically? How often?
- Have any combustible materials been used in stairwell construction (e.g., carpeting, stair treads)?

Safety and Materials Handling

- Do you hold regularly scheduled safety training sessions for your employees?
- Do you maintain copies of material safety data sheets (MSDSs) for all chemicals stored on the premises?
- Are your employees properly trained to interpret MSDS information?
- Are combustible materials stored in an "out" building?
- If not, are they stored in vented, fireproof storage cabinets?
- Are paints, mineral spirits, and cleaning solvents disposed of properly?
- Are storage containers for combustibles kept clear of critical building system controls?
- Are soiled or solvent-soaked rags kept in self-closing metal storage receptacles?
- Are occupants (residents, commercial tenants) reminded periodically about proper methods for storing, handling, and disposing of hazardous materials in their premises?
- Do commercial tenants maintain MSDSs for chemicals stored and used within their premises?
- Are commercial tenants' leased premises inspected periodically by OSHA for workplace safety and hazardous materials compliance?

Maintenance Shop/Building Storage Areas

- Is the room kept neat and clean? Is it kept clear of debris and spills?
- Are combustible materials stored properly in approved cabinets?
- Is a fire extinguisher provided in the room?
- Does the room have adequate ventilation?

Other Building Elements

- Is the Dumpster floor area kept clear of debris and spills?
- Is the trash chute cleaned regularly and kept free of material buildup?
- Are all draperies and building ornamentation made from fire retardant materials?

- Are building corridors kept clear of debris and spills?
- Are restrooms kept clear of debris and spills?
- Are windows checked periodically to ensure that they open and close properly and fasteners are in good operating condition?
- Are window systems checked periodically to ensure that they are not deteriorating?
- Is installed window-washing apparatus and/or scaffolding properly attached to the concrete roof decking?

Operational Issues

- Does the building have an emergency procedures manual?
- Does the building have a safety committee?
- Do building staff receive appropriate training related to bloodborne pathogens, first aid, and other emergency response subjects?

Community Room

- What is the maximum occupancy of your community room? Is it posted?
- Are exits from this space kept clear of furniture, displays, storage boxes, and other obstacles?
- When positioning furniture for functions, are clear aisles maintained for quick and easy egress in an emergency?
- Is the range and/or microwave oven maintained in a clean and safe manner? Are orifices in gas ranges kept clear?
- Are there curtains or any other combustible materials near the range?
- Is there a properly sized and vented range hood?
- Is grease periodically cleaned from the hood and ductwork by on-site staff or an outside contractor?
- Has a Class B fire extinguisher been provided in the kitchen area?
- Are the coils on the refrigerator/freezer kept clean of dirt and lint?

Note: State and local governments generally establish inspection schedules as part of building codes. The Occupational Safety and Health Administration (OSHA) establishes requirements related to workplace safety. Use of this questionnaire should take into account the various regulatory requirements for inspection and testing. Also, a building's use and occupancy, including visitors, may determine the level of risk—the presence of children and/or elderly or disabled persons may increase some risks.

Emergency Procedures Planning Forms

This collection of forms can be used to document various aspects of the emergency planning process described in Chapter 1 and to maintain records of incidents, drills, and related expenditures. These forms are also provided as digital files in Excel format on the accompanying CD-ROM. Those files may be adapted to a management company's or a property's unique needs. For example, it may be desirable to include a column for recording accounting codes on the forms that apply to emergency expense records and cash expenditures. At some properties, it may be desirable to account for additional key service vendors such as heating oil suppliers. Lists of emergency supplies may be more extensive than shown in the form; the list in Chapter 1 includes additional suggestions. Insurance information might also include particulars related to fire and casualty and general liability coverages. The Emergency Incident Log may be used in conjunction with the Emergency Report Form in Chapter 7 to ensure that all important details—including identification of victims and witnesses as well as where the incident happened—are documented for each emergency that arises.

Here are the titles of the forms in the order of presentation. (These are also the file names for the forms on the accompanying CD-ROM.)

Emergency Response Team
Specialized Training/Skills Bank
Key Service Vendors
Emergency Response Overview (team members alphabetically)
Emergency Response Overview (team responsibilities alphabetically)
Emergency Supplies
Resident Profile
Insurance Information
Building Utility and Equipment Shut Offs
Fire Detection/Alarm Checklist
Critical Equipment and Materials
Computer and Information Management
Paper and Micrographics Business Records Management
Vendor Information
Emergency Expense Records
Cash Expenditures
Emergency Incident Log
Emergency Response Plan Review Dates and Drill Records
Evacuation and Plan Review Dates

Permission to reproduce these forms in *Before Disaster Strikes* and for readers of this book to use them has been granted by the copyright owner as stated on each form.

EMERGENCY RESPONSE TEAM

Name	Title/Dept.	Business Phone	Pager	Cellular Phone	Fax Number	Home Phone	E-Mail Address

Date: _____

By: _____

Updated: _____

This form may be reproduced pursuant to permission granted by David Mistick, CPM®.

SPECIALIZED TRAINING/SKILLS BANK

Training/Skill	Employee	Department/Office	Phone/Pager	Certification Yes/No	E-Mail Address

Date: _____

By: _____

Updated: _____

KEY SERVICE VENDORS

Vendor Type	Contractor / Vendor	Emergency Contact Phone Number	
Alarm Systems			
Computer Systems			
Disaster Restoration Contractor			
Electric Company			
Electrician			
Elevator Service			
Engineering Firm			
Environmental Services			
Fire Suppression System(s)			
Gas Company			
Glass Company			
HVAC Service			
Janitorial Supplies			
Locksmith			
Movers/Storage			
Office Equipment			
Office Supplies			
Phone System Service			
Plumber			
Printer/Business Forms			
Security Systems			
Sign Maker			
Snow Removal			
Steam Company			
Water Company			
Other Daily Operations Supplies			
Emergency Generator			

Date: _____

By: _____

This form may be reproduced pursuant to permission granted by David Mistick, CPM®.

250

EMERGENCY RESPONSE OVERVIEW
Cross-Reference List

Emergency Team Member (Alphabetical Order)	Critical Issue / Functional Responsibility

Date: _____ Updated: _____

By: _____

This form may be reproduced pursuant to permission granted by David Mistick, CPM®.

EMERGENCY RESPONSE OVERVIEW
Cross-Reference List

Critical Issue/Functional Responsibility (Alphabetical Order)	Emergency Team Member

Date: _____ Updated: _____

By: _____

This form may be reproduced pursuant to permission granted by David Mistick, CPM®.

EMERGENCY SUPPLIES

Item	Location	Quantity	Inspected By	Date
Blankets				
Bottled Water				
First Aid Supplies				
Flashlights/Batteries				
Rubber Boots				
Rubber Gloves				
Cotton Gloves				
Eye Protection				
Protective Clothing				
Dust Masks				
Respirators				
Brooms				
Mops				
Buckets				
Flat Shovels				
Trash Bags and Barrels				
Paper Towels				
Axe				
Crowbar				
Cordless Drill				
Circular Saw				
Hand Saw				
Wet/Dry Vacuum				
Nylon Rope				

Page One

This form may be reproduced pursuant to permission granted by David Mistick, CPM®.

EMERGENCY SUPPLIES, continued

Item	Location	Quantity	Inspected By	Date
Basic Tool Kit				
Fasteners				
Roll 6 Mil Plastic				
Ladders				
Staple Gun/Stapler				
Duct Tape				
Tarp				
Hard Hats				
12 Gauge Extension Cords				
Portable Quartz Lights				
Generator				
Gasoline				
Water Containers				
Cardboard Boxes				
Labels				
Markers				
Packing Tape				
Scissors				
Battery Operated Radio				
Two-Way Radios				
As Built Drawings				

Page Two

Date: _____   Updated: _____

By: _____

This form may be reproduced pursuant to permission granted by David Mistick, CPM®.

RESIDENT PROFILE
(Confidential)

Building Number: _____

Address: _____

Unit No.	Resident(s)	E-Mail Address	Phone	Age	No. of Children	Ages of Children	Physical Impair.	Special Assistance Needed	In Case of Emergency Contact (Name & #)

Date: _____

By: _____

Updated: _____

INSURANCE INFORMATION

Agency: _____

Contact: _____

Office Phone: _____

Home Phone: _____

Corporate Phone: _____

Coverage Type	Policy Number	Carrier	Coverage Amount	Renewal Dates	Additional Info. (Deductible, Etc.)
Contents					
Vital Records					
Electronic Equipment					
Business Interruption					
Structure					
Other					

Date: _____

By: _____

Updated: _____

This form may be reproduced pursuant to permission granted by David Mistick, CPM®.

256

BUILDING UTILITY AND
EQUIPMENT SHUT OFFS

Building/Address	Utility	Shut Off Location
	Gas Water Electric Fire Suppression • Sprinkler • Dry-Chemical • Other Boiler Sump Pumps Other	_____ _____ _____ _____ _____ _____ _____ _____ _____ _____
	Gas Water Electric Fire Suppression • Sprinkler • Dry-Chemical • Other Boiler Sump Pumps Other	_____ _____ _____ _____ _____ _____ _____ _____ _____ _____
	Gas Water Electric Fire Suppression • Sprinkler • Dry-Chemical • Other Boiler Sump Pumps Other	_____ _____ _____ _____ _____ _____ _____ _____ _____ _____
	Gas Water Electric Fire Suppression • Sprinkler • Dry-Chemical • Other Boiler Sump Pumps Other	_____ _____ _____ _____ _____ _____ _____ _____ _____ _____

(Typical)

This form may be reproduced pursuant to permission granted by David Mistick, CPM®.

FIRE DETECTION / ALARM CHECKLIST

Equipment	Yes/No	Location(s)
Main Fire Alarm Control Panel		
Fire Extinguishers		
Class A		
Class B		
Class C		
Automatic Sprinklers		
Fire Pump		
Smoke Detectors		
Heat Detectors		
Fire Alarm—Remote Panel		
Fire Alarm—Manual Pull Stations		
Standpipes		
Hose Stations		
FD Connections—Siamese		
Emergency Lighting		
Lighted Exit Signs		
Fire Doors		

Date: _____

By: _____

This form may be reproduced pursuant to permission granted by David Mistick, CPM®.

CRITICAL EQUIPMENT AND MATERIALS

Equipment/Room	Location	Access Required	Preventive Action Required
Emergency Generator			
Emergency Command Center			
Emergency Supplies			
Hazardous Materials Storage			
Phone System Equipment			
Satellite Equipment Room			
Computer Center			
Servers			
Workstations/PCs			
Elevator Control Room			
Copiers			
Printers			
Fax Machines			

Date: _____

By: _____

Updated: _____

COMPUTER AND INFORMATION MANAGEMENT
List in order of importance

Location	Equipment	Serial #	Security Level	Own/Lease	Service Agr. / Vendor	Warranty Expiration	Manager In Charge

Date: _____

By: _____

Updated: _____

PAPER AND MICROGRAPHICS
BUSINESS RECORDS MANAGEMENT
List in order of importance

Location or Office	Type of Information	Cabinet or Drawer	Security Level	Manager In Charge

Date: _____   Updated: _____

By: _____

This form may be reproduced pursuant to permission granted by David Mistick, CPM®.

VENDOR INFORMATION

Vendor	Business Phone	Contact	After Hours Phone	Contact

Date: _____

By: _____

Updated: _____

EMERGENCY EXPENSE RECORDS

Date	Purchase Order #	Vendor	Item/Service Purchased	Dollar Amount
			Sheet Total	$

Date: _____

By: _____

Updated: _____

CASH EXPENDITURES

By Whom	Cash / Check	Item Purchased	Dollar Amount
		Total	$

Date: _____

By: _____

Updated: _____

EMERGENCY INCIDENT LOG FOR _____

Date	Time	Type of Emergency	Discovered By	Cause and Origin	Resolution

Date: _____

By: _____

Updated: _____

EMERGENCY RESPONSE PLAN REVIEW DATES AND DRILL RECORDS
FOR THE YEAR _____

	Dates	Participants
Plan Review		
Next Review		
Next Review		
Next Review		
Next Review		
Plan Drill		
Plan Drill		

Date: _____

By: _____

This form may be reproduced pursuant to permission granted by David Mistick, CPM®.

EVACUATION AND PLAN REVIEW DATES

Emergency Preparedness Plan	Date	Evacuation Exercise Conducted	Date

This form may be reproduced pursuant to permission granted by David Mistick, CPM®.

267